STATES OF JUSTICE

States of Justice theorizes the ways in which states that are presumed to be weaker in the international system use the International Criminal Court (ICC) to advance their security and political interests. Ultimately, the book contends that African states have managed to instrumentally and strategically use the international justice system to their advantage, a theoretical framework that challenges the "justice cascade" argument. The empirical work of this study focuses on four major themes around the intersection of power, states' interests, and the global governance of atrocity crimes: first, the strategic use of self-referrals to the ICC; second, complementarity between the national and the international justice systems; third, the limits of state cooperation with international courts; and fourth, the use of international courts in domestic political conflicts. This book is valuable to students, scholars, and researchers who are interested in international relations, international criminal justice, peace and conflict studies, human rights, and African politics.

Oumar Ba is Assistant Professor of Political Science at Morehouse College in Atlanta. He earned a doctorate in political science from the University of Florida. His research interests lie at the intersection of global politics and international criminal justice, with a focus on the International Criminal Court, the global governance of atrocity crimes, cultural heritage in conflict, and the politics of knowledge production from Global South perspectives. The draft manuscript on which this book is based was the 2019 International Studies Association (ISA) Northeast Scholars' Circle honoree.

States of Justice

THE POLITICS OF THE INTERNATIONAL CRIMINAL COURT

OUMAR BA

Morehouse College

CAMBRIDGE
UNIVERSITY PRESS

CAMBRIDGE
UNIVERSITY PRESS

University Printing House, Cambridge CB2 8BS, United Kingdom

One Liberty Plaza, 20th Floor, New York, NY 10006, USA

477 Williamstown Road, Port Melbourne, VIC 3207, Australia

314-321, 3rd Floor, Plot 3, Splendor Forum, Jasola District Centre, New Delhi - 110025, India

103 Penang Road, #05-06/07, Visioncrest Commercial, Singapore 238467

Cambridge University Press is part of the University of Cambridge.

It furthers the University's mission by disseminating knowledge in the pursuit of education, learning and research at the highest international levels of excellence.

www.cambridge.org
Information on this title: www.cambridge.org/9781108738835
DOI: 10.1017/9781108771818

© Oumar Ba 2020

First published 2020
First paperback edition 2022

A catalogue record for this publication is available from the British Library

Library of Congress Cataloging in Publication data
Names: Ba, Oumar, 1977- author.
Title: States of justice : the politics of the international criminal court / Oumar Ba, Morehouse College, Atlanta.
Description: Cambridge, United Kingdom ; New York, NY, USA : Cambridge University Press, 2020. | Based on author's thesis (doctoral - University of Florida, 2017) issued under title: Outsourcing justice : Africa and the politics of the International Criminal Court. | Includes bibliographical references and index.
Identifiers: LCCN 2019059923 | ISBN 9781108488778 (hardback) | ISBN 9781108738835 (ebook)
Subjects: LCSH: International Criminal Court. | International criminal courts–Political aspects. | Jurisdiction (International law) | International criminal courts–Political aspects–Africa.
Classification: LCC KZ7312 .B3 2020 | DDC 345–dc23
LC record available at https://lccn.loc.gov/2019059923

ISBN 978-1-108-48877-8 Hardback
ISBN 978-1-108-73883-5 Paperback

To the memory of Mamadou Khalidou and to Abdoulaye Ba

Contents

Tables

Acknowledgments

This book project took shape during my graduate study years at the University of Florida's (UF) Department of Political Science. It was nurtured by a great number of teachers and mentors, to whom I will be forever grateful. Over many years, Aida Hozic has guided my journey through academia while constantly pushing me to reflect on myself as much as I reflect on my research subject. It is thanks to Aida that I learned to be comfortable in the margins from which I theorize international relations. I also extend my sincere gratitude to Leonardo Villalón: but for the funding opportunity that Leo offered me at the beginning of this journey, I would not have been able to enter the UF doctoral program. Ido Oren, Dan O'Neill, and Sharon Abramowitz, with their probing questions, helped push this work in directions that I had not anticipated and expanded my intellectual horizon. Laura Sjoberg and Badredine Arfi taught me how to think critically of international relations and international organizations and what these institutions do, beyond their intended purpose. At Ohio University, Andrew A. G. Ross guided my first steps in the study of international law and human rights and has ever since helped me find a footing within many scholarly circles. I am also thankful for the mentorship of Steve Howard and the late Patricia Weitsman.

Fieldwork for this book was generously funded by the UF Center for African Studies, the UF Department of Political Science, the UF College for Liberal Arts and Sciences, the UF Graduate School, and the UF Sahel Research Group. I owe a debt of gratitude to these institutions, their faculty, and their staff. In Uganda, Amanda Edgell and Dr. Charlotte Mafumbo were tremendously helpful in facilitating my research and connecting me with Ugandans who taught me so much about their country's history and politics. Tom Wolf knows the Kenyan political landscape like no other and pointed me in new directions. Sammy Gachigua made me feel at home in Nairobi, shared many cups of tea – with copious amounts of sugar and milk – and connected me with his colleagues around the country. Adama Bocoum provided me with valuable guidance in Mali, from Bamako to Djenné and Timbuktu. To all those who shared their stories with me and trusted me with their voices, I hope this work has remained faithful to your views and reflects the experiences that you shared with me.

Key insights of this work were gained through presentations and discussions with colleagues at various conferences of the International Studies Association (ISA), the ISA Northeast, and the African Studies Association. I am especially grateful to Anna Agathangelou, Andrew A. G. Ross, Steven C. Roach, Franziska Boehme, Jarpa Dawuni, Annie Bunting, and all the participants at the 2019 ISA Northeast Scholars' Circle. Roundtable discussions with, and tweets and blog posts from, a great number of colleagues have helped me probe deeper many of the themes discussed in this book. I'm also grateful to Tom Randall, Gemma Smith and Laura Blake at Cambridge University Press and to three anonymous reviewers.

Lina Benabdallah has been a constant source of moral and intellectual support for almost a decade now, and her companionship, wit, and humor have made every step of this journey more enjoyable. I cherish the shared memories with Lina – the moments of joy, doubts, and pain throughout these years. Leo Villalón and Fiona McLaughlin made Gainesville a welcoming home, which provided much social, moral, and intellectual support. Their generosity is without parallel. Abdoulaye Kane and Aissé (Ba) Diallo too sustained me through delicious food and cultural nourishment, re-creating a Fouta atmosphere in the heart of Florida. I have also benefited from tremendous support from "the gang" – my friends and colleagues at UF and Tanglewood Village. At Morehouse College, my colleagues Andrew Douglas, Matthew Platt, Levar Smith, Adrienne Jones, Dr. Aka, Kipton Jensen, Sam Livingston, and Fred Knight helped create a fruitful intellectual space, despite the institutional assaults on our profession and livelihoods.

When one grows up on the banks of the Senegal River, wherein the closest middle and high schools are more than 100 miles away, some may say that it takes a great deal of courage to go and stay in school. Others may call it resilience. But I believe my education has been made possible by the love and sacrifice of my parents, Khalidou Saïdou Ba and Aissata Nazirou Ly, who have not had a chance to get formal education themselves but who understood why it was necessary to provide such an opportunity for their children. Love and sacrifice also of extended family members and strangers, who took in other people's children. Without the sacrifices of my aunt Néné Couro, my grandmother Maam Poulo, my great-uncles Abass Sow and Hady Sow, my uncles Mahfouze Ly and Saikhou Oumar Ly, and countless others, I would not have made it this far. If there is any merit in this work, it is theirs.

Abbreviations

AAR	Agreement on Accountability and Reconciliation
ARLPI	Acholi Religious Leaders Peace Initiative
ASP	Assembly of States Parties
AU	African Union
CAR	Central African Republic
CDVR	Commission Dialogue, Vérité, et Reconciliation
CEI	Commission Électorale Indépendante de Côte d'Ivoire
CIPEV	Commission of Inquiry into the Post-Election Violence
CNDD-FDD	Conseil National pour la Défense de la Démocratie – Forces pour la Défense de la Démocratie
CONARIV	Commission Nationale pour la Réconciliation et l'Indemnisation des Victimes
DRC	Democratic Republic of Congo
EACJ	East African Court of Justice
ECCC	Extraordinary Chambers in the Courts of Cambodia
ECHR	European Convention on Human Rights
ECOWAS	Economic Community of West African States
FIDH	Fédération Internationale des Ligues des Droits de l'Homme
FPI	Front Populaire Ivoirien
HRW	Human Rights Watch
HSMF	Holy Spirit Mobile Forces
ICC	International Criminal Court
ICD	International Crimes Division (Uganda)
ICJ	International Court of Justice
ICTR	International Criminal Tribunal for Rwanda
ICTY	International Criminal Tribunal for the former Yugoslavia
IDP	internally displaced persons

IEC	Independent Electoral Commission
IR	international relations
LRA	Lord's Resistance Army
MLC	Mouvement de Libération du Congo
NATO	North Atlantic Treaty Organization
NGO	Nongovernmental organization
NRA	National Resistance Army
ODM	Orange Democratic Movement
OHCHR	Office of the High Commissioner for Human Rights Commission
OTP	Office of the Prosecutor
PDCI	Parti Démocratique de la Côte d'Ivoire
PNU	Party of National Unity
RDR	Rassemblement des Républicains
RLP	Refugee Law Project
SCSL	Special Court for Sierra Leone
SPLA	Sudan People's Liberation Army
TNC	Transitional National Council
UN	United Nations
UNESCO	United Nations Educational, Scientific and Cultural Organization
UNLA	Uganda National Liberation Army
UNSC	United Nations Security Council
UPDF	Uganda People's Defence Force
UPDLA	Uganda People's Democratic Liberation Army
WWII	World War II

1

Regimes of International Criminal Justice

INTRODUCTION

On 16 May 2014, the prosecutor of the International Criminal Court (ICC) requested an adjournment until the end of June in the trial of William Ruto and Joshua Arap Sang. Ruto is the deputy president of the Republic of Kenya. Alongside former journalist Sang, he was standing trial before the ICC for charges of crimes against humanity in the Kenyan post-electoral violence of 2007–2008. In a separate case, but stemming from the same context of political violence, the sitting president of Kenya, Uhuru Kenyatta, was also charged with the same crimes and his case was still at the pretrial phase at the ICC. The Office of the Prosecutor (OTP) had informed the judges of its intention to withdraw its own witness, code named P-025. Anton Steynberg, the lead trial lawyer for the OTP, wrote that Witness P-025 "was unable to accurately recall or give a coherent and consistent account of critical parts of the evidence the prosecution had intended to lead." In granting the requested adjournment, Presiding Judge Chile Eboe-Osuji issued a strong warning to the OTP: "The Chamber expresses very serious concern and dissatisfaction that we only had two days of testimony this session, a session that was scheduled to last four weeks, hearing witnesses," the judge said. "All available means must be employed by the prosecution to ensure this is not repeated." Judge Eboe-Osuji, visibly disappointed and annoyed, told the prosecutor that the chamber expected "to have witnesses lined up for testimonies" and the prosecutor to have "their ducks in a row" when the trial reconvenes.[1]

This episode encapsulates many of the issues and debates that animate the current state of international criminal justice, as embodied by the practice of

---

[1] The author was present at this audience while doing fieldwork research at the ICC in The Hague, in May and June 2014.

the ICC. The first permanent international criminal court was prosecuting both a sitting president of an African state and his deputy for crimes against humanity.[2] The preamble of the Rome Statute states the determination of the Court "to put an end to impunity for the perpetrators of [atrocity] crimes and thus to contribute to the prevention of such crimes." Yet this goal faces the challenges of pursuing justice for individual criminal accountability in a world where states remain the main actors. The daunting task of the prosecutor to bring witnesses to The Hague to testify against their own government officials is but one of the issues that the ICC faces with the lack of compliance that borders on obstruction from state parties to the ICC – when the investigation and prosecution target state agents. Then again, the ICC is a treaty-based court to which states become willing members by ratifying the Rome Statute, its founding document, which raises the question: What do states have to gain by joining such institution?

This book explores the following question: How do states respond to the widening adoption of human rights norms, accountability for atrocity crimes, and transnational regimes of criminal justice? In other words, what mechanisms and strategies do states develop in reaction to and within regimes of transnational criminal justice? And to what extent are weaker states in the international system able to use the ICC as leverage in the pursuit of their political and security interests? Consequently, what lessons can be drawn from such mechanisms in terms of the primacy of state's interests? This study attempts to answer these questions by focusing on four main issues that stem from the functioning of the ICC and its relationship with states: self-referrals, complementarity, compliance, and domestic politics.

How do states respond to the increasing transnational character of criminal justice and the diffusion of human rights norms and regimes that uphold individual criminal accountability following the perpetration of mass atrocities? Whereas it is often argued that such transnational regimes may erode state sovereignty, this study explores the ways in which states – especially those presumed to be weaker in the international system – use the ICC as leverage in their domestic conflicts and to empower themselves in the pursuit of their political and security interests. I postulate a dynamic process through which states and international courts are in a constant struggle over power and influence, within those international legal regimes, using a theoretical framework that explicates the patterns of behaviors that states adopt when engaging with the ICC.

---

[2] Former heads of states have been prosecuted by international courts in the past, but none of them was prosecuted while in office. In addition, those courts were ad hoc tribunals.

THE ICC AND REGIMES OF INTERNATIONAL CRIMINAL JUSTICE

The international community faced many dilemmas at the Rome Conference in 1998 while drafting the statute that created the ICC.[3] How does one balance state sovereignty with the powers vested in an international prosecutor to instigate investigations and prosecution of crimes that fall under the ICC jurisdiction? The Rome Statute was ultimately a work of compromise, widely adopted by the states, albeit with the opposition of some of the most powerful ones.[4] The ICC has jurisdiction over four types of crimes – genocide, war crimes, crimes against humanity, and crimes of aggression – which can be triggered by a state referral, a UN Security Council (UNSC) referral, or the prosecutor using her *proprio motu* powers.

The complementarity principle governs the general rule of the ICC's intervention in situations under its material, territorial, and temporal jurisdiction. It gives primacy to the state in which the crimes have been committed to investigate and prosecute them. In theory, this means that the ICC intervenes only when the state is *unwilling* or *unable* to fulfill its duty to investigate and prosecute. However, the reality of the ICC investigations and prosecutions suggest that both the ICC prosecutor and the states have manipulated the basic reading of the complementarity principle. As the discussion of the ICC cases will show, the unwillingness or inability of the state to investigate and prosecute has not always been taken into consideration either by states or by the ICC OTP.[5]

The use of the self-referral trigger mechanism raises the issue about whether African states that have referred situations in their territory to the ICC are outsourcing justice; in other words, these states forego their right and duty to investigate and prosecute crimes committed in their territory for the convenience of handing the task to an international court. Obviously, there may be many reasons guiding such actions, and certainly, such reasons may differ from one case to another. This warrants a closer inquiry to unveil the reasons that may guide such self-referrals by studying the process that led to the first case of self-referral, that of Uganda, and that of Côte d'Ivoire. This study also investigates in depth the ways in which Kenya and Libya have engaged with the ICC's intervention in the aftermath of the 2007–2008 postelection violence and the 2011 conflict, respectively.

---

[3] See the Rome Statute of the International Criminal Court, www.icc-cpi.int/nr/rdonlyres/ea9aeff7-5752-4f84-be94-0a655eb30e16/0/rome_statute_english.pdf.

[4] Many states, including the United States, Russia, China, India, and Turkey, are not parties to the ICC.

[5] For example, Akhavan (2010, 110) writes that Uganda, whose "judiciary is among the best in Africa" had a justice system and courts that were fully functional when its government referred the case to the ICC. Yet the OTP still proceeded with opening an investigation.

TABLE 1.1. *ICC situations under investigation as of December 2019*

ICC situations	Trigger mechanism	Situation referred to the ICC	Opening date of ICC investigations
Uganda	Self-referral	January 2004	July 2004
Democratic Republic of Congo (DRC)	Self-referral	April 2004	June 2004
Central African Republic (CAR) I	Self-referral	December 2004	May 2007
Côte d'Ivoire	Self-referral/*proprio motu*	April 2003	October 2011
Darfur	UNSC referral	March 2005	June 2005
Kenya	*Proprio motu*		March 2010
Libya	UNSC referral	February 2011	March 2011
Mali	Self-referral	July 2012	January 2013
CAR II	Self-referral	May 2014	September 2014
Georgia	*Proprio motu*		January 2016
Burundi	*Proprio motu*		October 2017
Bangladesh/ Myanmar	*Proprio motu*		November 2019

THE ICC AND AFRICAN STATES

Since the entry into force of the Rome Statute on 1 July 2002, all the situations currently under investigation at the ICC are located on the African continent and concern African individuals, except for the situations in Georgia and Bangladesh/Myanmar.[6] This has largely animated the debate about the ICC and its apparent focus on African states. Whereas Henry Kissinger (2001) portrays the ICC and universal jurisdiction as "pitfalls," it is also clear that the ICC does nothing more than what any state could do by itself under current international law (Bassiouni 2001). To a large extent, the ICC is still constrained and depends on its state parties for funding, prosecution, and enforcement;

---

[6] It is important to note that, as of December 2019, however, there are nine situations that are under preliminary examination: Afghanistan, Colombia, Guinea, Iraq/United Kingdom, Nigeria, Palestine, The Philippines, Ukraine, and Venezuela. Upon conclusion of the preliminary examination phase, the prosecutor considers jurisdiction, admissibility (complementarity and gravity), and interests of justice in deciding to proceed or not with an investigation or requesting an authorization from the Pre-Trial Chamber in the case of a *proprio motu* trigger mechanism. For a current list of ICC situations under investigation or preliminary examination, see www.icc-cpi.int/pages/pe.aspx.

therefore, power politics are a fundamental component of the international criminal justice regime (Bosco 2014). African states were especially eager for the establishment of a permanent international court. In fact, forty-seven out of the fifty-four African states took part in the 1998 Rome Conference during which the ICC was created (Manirakiza 2009). As Moghalu (2006) explains, Africa's early support for the ICC is related to the fact that some of the weakest states in the international system are located on the continent. Soon after the ICC started its first investigations that targeted state officials in Africa, however, the working relationship between the ICC and many African states became strained. The main criticism regarding the ICC is that the Court is biased and unfairly targeting Africans because of its quasi-exclusive focus on the African continent. However, a counterargument to that charge may be that Africa's judicial systems are weak, which would explain the ICC's involvement in fighting against impunity for atrocity crimes on the continent. In any case, African states and the ICC are involved in a deeply complicated, contentious, and entangled relationship around international justice (Anghie 2005; Clarke 2009, 2015; Grovogui 2013; Ba 2017). This section provides a brief sketch of the main criticisms and counterarguments regarding the ICC's involvement in African situations.

The ICC as a Biased Court

Many critics argue that the ICC is biased and question its impartiality. For example, Mamdani (2009) has addressed the consequences of the implication of the ICC in the conflict in Darfur, pointing out the role that great powers politics play in ICC interventions. Schabas (2013, 545) argues that the ICC "has failed to live up to its expectations" due in part to its deference to the Security Council and "its inability or reluctance to take on hard cases that threaten powerful states." Similarly, Goldsmith (2003) contends that the ICC, as designed, is a self-defeating institution that will be incapable of punishing serious human rights violators, whereas Clarke (2009) explains that the current spectacle that the ICC enacts is part of a long history of "fictions of justice" embedded in the fusion of political and moral economies of neoliberal regimes.

The ICC therefore faces a legitimacy gap that can only be filled when the Court creates the impression that core crimes under its jurisdiction will be prosecuted "regardless of whom commits them, be they citizens of impoverished failed states or great powers" (Struett 2008, 165). Yet the ICC is inherently a political institution that makes the distinction between friends and enemies of the international community (Nouwen and Werner 2011). Thus, the Court becomes a weapon used in political struggles wherein warring parties and political adversaries brand each other. Mamdani (2009) has also argued that ICC's involvement in African conflicts has made their peaceful resolution more elusive.[7] Mamdani (2009, 284) concludes, "The ICC is rapidly turning into a Western court to try African crimes against humanity. Even then, its approach is selective: it targets governments that are adversaries of the United States and ignores U.S. allies…"

As expected, critics of the ICC also abound among African political elites (Ba 2017). For example, Rwandan president Paul Kagame, calling the ICC a "fraudulent institution" (cited in Lamony 2014), explained that "Rwanda cannot be party to ICC for one simple reason … with ICC all the injustices of the past including colonialism, imperialism, keep coming back in different forms. They control you. As long as you are poor, weak, there is always some rope to hang you." Jean Ping, then president of the African Union Commission, has said that "the international justice system seems to fight impunity only in Africa, as if there was nothing happening also in Iraq, Gaza, Colombia, or the Caucasus" (cited in Manirakiza 2009, 32).

The African Union (AU) has adopted a defiant stance toward the ICC and has consistently appealed to its members not to enforce ICC rulings. For example, after the Court issued a warrant for the arrest of President Bashir of Sudan in 2009, the AU justified its decision not to cooperate with the ICC by what it called the "publicity-seeking approach of the ICC Prosecutor" and had asked for deferment of Bashir's indictment (African Union 2009a).[8] Amid the indictment of both the president and deputy president of Kenya, the AU convened an extraordinary session in October 2013 to discuss "Africa's Relationship with the International Criminal Court (ICC)." Although the AU Assembly stopped short of calling for its members to withdraw *en masse* from the Court, it has nonetheless reiterated its "concern on the politicization and misuse of indictments against African leaders by ICC" and called on the UNSC to defer the Kenya and Sudan cases (AU 2009b). The UNSC did not grant the requested deferral, however, which led the AU to ask that any of its members that wish

---

7 Specifically, Mamdani (2009) contends that, had the ICC existed at the time, there would have been no peace and reconciliation in South Africa in 1990. The ICC would have also prevented the peace process in Mozambique that allowed the RENAMO, the armed opposition backed at the time by the apartheid regime of South Africa, to sign a peace agreement and benefit from amnesty. Referring to the situation in Darfur and the warrant for the arrest of President Bashir of Sudan, Mamdani (2009, 273) writes, "More than the innocence or guilt of the president of Sudan, it is the relationship between law and politics, including the politicization of the ICC, that poses a wider issue." On the ICC and the politics of peace and justice, see Vinjamuri (2015).

8 This refers to the ICC's first chief prosecutor, the Argentinian Luis Moreno-Ocampo.

to refer a case to the ICC to inform and seek advice from the AU (AU 2013). Therefore, it is clear that many African leaders and Pan-African organizations are unhappy with the ICC. Paradoxically, it is also noticeable that some African states chose to engage with the ICC by using the state referral trigger mechanism, which this study argues is used as a tool for the advancement of states' political and security interests.

Africa's Weak Judicial Systems

Others cite the atrocities committed in many African states and the weakness of local judicial systems as explanatory factors for the ICC's focus on Africa. It is important to note that the focus on the African continent is a discussion mostly about the OTP. The OTP is in fact the driving force behind the selection of situations and cases and conducts the investigations and prosecutions. Therefore, the OTP's work is the most noticeable and publicly visible feature of the Court. The prosecutor's discretionary power, as James Goldston (2010, 387) argues, is "grounded in law and evidence, but, of necessity, taking into account broader considerations of strategy and policy, even while refraining from 'politics.'" This at least has been the official response from the OTP to the criticism that its policy is infused with political calculations. Those in favor of the Court's interventions in Africa often stress the fact that the victims of these atrocity crimes are Africans. Desmond Tutu (2013) has argued:

> Those leaders seeking to skirt the court are effectively looking for a license to kill, maim and oppress their own people without consequence. They believe the interests of the people should not stand in the way of their ambitions of wealth and power; that being held to account by the I.C.C. interferes with their ability to achieve these ambitions; and that those who get in their way—the victims: their own people—should remain faceless and voiceless. (Tutu 2013)

Mutua (2016, 49) makes a similar argument, explaining that "[r]epressive African leaders grouped in the AU – a club of dictators – have no moral standing to attack the ICC, an institution built through a participatory global consensus to combat impunity and bring justice which elites deny victims at home."

The criticisms and counterarguments matter greatly in the current debate about the relationships between the ICC and Africa, which revolves around issues of sovereignty versus international institutions and regimes and what some Africans view as a Western tool for their subjugation. However, I argue that these critiques do not take into consideration the fact that most of the ICC cases in African states were initiated by the states themselves, when their respective governments approached the Court to self-refer cases to the ICC prosecutor. This illustrates the fact that the ICC was in any case bound to be a political tool at the hand of states – not only great powers, but also African states – in their attempt to settle scores. The paradox then is that the ICC was created to deliver justice by pursuing individual criminal accountability in a world made of states, thus making the OTP vulnerable to manipulation and influence from both powerful and less powerful states in the international system. The focus on the latter group is one of the main contributions that this book makes to the study of international criminal justice and international relations.

WHY AND HOW DO WEAKER STATES USE
INTERNATIONAL COURTS STRATEGICALLY?

David Bosco (2014) examines the work of the ICC in light of great power politics, focusing on the relationship between the Court and major powers. He argues that both the Court and major powers have given some ground and learned to accommodate each other, avoiding a direct clash between power and international justice. On the other hand, there also needs to be more research that systematically examines the relationship between the ICC and states that are not major powers in the international system, especially those states that have engaged with the Court in the past two decades. Some scholars have examined case studies between the ICC and some of those states along the lines of some of the themes that this study focuses on (Nouwen 2014; Kersten 2016b; Clark 2018).[9] This book goes beyond those examinations by developing a theoretical framework that explicates the range of behaviors seen or to be expected between the Court and states that engage with it. This work therefore does not just focus on the ICC and Africa but also aims to elucidate the range of possible trajectories in the engagement between the Court and states that are presumed weaker in the international system.

Many states have engaged with ad hoc and hybrid international courts; however, with limited material, territorial, and temporal jurisdiction, there is a gap in the literature regarding the ICC and its engagement with such states along the four themes that this book focuses on: (1) the strategic use

---

[9] Nouwen (2014) focuses on complementarity and the catalyzing effects of ICC intervention in Uganda and Sudan. Kersten (2016b) studies the effects of ICC intervention on peace, justice, and conflict processes, focusing on Libya and northern Uganda. Clark (2018) studies the multi-level impact of the ICC's intervention in Uganda and DRC.

of self-referrals, (2) complementarity between national and international justice systems, (3) limits of state compliance with international courts, and (4) the strategic use of international courts in domestic politics. Studying the relationship between the ICC and nonmajor powers along these themes is important because international courts derive their power and legitimacy not only from major powers but also through their engagement with less powerful states (and various civil society organizations and nongovernmental organizations [NGOs]) around the world. In this study, I focus on those states' patterns of behavior and the ways in which they shape, contest, and sometimes subvert norms of international justice that they use strategically in pursuit of their interests through their engagement with the ICC.

Although this project must engage with the ICC–African states relationship, the main focus is not an analysis of such a relationship, which has been studied at length in the literature (Allen 2006; Branch 2007; Clarke 2009; Hansen 2012; Nouwen 2014; Clark 2018). Rather, this book focuses on how states use the ICC for their own interests. It's important to emphasize, however, that I'm more interested in how states that appear weaker in the international system actively engaged with the Court through one or a combination of the three trigger mechanisms (state referral, UNSC referral, *proprio motu*). The aim is instead to analyze states' behavior when they engage with the ICC, and the analytical framework is drawn around the four major themes and the selection of cases: self-referrals (Uganda), compliance (Kenya), complementarity (Libya), domestic politics (Côte d'Ivoire).

Ultimately, this work provides a generalizable framework of states engaging with the ICC to advance their own political interests. There are important theoretical and policy implications to the findings of the book. It expands our understanding of how states that are weaker in the international system engage strategically with the ICC. This is important and timely given that many current situations under preliminary examination or investigation are located in such states, in Africa and beyond (Burundi, Mali, Gabon, Guinea, Philippines, Georgia, Ukraine, Afghanistan, Palestine, Bangladesh, Myanmar, Venezuela). Therefore, this project goes beyond the ICC-Africa debate. It posits a dynamic relationship between states and international courts that goes beyond the mere act of ratifying a treaty or joining a court. I argue that the Court's intervention (or call to intervene) in a situation leads to a behavior and the adoption of strategies that are adjusted to the political or security aims of the state. In other words, states devise strategies to initiate such engagement in the pursuit of their own political, domestic, and/or security interests. This is more important given that the focus here is on states that do not wield global power or influence. This study also covers all trigger mechanisms of ICC jurisdiction and brings together four major themes in the ICC's engagement with nonmajor powers in the system while theorizing how weaker states use the Court to advance their interests by various means and strategies.

I argue that the use of the self-referral mechanism to invite the ICC to investigate breaches of international law is based on states' political calculations of the costs and benefits associated with engaging with the Court. It appears that political elites in the countries that have used the self-referral mechanism have deferred to ICC jurisdiction to advance their own agendas by inviting the Court to remove or incapacitate their local adversaries – whether political opponents or rebel leaders. These states abandoned their responsibility to investigate and prosecute the alleged crimes committed in their territory and preferred handing the task to the ICC. At the superficial level, it may look like the states are deferring to an international court because the latter is better equipped to investigate and prosecute atrocity crimes. However, when one looks closely, the use of self-referrals stems actually from strategic calculations that aim at giving the state political and military leverage against its opponents, whom the state is having the ICC prosecute, as Uganda and all the other self-referral cases illustrate. Self-referrals tend to stem from governments facing a precarious situation that seek to assert legitimacy, whether in the wake of a postcoup transition or after highly contested electoral results.

Whereas the complementarity principle sought to make the ICC the court of last resort, the ICC has often been used as the court of first resort or even of only resort. Thus, self-referrals offer states the means to use the ICC as a "bad bank" (Jessberger and Geneuss 2012, 1089) by "exposing dangerous rebels internationally so as to dispose of them through the judicial process of the ICC" (Cassese 2006, 436). States that self-refer to the ICC "outsource" their obligation to investigate international crimes (Jessberger and Geneuss 2012, 1089). The Libyan situation also illustrates the challenges of the use of Article 17 of the Rome Statute, related to complementarity and primacy given to national courts, in lieu of the ICC. But the case of Libya also shows the strategic interpretation and use of the complementarity clause in ways that advance both the interests of the Libyan state and the ICC as an institution. Concerning nonparty states, if the ICC jurisdiction is triggered by a UNSC referral, as in the Libya and Sudan cases, the states develop mechanisms that challenge the ICC jurisdiction or withdraw cooperation that is necessary for successful investigations.

How do states react when their agents become targets of international legal prosecutions? In the Kenyan situation, where both the sitting president and deputy president have been indicted with crimes against humanity by the ICC, the state has developed mechanisms that make such prosecution difficult. International courts lack enforcement capacity and hence must rely on the compliance of the states that have agreed to the Court's jurisdiction and the cooperation of states in general, and this study shows that compliance and cooperation are dynamic tools that states wield depending on where their relationship with the Court stands at any given moment. Finally, the ICC involvement with domestic political conflicts opens new areas of inquiry for international relations scholars at the intersection of international criminal law and domestic politics. In the case of Côte d'Ivoire, where a new government has surrendered a former president to the ICC and where the ICC faces criticism of one-sided investigation, one sees how the ICC is also the stage for domestic political struggles.

To that end, this study sheds light on the intersection of state power and interests vis-à-vis international human rights norms and regimes of transnational criminal justice. The findings of this study contribute to the literature on international criminal justice and human rights norms diffusion, adoption, and/or perversion. This study also offers a critical reading of transnational legal processes that challenges the conception of an international criminal justice regime as an unmitigated good. When reading the international criminal justice regime through a critical lens, it is noticeable that the literature has addressed the ways in which powerful states use the system to their advantage. However, there is still a lack of understanding or acknowledgment of the ways in which weaker states use the regime for their own (political) interests.

THEORETICAL FRAMEWORK, RESEARCH DESIGN, AND METHODOLOGY

This book constructs an analytical account of nonmajor powers (or "weaker" states in the international system) engaging strategically with the ICC in ways that advance their own political and security interests – or at least those of their elites. The theoretical ambition of the book is grounded on an empirical analysis, and I use an abductive analytical framework to develop new theoretical insights. As Timmermans and Tavory (2012) show, induction does not logically lead to construction of novel theories. One may draw from theory of inference and meaning, however, using abduction rather than induction or deduction,[10] as a guiding principle for empirically based theory construction

---

[10] In summary, deductive reasoning begins with a rule and a prediction of what the observation would be. The researcher then proceeds through a case study to arrive at an observed result that either confirms the rule or falsifies it. By contrast, inductive reasoning makes generalizations from specific observations.

(Timmermans and Tavory 2012). Many researchers have recently pointed toward abduction for the ultimate goal of grounded theory and the construction of new theories (Haig 1995; Coffey and Atkinson 1996; Kelle 2007; Reichertz 2007; Timmermans and Tavory 2012). When using an abductive analytical process, the researcher seeks to find the "best" explanation that elucidates surprising facts or puzzles and thus leads to new theoretical insights. In sum, an abductive research process is therefore a qualitative data analysis aiming at generating novel theoretical insights derived from empirical findings in relation to or in contrast with extant theories. It allows the researcher to enter the field with a very broad theoretical base and, through "a dialectic of cultivated theoretical sensitivity," develop new concepts to account for empirical materials (Timmermans and Tavory 2012, 180).

This study uses an analytical framework with an interpretive epistemology, an approach that stresses "understanding of the social world through an examination of the interpretation of that world by its participants" (Bryman 2012, 380). This process uncovers meanings attached to actions through an analysis of discourse and arguments found in a number of selected cases. This method does not aim to uncover causal mechanisms leading to generalizations but rather to achieve a high level of explanatory power. The research design in this book is developed first through an extensive literature review on international criminal justice, international law, international relations, state behavior, comparative politics, and peace and conflict studies. The framework is then used to study the dynamic processes between the ICC and nonmajor states along the four main thematic areas: self-referral to the ICC, state compliance with the Rome Statute, complementarity between local and international justice systems, and domestic politics. The empirical data and insights gained from fieldwork research were then mapped into the framework, which in turn led to more refinement and research for more relevant data and insights. Finally, going beyond the four major case studies, insights from other states' engagement with the ICC are then examined to illustrate whether or not they conform to the patterns of behavior explicated initially in the framework.

SOURCES FOR EVIDENCE

This book draws on official court documents and filings, memoirs, and personal accounts and also on the extensive literature on the ICC, international criminal justice, international relations, and comparative politics. Primary sources include local newspapers from the states covered in the case studies. The book is also built upon interviews with ICC officials, government officials, local journalists, NGO workers, human rights activists, victims of political violence, and various legal experts in The Hague and countries in which the ICC has had investigations. I conducted about sixty semistructured interviews in total of four countries.

More precisely, I conducted in-depth semistructured interviews in The Hague, Kenya, Uganda, and Mali. In Kenya, I conducted fieldwork research in Nairobi and also in the Rift Valley towns of Nakuru, Eldoret, and Kisumu. These sites were at the epicenter of the 2007–2008 political violence. I also conducted interviews in Kampala and Gulu, which is the main city in Acholiland, where the Lord's Resistance Army (LRA) fought against the Ugandan government forces for over two decades. In Mali, interviews were conducted not only in Bamako but also in the northern cities of Timbuktu and Djenné. In all these cases, these interviews were conducted with ICC officials, lawyers, human rights activists, government officials, law experts, journalists, local citizens, researchers, and victims of political violence. These interviews were complemented by participant observation at the ICC. In The Hague, I observed the ICC in operation, watching various proceedings at different stages of the trials of Thomas Lubanga, Germaine Katanga, and Ruto/Sang. I also observed proceedings of the Libyan admissibility challenge at the ICC.

THE SELECTION OF CASE STUDIES

The research for this book rests on the examination of four main themes that highlight the behavior of states that have engaged with the ICC, leading to the selection of four cases that cover all three available trigger mechanisms of ICC jurisdiction and one "mixed" case. It is worth noting that the selection of the cases was not guided by a best-case scenario for the argument. It was instead based on making sure that the study covers all three available trigger mechanisms under ICC jurisdiction. Indeed, as stipulated in the Rome Statute, ICC jurisdiction is triggered through three mechanisms: state referral (wherein a state party refers a situation to the ICC), a UNSC referral, or the ICC prosecutor acting on her own volition (using her *proprio motu* powers).

Whereas some version of randomization is typically used for case selection in large-N research, random sampling would be inadequate for studies where the sample is small, such as this one. For a selection of case studies that encompass all trigger mechanisms of ICC jurisdiction, there is no guarantee that a few cases, chosen randomly, would provide insights on the research questions addressed by this study. Hence, as Gerring (2008, 645) argues, case selection for very small samples must employ "purposive (nonrandom) selection procedures." As such, this book's methodology uses the "typical case" technique, which by definition has a high degree of representativeness (Gerring, 2008, 648–650).

For self-referrals, the situations where the ICC opened an investigation are, in chronological order, Uganda (January 2004), CAR I (May 2004), DRC (June 2004), Mali (July 2012), and CAR II (May 2014) (See Table 1.1).[11] The choice of Uganda's self-referral as a main case study is justified by the fact that it was the first one submitted to the ICC.

Regarding UNSC referrals, there have been only two such cases to date: Darfur (Sudan) and Libya. Because this study is concerned with how states engage with the Court to advance their interests, the choice of Libya as the main case study is more pertinent. Unlike Sudan, Libya decided to engage with the Court through an admissibility challenge. Nonetheless, the Sudan referral is also discussed in terms of the ICC-UNSC relationship, alongside the failed attempt to refer Syria and North Korea to the ICC. The Sudan case is also discussed in the final chapter of the book.

To date, there has been five *proprio motu* cases that led to the ICC opening an investigation: Kenya (March 2010), Côte d'Ivoire (October 2011), Georgia (January 2016), Burundi (October 2017) and Bangladesh/Myanmar (November 2019). Here too, I follow the same logic, focusing on the Kenyan case because it was the first *proprio motu* investigation at the ICC.

Finally, there is one peculiar situation that I argue is a combination of two trigger mechanisms, Côte d'Ivoire, which explains the need to examine this situation closely as a case study. Côte d'Ivoire accepted ICC jurisdiction through an ad hoc declaration in 2003, akin to a self-referral (but for nonparty states). Then, the ICC prosecutor opened a preliminary examination that did not lead to an investigation. Using that 2003 ad hoc declaration, the ICC prosecutor opened a *proprio motu* investigation in October 2011 while Côte d'Ivoire was still not a state party to the Court.

The situations still under preliminary examination – but as yet have not led to the opening of full investigation – were not selected as case studies, although they will be factored in the analytical framework. Nine situations are currently under preliminary examination: Afghanistan, Colombia, Guinea, Iraq/United Kingdom, Nigeria, Palestine, Philippines, Ukraine, and Venezuela.[12]

---

[11] The state referrals that have not led to the opening of an investigation yet are excluded from this list. The Gabon situation is discussed in Chapter 7. It is also worth noting that Venezuela is currently under preliminary examination resulting from a referral by a group of state parties to the Rome Statute: Argentina, Canada, Colombia, Chile, Paraguay, and Peru. See www.icc-cpi.int/venezuela

[12] Preliminary investigation for the Gabon was recently closed with a decision not to proceed with an investigation. See Chapter 7.

OUTSOURCING JUSTICE: FROM STATE-PARTY
REFERRAL TO SELF-REFERRAL

Self-referrals to the ICC ushered in a "revolution" in global justice (Akhavan 2010). A debate about the legal underpinnings and political implications of self-referrals started shortly after Uganda referred a situation in its northern territory to the ICC in 2003. While some scholars questioned the admissibility of self-referrals and whether that conformed to the legal procedures of the Court, the ICC Appeals Chamber in the Katanga case ruled that self-referrals are legally acceptable.[13] But this legal ruling does not foreclose the political questions surrounding the fact that self-referrals offered states a convenient way to dispose of nonstate actors such as rebels, warlords, or even political adversaries (van der Wilt 2015).

During the negotiations that led to the adoption of the Rome Statute, however, no one seriously thought that states would self-refer to the ICC. As Arsanjani and Reisman (2005, 386) write, "no one – neither states that were initially skeptical about the viability of an ICC nor states that supported it – assumed that governments would want to invite the future court to investigate and prosecute crimes that had occurred on their territory." Instead, Article 14 of the Rome Statute about state referrals was thought as a referral mechanism initiated by an interested state about *another* state (Kress 2004; Akhavan 2010). However, states hardly serve as watchdogs for other states regarding human rights abuses (Akhavan 1995, 236–237). Therefore, during the drafting of the Rome Statute, state referral was thought to be the least likely trigger mechanism to lead to prosecution. As Schabas (2011a, 159) notes "It was frequently pointed out that States were notoriously reluctant to complain against other States on a bilateral basis, unless they had bilateral interests at stake. They would not, however, be likely to act as international altruists." Therefore, all instances of state referral to the ICC have been self-referrals, except for the recent Venezuela situation. This means that states used Article 14 of the Rome Statute not to refer other states but to refer *themselves* to the Court.

The state referral became the trigger mechanism for the first three cases before the Court: Uganda, DRC, and CAR. The Côte d'Ivoire's self-referral was a bit different because the state did not ratify the Rome Statute but accepted ICC

---

[13] See *Prosecutor v. Germain Katanga and Mathieu Ngudjolo Chui*, Judgment on the Appeal of Mr. Germain Katanga against the Oral Decision of Trial Chamber II of 12 June 2009 on the Admissibility of the Case, ICC-01/04-01/07-1497, Appeals Chamber, 25 September 2009. Former militia leader Katanga's defense team had argued that the Democratic Republic of Congo is able to prosecute him, and therefore his case before the ICC should be inadmissible.

jurisdiction in 2003 through an ad-hoc declaration under Article 12(3), "which in substance amounted to a self-referral" (Akhavan 2010, 106). Finally, Mali also self-referred to the ICC in 2013, and so did Gabon in 2016. The state referral mechanism did not operate as expected because these were not interstate referrals. However, the use of the term *self-referral* is also misleading. In fact, while referring their "situations" to the ICC, these states did not intend that the ICC investigation and prosecution be directed against their agents. In fact, all these states "sought to induce the Court to prosecute rebel groups operating within their own borders" (Schabas 2011a, 160) or to target political adversaries. For instance, in its referral letter, the government of Uganda mentioned specifically the "situation concerning the Lord's Resistance Army," which later prompted the OTP to inform the Ugandan authorities "that we must interpret the scope of the referral consistently with the principles of the Rome Statute, and hence we are analyzing crimes committed within the situation of northern Uganda by whomever committed them."[14] Self-referral provides states an avenue to gain immunity for their government officials while at the same time having the ICC prosecute their political adversaries or the rebel leaders operating in their territory. Finally, self-referrals allow unelected, interim, or illegitimate governments to assert their power. Ultimately, all the self-referral situations show a history of one-sided investigations and prosecutions from the ICC OTP. An in-depth analysis of the Uganda situation exemplifies these arguments.

In late 2003, the ICC prosecutor announced that Uganda, as an ICC member state, had referred a "situation" to him (ICC 2004d). After a preliminary examination, Prosecutor Ocampo announced on 28 June 2004 that there was "a reasonable basis to proceed with an investigation (ICC 2004c)." The warrants for the arrest of five LRA leaders were unsealed in October 2005, which led them to seek a peace settlement with the government of Uganda during negotiations that were held in Juba from 2006 to 2008. The discussion regarding the ICC involvement in Uganda has focused mostly on the motives of the Court and the Ugandan government, and its consequences on the stalemate of the peace negotiations and the protraction of the conflict.

Although the warrant for the arrest of the LRA leaders triggered the cessation of hostilities and the initiation of peace negotiations, it also prevented the completion of the peace accords because the LRA commanders insisted that the warrants for their arrest be annulled before they sign the Juba peace accords. Hence, President Museveni of Uganda, who had triggered the ICC intervention, asked Prosecutor Ocampo to withdraw the warrants and

---

[14] See Office of The Prosecutor, "Letter to the ICC President," ICC-02/04-1 06-07-2004 4/4, 17 June 2004, www.icc-cpi.int/CourtRecords/CR2007_02419.pdf.

promised immunity to the LRA commanders (Schabas 2011a, 42). This move by the Ugandan president clearly shows that self-referral to the ICC was destined to further his own interests, mainly to guarantee his political survival. As stated earlier, the focus of this argument is on state leaders and elites and how they use the international criminal justice regime to further their own interests, and how they switch their strategy when the demands for their political interests warrants it. The case in Uganda is a potent illustration of the selective investigations and prosecution with which the ICC OTP operates. In fact, despite the allegations of atrocities committed by the Ugandan armed forces, the ICC prosecutor investigated only the LRA commanders.

FAILURE OF THE COMPLEMENTARITY PRINCIPLE

Article 17 of the Rome Statute stipulates that, under the principle of complementarity, a case is admissible before the Court only when the state responsible for prosecution can be shown to be unwilling or unable to investigate and prosecute it. In the early years of the Court's operation, Prosecutor Ocampo stated, "As a general rule, the policy of the OTP will be to undertake investigations only when there is a clear case of failure to act by the State or States concerned" (ICC OTP 2003a, 2003b, 2). The complementarity principle was thus intended to recognize the primary responsibility of states to exercise criminal jurisdiction, which also means that states can introduce an admissibility challenge to the ICC to prove their willingness and ability to investigate and prosecute crimes that would otherwise fall under the jurisdiction of the Court (Stahn 2015a).

When the UNSC issued a resolution that referred the situation in Libya to the ICC, the OTP reacted with lightning speed, opening an investigation only a couple of days after the referral, on 2 March 2011, which made the preliminary examination the fastest one in the history of the Court (Stahn 2012, 329).[15] Soon after the referral, on 16 May 2011, Ocampo requested that arrest warrants be issued against the "Tripoli Three": Muammar Gaddafi, Saif Al Islam Gaddafi, and Abdullah Al-Senussi.[16] After the fall of the Gaddafi regime, the new government of Libya – the Transitional National Council

---

[15] By comparison, the preliminary examination in Darfur, the other UNSC referral, lasted roughly two months. The preliminary examination in the Afghanistan situation lasted more than a decade.

[16] Al Senussi was head of Libyan intelligence services under the Gaddafi administration. The ICC later issued warrants for the arrest of Al-Tuhamy Mohamed Khaled (unsealed on 24 April 2017) and of Mahmoud Mustafa Busayf Al-Werfali on 15 August 2017. Both defendants remain at large.

(TNC) – introduced an admissibility challenge before the ICC, based on Article 17 of the Rome Statute on complementarity. Libya essentially argued that it was willing and able to prosecute Saif Gaddafi and Al-Senussi.[17] After long and drawn-out proceedings between Libya and the ICC, the Court had decided that Gaddafi must be tried in The Hague, but Al-Senussi may be tried in Libya. The Libyan cases illustrate ICC inconsistency in matters of complementarity.

ICC investigations that are triggered by a UNSC resolution show a collusion between the political and the legal in international relations. Does the relationship between the UNSC and the ICC allow for a dissociation between the two spheres? For instance, the former prosecutor of the International Criminal Tribunal for the Former Yugoslavia (ICTY) Louise Arbour has called for a greater separation between the ICC and the UNSC, noting that "international criminal justice cannot be sheltered from political considerations when [it is] administered by the quintessential political body" (cited in Stahn 2012, 327). The situations in Sudan and Libya are the only two ICC cases so far that were triggered by a UNSC resolution. Although both the situations in Sudan and Libya stem from the same trigger mechanism, they evolved in different directions and have resulted in two different outcomes. In the case of Sudan, the main suspects are President al-Bashir and other high-ranking officials; in Libya, the ICC prosecutor initially targeted three individuals who are no longer in power.

THE LIMITS OF STATE COMPLIANCE

The Preamble of the Rome Statute states that the States Parties "[affirm] that the most serious crimes of concern to the international community as a whole must not go unpunished … [and they are determined] to put an end to impunity for the perpetrators of these crimes and thus to contribute to the prevention of such crimes." To accomplish that mission, the Court must rely on the compliance and cooperation of states parties to the Rome Statute at every step, from the initial investigation to arresting the perpetrators, to conducting the trials, and to housing the prisoners. However, compliance and cooperation of states with the ICC are not a given. In fact, by ratifying the Rome Statute, states delegate their power and privileges to an international institution whose main purpose is to limit the sovereignty of said states. This delegation of power and privileges to an international court poses challenges to a state when its officials are sought after by the Court.

[17] The case against Muammar Gaddafi had become moot following his death.

Going beyond the literature on delegation of powers, this study focuses on the processes that sustain or challenge such delegation of power and contends that delegation of power is a dynamic process that does not stop at the door of treaty ratification. What happens next in the dynamic relationship between the principal (the state) and the agent (the Court)? How do the ICC and the state manage such expectations and rules amid changing conditions in international politics? How does a state that vested powers in the international court and later becomes target of investigations manage such a relationship?

Using the example of the Kenya cases before the ICC, I explore the instances that lead a state to renege on its commitment to cooperate with an international court and to comply with its requests. For the ICC to be operational, it must rely on the willingness of states to comply with the Rome Statute and to assist the Court in its investigation and prosecution. Ultimately, I contend that the need for and limits to state cooperation may be one of the most enduring challenges to the delivery of international criminal justice.

In the Kenyan situation, the ICC prosecutor used his *proprio motu* powers, which means opening an investigation on his own volition, without a state or UNSC referral. Prosecutor Ocampo acted on his own initiative to start a preliminary examination related to the 2007 postelection violence in Kenya. Upon presenting the preliminary findings to the Pre-Trial Chamber, the latter gave the prosecutor a motion to proceed, which allows the opening of a full investigation. As a state party to the Rome Statute, Kenya is obligated to cooperate with the Court. Yet Uhuru Kenyatta and William Ruto, president and deputy president of Kenya, respectively, were the main suspects, accused of crimes against humanity. Because their prosecution started prior to their election, Kenyatta and Ruto had used their indictment as a political platform and joined forces to run on the same presidential ticket. Kenyatta's trial was set to begin in October 2014, but the case against him was later dismissed following the prosecutor's inability to gather enough evidence. Ruto's trial started in September 2013 and lasted until April 2016, when the case was terminated.

The Kenyan state has developed mechanisms to challenge the indictment of its president and deputy president by seeking support from the AU, which sought a UNSC deferral and proposed an amendment to the Rome Statute that would grant immunity to sitting heads of state. While pretending to cooperate and comply with the ICC as a state party to the Rome Statute, Kenya has used extensive measures to obstruct the work of the ICC prosecutor and basically to torpedo the cases.

THE COURT IS THE POLITICAL ARENA

The situation in Côte d'Ivoire involves the prosecution of three individuals: former president Laurent Gbagbo; his wife, Simone Gbagbo; and Charles Blé Goudé, a former official in Gbagbo's administration. Côte d'Ivoire held a presidential election in November 2010, the aftermath of which triggered six months of unrest and human rights abuses. Gbagbo had refused to leave office despite having lost the election to his opponent, Alassane Ouattara. In the violence that followed the struggle for power, at least 3,000 people were killed by forces on both sides, along political, ethnic, and religious lines (Human Rights Watch 2013).

Although the situation in Côte d'Ivoire is officially a *proprio motu* case, Côte d'Ivoire was not a member at the time it acceded to ICC jurisdiction. One may then ask, What leads a state that did not join the ICC to extend nonetheless an invitation to the ICC prosecutor to open an investigation in relation to its political crisis? The Ivoirian state first recognized the jurisdiction of the ICC in a letter signed by then-minister of foreign affairs Bamba Mamadou on 18 April 2003, following the first Ivoirian civil war. That ad hoc declaration was dormant, however, because the ICC prosecutor did not take steps to conduct an investigation. After the 2010 elections and the conflict that ensued, president-elect Ouattara sent a second letter to the ICC on 14 December 2010 in which he "confirms the declaration of 18 [April] 2003" and engages Côte d'Ivoire "to fully cooperate and without delay with the ICC, especially regarding all the crimes and abuses perpetrated since [March] 2004."[18]

Despite this invitation letter that Ouattara sent to the ICC in 2010, Côte d'Ivoire did not ratify the Rome Statute until 15 December 2013, even though the Ouattara administration had arrested Gbagbo and handed him over to the ICC in November 2011. Therefore, the situation in Côte d'Ivoire raises many important questions. For example, what leads a nonparty state to the Rome Statute to accept ICC jurisdiction through an ad hoc declaration? Why did the ICC prosecutor not open the investigation in 2003? What led the Ouattara administration to issue a second invitation letter to the ICC prosecutor in 2010? Why did the Ivoirian state hand over Gbagbo and Blé Goudé to the ICC but refuse to surrender Simone Gbagbo? Why did the ICC prosecution in Côte d'Ivoire target only Gbagbo loyalists despite the fact that, as Human Rights Watch (2013) reports, both pro-Gbagbo and pro-Ouattara forces are implicated in "war crimes and likely crimes against humanity"? The answers

---

[18] See the referral letter here: www.icc-cpi.int/NR/rdonlyres/498E8FEB-7A72-4005-A209-C14BA374804F/0/ReconCPI.pdf.

to these questions lie in the fact that the Ivoirian state had transposed its domestic political crisis to the ICC, ultimately using the Court as a bad bank to handle its two most virulent political adversaries.

BOOK OUTLINE BY CHAPTER

As an introduction to the book, Chapter 1 has laid out the four major themes around the intersection of state power and international criminal justice that this book explores: the strategic use of self-referrals to the ICC, complementarity between national and international justice systems, the limits of state compliance with international courts, and the use of international courts in domestic political conflicts. Each of these major themes revolves around the ICC and its relationship with states. The four empirical cases – Uganda, Libya, Côte d'Ivoire, and Kenya – built around these major themes cover all available trigger mechanisms of ICC jurisdiction.

Chapter 2 discusses my theoretical argument in depth. As a discipline, international relations, especially from the realist perspectives, has long viewed international law and regimes of international justice as epiphenomenal. As a practice, law is often presumed to be meaningful only when backed by enforcement that is carried out by a legitimate authority. Following this logic, international law cannot meaningfully exist in a world where there is no world state. But what explains the dramatic rise of international courts not only in terms of their numbers but also their relevance and the widening of their jurisdiction and competency? In other words, why would states, whether democratic or not, favor establishing or joining international regimes whose main purpose is to constrain their domestic sovereignty? One must study, against a utilitarian frame, a state's behavior in shaping, reshaping, and sometimes subverting norms of international justice that they use strategically in pursuit of their interests.

Chapter 3 explores the ways in which states subvert international legal institutions and norms in pursuit of their own security and political interests. Specifically, Chapter 3 argues that the use of self-referrals to the ICC stems from political calculations that allow political leaders to advance their own domestic and international agendas at the expense of furthering the goals of the international justice regime. However, stating that actors, whether politicians, ICC officials, community leaders, or NGOs, use self-referrals, cooperation (or the lack thereof), or the complementarity principle selectively with the ICC for the advancement of their political goals is self-evident. As Nouwen (2014, xvi) notes, it is obvious that "African states have engaged in political calculations to avoid the costs and maximize the benefits of cooperation with the

ICC. These governments have sought – and often succeeded – in deflecting or coopting the ICC as an instrument for dealing with local adversaries…" But the topics that we know less about – and to which Chapter 3 of this book contributes – is how states do so, and what are the effects of such calculations on the norms of international criminal justice? Hence, Chapter 3 is a story of political calculations, political power and security interests, and the agency of (African) states in creating and shaping the delivery of international justice (Clark 2011).

Chapter 4 points to the inherently political character of international justice and shows the working paradox between the UNSC and the ICC. The UNSC is the institution that allows the ICC to gain jurisdiction over states that have not ratified the Rome Statute, and Chapter 4 also asks whether international treaties such as the Rome Statute apply to states who are not signatories. Finally, the example of Libya is studied in detail to highlight the ways in which a non-ICC member chose to engage the Court by introducing an admissibility challenge and how the Court responded to the challenge to show the inconsistency of its ruling, which also brings back the political dimension of international justice.

Chapter 5 highlights how the need for compliance and cooperation constrains the ability of the ICC to accomplish its mission. By ratifying the Rome Statute, states delegate their power and privileges to an international institution whose main purpose is to limit the sovereignty of said states; this raises questions about why states choose to delegate those powers. Chapter 5 empirically tests the actions of states that, after having willingly delegated some of their powers and privileges to the ICC, have its officials or nationals become the target of an investigation. Chapter 5 uses the Kenyan example to study whether the actions of state parties to the Rome Statute are consistent with their avowed compliance and cooperation with the ICC, and it outlines the limits of state cooperation in the area of international criminal justice.

Chapter 6 shows how the ICC becomes a transposed arena where domestic politics are meted out and enmeshed with the rule of law and legal procedures. The situation in Côte d'Ivoire is a prime example of the ICC becoming involved in a highly politically charged crisis that was set off by contested electoral results in December 2010. The Ouattara administration outsourced justice to the ICC for the purpose of handling adversaries, following the lead of other states who had previously used the self-referral mechanism.

Chapter 7 concludes this study and this book. A strategic use of international courts by weaker states in the system becomes a mechanism through which African states have taken advantage of the ICC. Such strategic use of the international justice system does not necessarily violate international law, but it does feature new readings of the law and introduces new norms of behavior that deviate from the spirit of the law in the first place. That states use international institutions at their disposal to advance their interests is not in itself noteworthy; the fact that weaker states in the international system are able to use the international justice system for such ends is what I argue to be worthy of studying. This instrumental use of norms of international justice shows that the argument of "justice cascade" (Sikkink 2011) may not be as convincing as previously thought. The supposedly widespread adoption of norms of individual criminal accountability and prosecutions in the wake of massive violations of human rights may actually just be symptomatic of an *instrumental* adoption. Chapter 7 also analyzes other ICC situations (DRC, CAR, Mali, Sudan, Burundi, and the Philippines) and South Africa's and Gambia's attempts to withdraw from the Court to highlight the ways in which these cases also support the arguments developed in this book's analytical framework.

CONCLUSION

Since the entry into force of the Rome Statute in 2002, the ICC has, without doubt, spearheaded a new era in the global governance of atrocity crimes and criminal justice. As a relatively new institution, the ICC departed from former UN ad hoc tribunals, which were created in the aftermath of conflicts and with both limited temporal and territorial jurisdiction. Those tribunals also were often criticized as "victor's justice" (De Vos, Kendall, and Stahn 2015). To that extent, the current global phase of justice is characterized by an increasing "judicialization" wherein judgment is now more centralized by an international regime personified by the ICC as its main actor. Around the world, in places as varied as Afghanistan, Colombia, Georgia, and Ukraine, the work of the ICC has been "vernacularized" to varying degrees, circulating among alternate and often competing conceptions of what qualifies as an appropriate response to mass atrocities (Mégret 2015).

The growing "tribunalization of violence" (Clarke 2009, 45) reverberates in both domestic and global political arenas. And while trying to include "the local" in its approaches, the ICC becomes also "vulnerable to some of the dilemmas that other liberal and emancipatory projects face in their engagement with 'the local', such as paternalistic and missionary features, perpetuation of structural inequalities or distorting effects of de-localisation"

(Stahn 2015b, 50). Nevertheless, as Stahn argues, the ICC is different from former hegemonic projects of the nineteenth and twentieth century in the sense that it is not dependent on a few powerful Western states but results rather from the success of the power of small states in international law and the push from civil society organizations. This book highlights the role of those "small states" as main actors in international justice regimes, and especially their ability to use the institutions effectively to achieve their goals.

2

States of Justice

International relations as a discipline – especially from the realist perspective – has long viewed international law as epiphenomenal. With the presumption that law is meaningful in practice only when backed by enforcement and coercion, it follows that an absence of an enforcer at the international level makes international regimes of justice epiphenomenal. Hence, following this logic, international law cannot meaningfully exist in a world where there is no world-state. However, as Alter (2014, 68) asserts, at the end of the Cold War, there were only six permanent international courts, which had collectively issued 373 binding judgments between 1945 and 1989. Thus, it is puzzling to note that, by the year 2014, there were at least twenty-four permanent international courts, which had issued some 37,000 binding legal documents (Alter 2014, 68). What explains the dramatic rise of international courts, not only in terms of their numbers but also in terms of their relevance, and the widening of their jurisdiction and competency? This chapter first describes the rise of international legalism and proceeds to explore the tensions between international legal regimes and state sovereignty. It then problematizes states' interests and the ways in which they shape, reshape, or subvert international legal institutions and norms, which presents a challenge to the "justice cascade" literature. And finally, the chapter provides a novel theoretical framework that systematically analyzes the relationship between the International Criminal Court (ICC) and the states that are not major powers in the international system and highlights the ways in which these states pursue their interests within the regimes of international justice.

THE RISE OF INTERNATIONAL LEGALISM

Unlike the previous generation of international courts that functioned mostly as dispute settlement mechanisms,[1] the new wave of post-Cold War international courts has jurisdiction over economic, social, and cultural rights, and crimes associated with mass violence. The rapid growth of international courts signifies the increased relevance of international law and legalism, in a context where courts and judges shape major political events. Long gone are the days when scholars' interests in international courts focused mostly on the ICJ, which functions largely as an arbitration process between two willing parties. International relations and international law scholars are now confronted with an ever-increasing complexity and entrenchment between law and international politics within the post-Cold War supranational judicial institutions. These international courts have altered domestic and international politics in profound ways.

For instance, as Alter (2014, 3) writes,

> since the end of the Cold War, the rulings of international judges have led Latin American governments to secure indigenous peoples' land rights; the United States Congress to eliminate a tax benefit for American corporations; Germany to grant women a wider role in the military; Niger to compensate a former slave for her entrapment in Niger's family law justice system.

International courts have indeed become agents of policy change, whose judgments influence states and other actors beyond the parties to a dispute (Helfer and Voeten 2014). At the domestic policy level, judgments from international human rights courts, such as the European Court of Human Rights, often gain strong local support and attract democratic institutions that are dedicated to implement them at home (Hillebrecht 2012, 2014). Knowing that the adjudication of such matters falls exclusively within the domestic affairs of states, one may ask how international courts are able to make states abide by their rulings in the absence of an enforcing authority. In other words, how do we get to a place where "governments bend over backward not to be seen as violating the law" (Alter 2014, xvi)? And why does it matter to states to be viewed as abiding by the rule of law and supporters of international legal regimes?

INTERNATIONAL LEGAL REGIMES AND STATE SOVEREIGNTY

Krasner (1983, 186) defines "regimes" as "sets of implicit or explicit principles, norms, rules, and decision-making procedures around which actors' expectations converge in a given area of international relations." There is a "demand

---

[1] Examples of such courts include the International Court of Justice (ICJ) and the International Tribunal for the Law of the Sea.

for international regimes" (Keohane 1982), which may also be viewed as "institutions with explicit rules, agreed upon by governments, that pertain to particular sets of issues in international relations" (Keohane 1982, 4). Yet, from a constructivist perspective, regimes are viewed as "governing arrangements constructed by states to coordinate their expectations and organize aspects of international behavior in various issue-areas" (Kratochwil and Ruggie 1986, 759). It derives from these definitions that the international criminal justice regime is a set of norms, rules, and regulations, spearheaded not only by states but also by a wide range of transnational nonstate actors and institutions.

International institutions and human rights–based regimes of international justice are designed to hold states and individuals accountable for both international and internal activities. These regimes also empower citizens to challenge their governments before international courts or fora. As such, they pose a challenge to Westphalian sovereignty in international relations theory. The puzzling question then is why states, whether democratic or not, would favor establishing or joining international regimes whose main purpose is to constrain their domestic sovereignty? Or as Simmons (2009, 4) asks, "Why would an individual government choose to commit itself internationally to limit freedom of action domestically?" This question is even more puzzling given the fact that 84 percent of the international courts that exist as of 2014 allow nonstate actors to initiate litigation against states (Alter 2014). Whereas old-style courts lacked compulsory jurisdiction (requiring consent of the defendant state) and functioned as voluntary interstate dispute settlement mechanisms, new-style internationalized courts have compulsory jurisdiction and allow nonstate actors, such as international commissions, prosecutors, international actors, and private litigants, to initiate litigation.

In response to Simmons' question about why a state would choose to commit itself internationally to limit freedom of action domestically (2009, 4), realist scholars have argued that states join international human rights regimes in response to coercion. Liberalism and its various strands, on the other hand, argue that governments are convinced to adopt human rights norms. Therefore, the extant theories of international human rights cooperation focus on two elements: coercion and normative persuasion (Moravcsik 2000). The latter stresses the idealistic and altruistic foundations for the creation and sustaining of international human rights regimes (Moravcsik 2000, 223). Thus, both realist and idealist theories argue that states, interest groups, and public opinion in established democracies lead the effort to form and enforce human rights regimes.

However, Moravcsik (2008) argues that this is not the case because established democracies – in postwar Europe, for instance – opposed binding human rights regimes and did not coerce or induce other states to accept them. Between these two positions, a new theoretical starting point emerges: the domestic political self-interest of national governments (Moravcsik 2000). Governments will resort to creating international human rights regimes when "reducing future political uncertainty [outweighs] the sovereignty costs of membership" (Moravcsik 2000, 220).[2] In other words, governments create these human rights and international regimes or join them to tie the hands of their successors and reduce uncertainty. This certainly poses a challenge to any rigid conception of Westphalian sovereignty. However, imagining sovereignty on fixed grounds is problematic in any case. As Grovogui (2008, 263, emphasis added) argues, "Sovereignty is first and foremost an historical abstraction intended to convoy an organizing principle of the international system. It thus serves to order a set of *changing* internal and external relationships between and amongst *unequal* political agents."[3] Grovogui (2002; 2008) contends that contestations about the nature of the moral order underlying sovereignty resulted in political settlements that generated a succession of regimes of sovereignty that, at times, have competed and coexisted.[4] For instance, these regimes of sovereignty are visible in the "post-conflict" discourse and framework within which the ICC intervenes. At the end of the Cold War, in the face of the perceived threats that weak and failed states represented for others, the notions of "shared," "pooled," and "conditional" sovereignty emerged as possible solutions to failures of statehood (Krasner 2004). Thus, as Hozic (2014, 27) asserts, "[M]alleable notions of sovereignty matched the malleable definition of conflict and the malleable concept of intervention."

However, although human rights regimes are prominent in the liberal global agenda, states do put in place mechanisms that try to limit their reach and effectiveness, given that the global codification of rights limits the sovereignty of states in principle (Grugel and Piper 2007).[5] The rising international legalization impacts state behavior and human rights–based international

---

[2] Moravcsik (2000, 229) posits a "republican liberal" explanation that argues that human rights regimes are a result of instrumental calculation about domestic politics. Governments delegate power to human rights regimes in order to limit political uncertainty, for example, to constrain the behavior of future national governments, which is the reason why, according to Moravcsik, the strongest support for binding human rights regimes came from new and potentially unstable democracies and not from the established ones.

[3] See also Gerry Simpson (2004) for a discussion of the power hierarchy in the sovereignty of the states.

[4] Grovogui (2008, 263) defines a "regime of sovereignty" as "a manner, a method, and a system of organization of sovereignty in time and space."

[5] Grugel and Piper (2007) argue that the global codification of rights creates a kind of constitution that can be used as a vehicle for making claims and legitimizes nonstate action on behalf of vulnerable groups.

regimes. As Simmons (2009, 3) explains, from the end of World War II (WWII) to the turn of the century, "governments have committed themselves to a set of explicit legal obligations that run counter to the old claim of state sovereignty." How did the supremacy of sovereignty give way progressively to its contestation? International institutions and regimes affect domestic politics, and treaties to which states adhere alter the political agenda of domestic elites and galvanize social movements (Simmons 2009), leading to a balancing act between norms and demands of international justice and states' interests.

BALANCING NORMS OF INTERNATIONAL
JUSTICE WITH STATES' INTERESTS

Realism assumes that states are the most important actors in the international system, and they are unitary and rational in pursuit of their self-interests. But one may ask, where do states' interests and preferences come from, and how do states know what they want? (Finnemore 1996). The ways in which states work within the international criminal justice regime suggest that their interests are the reflection of the interests of their elites. This position, derived from what Moravcsik (2008) called the "New Liberalism," is fundamentally different not only from realism but also from liberal institutionalism. If, as Moravcsik (2008) suggests, states' preferences and interests reflect the preferences and interests of a subset of the state, then the state is not an actor *per se* but an institution susceptible to be captured by coalitions of social actors. Thus, some norms developed to reflect the preferences of such domestic coalitions spill over in the international arena. Following the same reasoning, Bass (2000, 18) argues that liberal ideals make liberal states take up the cause of international justice.[6] Therefore, war crimes legalism, for example, encompasses the process by which domestic norms are transferred to international politics. To that extent, the ICC fits in the long and arduous process of building an international justice regime that holds individuals accountable and responsible for international crimes in a world made of states.

Following WWII, the Nuremberg trials consecrated the idea of individual responsibility for war crimes, which opened a new era in the international justice regime. The Nuremberg trials set a precedent for the possibility of prosecuting state officials for crimes committed against humanity regardless of where they were committed. The massive human rights violations that

---

[6] Bass (2000, 19) notes that every international war crimes tribunal was established by liberal states (in Leipzig, Constantinople, Nuremberg, Tokyo, The Hague, Arusha, and so forth). But this argument doesn't account for why some liberal states opposed the creation of the ICC.

occurred during the spike in ethnic conflicts and civil wars at the end of the Cold War led to the creation of ad hoc tribunals such as the International Criminal Tribunal for the former Yugoslavia (ICTY), the International Criminal Tribunal for Rwanda (ICTR), and the Special Court for Sierra Leone (SCSL). Other international or hybrid ad hoc tribunals have also been implemented for Cambodia, Timor-Leste, Lebanon, and Kosovo, to name a few. The necessity to address the "tribunal fatigue" eventually led to the establishment of the ICC, the first permanent international criminal court (Cassese 2012, 18). But the creation of the ICC is also a reflection of the rise and wide adoption of norms of international justice.

TAKING NORMS SERIOUSLY

Human rights norms and international criminal justice legalism pose a challenge to state sovereignty and rationalist understandings of international relations and states' interests (Krasner 1999). Finnemore (1996, 22) defines "norms" as "shared expectations about appropriate behavior held by a community of actors." Working intersubjectively, international norms shape and construct states' identities and interests by activating transnational advocacy networks that in turn help advance the norms (Sikkink 1996; Finnemore and Sikkink 1998). Norm entrepreneurs take upon themselves the task of starting the process that sets off the "norms cascade," which occurs in three steps: emergence, diffusion, and internalization (Finnemore and Sikkink 1998).

Katzenstein (1998, 19) conceptualizes "norms" as "social facts, which define standards of appropriate behaviour and express actors' identities." Actors, whether states or otherwise, do not start with a "blank sheet," as actions are ingrained in preexisting beliefs, ideas, and norms that point toward appropriate behavior (Checkel 2001; Meyer 2005; Goodin 2011). Regardless of how actors (including states) want to pursue utilitarian interests, their actions are not divorced from the social and cultural context in which they exist. It is against this frame that one must study states' behavior in shaping, reshaping, and sometimes subverting norms of international justice, which they use strategically in pursuit of their interests. This book argues that states – including those presumed to be weaker in the international system – ultimately develop strategies to use international legal regimes, institutions, and norms to pursue their security and political interests.

INTERNATIONAL SOCIALIZATION

Although African states have been socialized in engaging with international courts and integrating human rights normative discourse and practices, a careful analysis of the engagement with the ICC shows that such socialization is embedded in strategic calculations on the part of the states. These strategic calculations take into consideration the costs and benefits of such engagements in deciding the extent of and the limits to such compliance and cooperation with the ICC and the adoption of norms of international criminal justice. In fact, the adoption of norms of international criminal justice and cooperation with international courts is characterized in self-interested political preferences and strategic instrumental action. As Schimmelfennig (2005, 832) argues, "[States] conform with international norms if it increases their political utility, and on the condition that the costs of adaptation are smaller than the benefits of external rewards or the costs of external punishment. In addition, actors manipulate the norms strategically to avoid or reduce the costs of socialization." For instance, while explaining the international socialization of Central and Eastern European countries to liberal human rights and democracy norms through a rationalist approach, Schimmelfennig (2005, 829) argues, "The higher the domestic political costs of adaptation to international human rights and democratic norms, the less likely target governments will conform with them." The empirical chapters in this book show that while working within the international criminal justice regimes, weaker states in the international system adopt the norms, contest them, or reshape them in ways consistent with their political and security interests.

How do they develop their interests, and what are the ways in which those interests change? A constructivist approach to international relations helps us understand the social structure in which states are embedded, wherein networks of transnational social relations shape states' preferences (Checkel 1998). "States do not always know what they want," Finnemore (1996, 128) writes. Instead, "States are *socialized* to want certain things by the international society in which they and the people in them live" (Finnemore 1996, 2). Given that international norms and values change, the normative context in which states operate is also subject to change. Indeed, states make international organizations just as much as those organizations too constitute and reshape states.[7] In other words, international institutions such as the ICC may affect states' preferences in profound ways. This brings us to the "justice cascade" argument (Sikkink 2011).

---

[7] For instance, Finnemore (1996) shows how the United Nations Educational, Scientific and Cultural Organization (UNESCO) taught states that a science bureaucracy was a necessary component of the modern state. The International Committee of the Red Cross taught states that the first Geneva Convention was in their interests; in the 1960s and 1970s, alleviation of poverty and meeting of basic human needs became part of development policy because the World Bank taught that to states.

THE "JUSTICE CASCADE"

In a number of earlier publications (Sikkink and Walling 2007; Lutz and Sikkink 2001; Finnemore and Sikkink 1998; Keck and Sikkink 1998) and especially in her book *The Justice Cascade*, Sikkink (2011) contends that transnational emulation and normative socialization of states echoed the works of domestic activists and norm entrepreneurs, from the 1970s onward. The resulting effect, which Sikkink (2011, 5) calls the "justice cascade," is defined as the emergence of "an interrelated, new trend in world politics towards holding individual state officials, including heads of state, criminally accountable for human rights violations." Whereas sovereign immunity for heads of states and other officials had been the prevailing norm, that model eroded in the post-WWII era as state accountability started to take root in human rights regimes. Later, through prosecution for massive violations of human rights, the individual criminal accountability norm emerged, and all three coexist today (Sikkink 2011). International tribunals, which had been dormant after World War II, partly due to the Cold War, were resurrected by the UN Security Council in the wake of the wars in the former Yugoslavia and the genocide in Rwanda in the early 1990s. This, in turn, had the effect of leading to the establishment of domestic and hybrid tribunals elsewhere. Sikkink (2011) situates the emergence of the latest norm of individual criminal responsibility for atrocity crimes in the role that individuals, nongovernmental organization (NGO) activists, and states have played in creating and diffusing the norm of individual criminal accountability in the wake of human rights abuses, which, in essence, is the "justice cascade" argument.

More specifically, the sources of the justice cascade can be traced back to transition periods from military dictatorships to democracy both in Southern Europe and Latin America during the 1970s. Constructivist scholarship points to a normative shift from blanket amnesties for human rights abuses to demands for individual criminal responsibility. A progressive delegitimization of amnesties had the effect of holding former state officials individually accountable for past human rights abuses, notably in Latin America. According to Sikkink (2011), a transnational justice network was responsible for these changes, by socializing states into adopting the norm of the duty to prosecute past human rights abuses and international crimes. These transnational advocacy networks persuaded the countries emerging from dictatorships that not only were amnesties in violations of the rights of the victims but they would also set the stage for further violations of human rights (Sikkink 2011). Therefore, prosecutions were necessary, they argued, not only as a matter of moral and legal duty but also as an instrument to consolidate peace and democracy and prevent future atrocities. Finally, Sikkink (2011) contends that trials for human rights abuses lead to lower levels of repression in those countries, that prosecutions work when balanced with truth commissions, and that prosecutions deter human rights violations and create greater political stability. Therefore, for Sikkink (2011, 169), trials have both deterrent effects and socializing functions. However, my findings show that the "justice cascade" argument may have exaggerated the normative and positive effects of prosecution for human rights abuses.

TEMPERING THE JUSTICE CASCADE: A CRITIQUE

We may ask whether there is really a justice *cascade*, and if so, is it truly global, as Sikkink (2011) suggests? As the data that Sikkink (2011) provides show, there is a wide adoption of the norm of individual criminal accountability in Latin America that materialized in the use of trials to prosecute perpetrators of human rights abuses. Latin America, however, seems to be a cluster of cases that are not representative of other regions around the world that have also experienced widespread human rights abuses. In Asia, for instance, outside of Cambodia, which has established the Extraordinary Chambers to reckon with the Khmer Rouge regime,[8] the claim of a widespread adoption of this norm is flimsy. The Middle East also seems to be outside of this cascading of justice. One could argue that African states, constituting the largest regional bloc in the ICC membership, show a widespread adoption of the norm of individual criminal accountability in the face of international crimes. But as I argue in this study, such claims rest on shaky grounds, considering the ways in which these states, although appearing to have adopted the norm, nonetheless devise strategies to circumvent it and bend the rules to fit their calculations. Joining the ICC and working with international tribunals can be a mere cost-benefit analysis for states that are eager to find avenues to prosecute their enemies and at the same time shielding their agents.

Moreover, whereas Sikkink (2011) argues that "foreign prosecutions and international tribunals can be cost-effective alternatives to military intervention," Rodman (2015) shows that the SCSL was able to prosecute former Liberian president Charles Taylor and hold other rebel leaders accountable only because of an interventionist commitment from Western powers and

---

[8] The Extraordinary Chambers in the Courts of Cambodia (ECCC) is an internationalized hybrid tribunal established to prosecute crimes committed by the Khmer Rouge regime between 1975 and 1979. See https://eccc.gov.kh/en.

West African regional organizations to a military victory over rebels in Sierra Leone and a regime change in Liberia. Hence, as Rodman (2015, 39) argues, "Taking criminal accountability seriously requires an interventionist rather than a consent-based approach to conflict resolution." Therefore, the experience of the SCSL shows the limits of the norm diffusion argument when addressing accountability in ongoing conflicts (Rodman 2013). The fall of the president Jammeh regime in Gambia and the subsequent creation of a truth and reconciliation commission owe much to the Economic Community of West African States' (ECOWAS) commitment to a military intervention that started in January 2017 to push Jammeh out (Hartmann 2017; Odigie 2017).

Furthermore, as McAuliffe (2013, 109) contends, the justice cascade argument "has been accepted uncritically by a number of scholars."[9] However, one can also argue that the demand for justice has not translated into an increased willingness of states to engage in risky accountability processes (McAuliffe 2013; Olsen, Payne, and Reiter 2010). In fact, Olsen, Payne, and Reiter (2010, 101–103) argue that "the *relative* frequency of prosecutions and amnesties has remained stable" and that the increased number of prosecutions is simply due to a greater number of transitions since the late 1970s. As such, any increases in the implementation of trials merely reflect global democratization trends, not an adoption of the norm of individual criminal accountability and socialization of states, as the justice cascade argument would posit (Olsen, Payne, and Reiter 2010, 101).

It is therefore possible that what has been uncritically accepted as the justice cascade may merely be an "advocacy cascade" (McAuliffe 2013, 106). Such conflation may be due to the fact that transitional justice and its virtuous effects are oftentimes presented in idealistic terms by scholars, which make its positive effects presumed but not proven (van de Merve, 2009, 121). As McAuliffe (2013, 106) writes, "Amongst advocates and activists in particular, one sees in the literature an emotional commitment to transitional justice that generally foregoes doubts about its overall efficacy even where isolated shortcomings are accepted. Policy has hitherto proceeded less from analysis to conclusions than from commitments to action." And indeed, as Vinjamuri and Snyder (2004, 345) have pointed out, "[T]he commitment to advocacy has come at the expense of progress in empirical research." Even Sikkink (2011, 7) admits that her scholarship in *The Justice Cascade* is based on a mix of qualitative analysis of a database that she developed with a treatment of what she called her own "personal and scholarly journey." Such approach may be

---

9 See, for instance, Barahona de Brito (2010), Sriram (2003), Huneeus (2007), Levy (2010), and Roht-Arriaza and Mariezcurrena (2006).

problematic in the field of transitional justice wherein advocacy is often pre-sented in heroic terms (McAuliffe 2013, 107). Indeed, Sikkink and other human rights scholars, as Coomans, Grünfeld, and Kamminga (2010, 18) write, "tend to passionately believe that human rights are positive. Many of the scholars are activists or former activists in the field of human rights. Although seldom stated, the explicit aim of their research is to contribute to improved respect for human rights standards.... [T]here is little room for research challeng-ing the conventional wisdom that such systems be applauded." Sikkink (2008, 229) admits that scholars of human rights have not found satisfactory ways to combine ethical commitments with empirical research, which should lead to even more critical analysis of the empirics of the justice cascade argument.

It is in consideration of these limitations on the ethical commitments of human rights scholars that one must assess the claim that criminal prosecu-tions have had a deterrent effect on the perpetration of atrocity crimes. Even in the case of the ICC, its record of prosecuting individuals for war crimes and crimes against humanity since 2002 has not had the deterrent effect that many expected even on the African continent, where the overwhelming majority of its cases are located. The fact that the ICC had to open two situations under investigation in the Central African Republic (CAR I opened in 2007 and CAR II in 2014) shows that the threat of being prosecuted in The Hague does not necessarily deter would-be perpetrators in conflict settings. Therefore, a deep skepticism about the "Human Rights Imperium" is warranted (Hopgood 2013). In this ritualization of international justice, where its unmitigated good is taken for granted, Hopgood (2013, Loc 3488) contends, "The ICC ... will be used by states to solve political problems, not to change the world." However, whereas the organized hypocrisy of the international justice system is often leveled as a critique of Western powers, this study shows the ways in which African (and other weaker) states as well are trying to maximize their benefits by collaborating with the ICC when it suits their goals or stonewalling the court despite the compliance that their ICC membership requires, when their agents are targeted for prosecution.

WHEN NORM SUBVERSION BECOMES STRATEGIC

This book points to the ways in which weaker states in the international system use norms and the international justice regime instrumentally. It is understood that international institutions socialize states to adopt new politi-cal goals, values, and interests (Finnemore 1996). In asserting that norms shape interests, however, Finnemore (1996) overlooks the fact that interests, derived from outside of the norms, reshape those norms in the sense that they violate them, or subvert them, or in any case, engage with them in novel ways. This book argues that while interacting with international organizations, states rearrange those values to retrofit them with their interests derived from political calculations and cost-benefit analyses. Focusing on norms of international criminal justice, the theoretical framework of this study shows the ways in which states that have come to establish some working relationship with the ICC adopt discursive strategies and courses of actions that allow them to pursue their interests, even when such strategies mean that they will subvert the norms while doing so. In that regard, this analysis takes Finnemore's argument a step further by looking at not only the ways in which states construct their interests through their social relations with one another and with international institutions but also how those interactions unearth new interests that too are pursued, even if they do not match with the earlier goals that states may have had.

While the argument about trials and prosecutions of state leaders for human rights abuses has gained ground (Sikkink and Walling 2007; Sikkink 2011), other works in transitional justice have shown that criminal prosecutions and states' collaboration with international courts do not necessarily advance the rule of law or norms of human rights. In the case of the ICTY, for example, Subotic (2009) shows that political elites "hijack" the transitional justice process for the advancement of their own goals. Thus, this is one area where transitional justice helps us better understand the ways in which, at the domestic level, norms can be hijacked and geared toward purposes for which they were not intended. Subotic (2009) argues that compliance with international norms becomes a strategic, even subversive, choice for states that do not have much interest in following them. Focusing on Bosnia, Serbia, and Croatia, Subotic (2009, 167) finds that "under specific domestic conditions, compliance with international norms becomes a political strategy that allows states to go through the motions of fulfilling international demands while in fact rejecting the profound social transformation these norms require." This book argues that the strategies that Subotic (2009) has identified in the case of the Balkans are also present in the relationships between states (from the African continent and beyond) and the ICC. The concepts of norm hijacking and hijacked justice that Subotic (2009, 184) has developed regarding the Balkans are also applicable to the relationships between the ICC and African states. This study contends that African states that have so far engaged with the ICC did not refer cases or cooperate with the court because they believed in advancing the norms of individual criminal responsibility in the face of mass atrocities. Rather, they have strategically used the international justice system to advance their political and security interests. Furthermore, in the cases of UN Security Council (UNSC) referral and the prosecutor's *proprio motu* initiative, this analysis provides opportunities to better explain and understand the ways in which states deploy resistance to or accommodation toward the international criminal justice regime.

STATES OF JUSTICE: A THEORETICAL FRAMEWORK

This study provides a theoretical framework that systematically analyzes the relationship between the ICC and states that are not major powers in the international system. The focus here is on states that have "engaged with" the court during its almost two decades of operation. This framework, however, also illuminates possible scenarios by identifying patterns of state behavior that would apply to potential interactions between other states and the ICC in the future. The relationship between these states and the ICC revolves around four themes: (1) the strategic use of self-referrals, (2) complementarity between national and international justice systems, (3) limits of state compliance with international courts, and (4) the strategic use of international courts in domestic politics. In fact, states that appear weaker in the international system actively engage with the court through one or a combination of the three trigger mechanisms: state referral, UNSC referral, *proprio motu*. From that point, the relationship between the court and the state is dynamic, as the latter adopts a pattern of behavior that seeks at any time to advance its political and security interests. This framework is generalizable and is useful to examine the behavior of other states in and outside of the African continent where the ICC prosecutor has opened either investigations or preliminary examinations.

The theoretical ambition of this book is grounded in an empirical analysis, using an abductive analytical framework to develop new theoretical insights. This analytical framework uses an interpretive epistemology, an approach that stresses an understanding of the social world by uncovering meanings attached to actions. This method does not aim to uncover causal mechanisms but rather achieve a high level of explanatory power.

This framework (Table 2.1) captures the universe of cases at the ICC and the related state's pattern of behavior. It encompasses all trigger mechanisms to ICC intervention available: state referrals, UNSC referrals, and the Office of the Prosecutor's (OTP) use of *proprio motu* powers. Depending on which trigger mechanism activated ICC jurisdiction in a specific case and the political risks to the state associated with the investigation, states develop a range of strategies in pursuit of their strategic interests in their relationship with the court. If, for instance, the OTP's preliminary examination and investigation focuses on state agents, the state develops strategies and tactics to impede or

TABLE 2.1. *States of justice: A theoretical framework*

Triggers	OTP focus	State behavior	Outcome
State referrals	State officials	Noncooperation	Selective investigation and prosecution
	Other	Compliance/ cooperation	
UNSC referrals	State officials	Noncooperation	Stalemate
	Other	Admissibility challenge	
Proprio motu	State officials	Noncooperation	Selective investigation and prosecution
	Other	Compliance/ cooperation	

hinder the cases. On the other hand, in the cases where the primary targets for investigation and prosecution are "Other" (rebel leaders, warlords, or political opponents, for instance), the state's compliance and cooperation are to be expected. Given that the OTP is by design allowed to (and, in fact, should) investigate all parties in the conflict, the outcome is selective investigation and prosecution. The investigations and the prosecution are likely to fail or end in a stalemate without the state's cooperation.

State's behavior is, therefore, a major factor impacting the outcome of cases at the ICC. The noncompliance behavior encompasses a range of tactics that states adopt, which are discussed in depth in the empirical case studies.

Despite being a relatively new institution, the ICC has become one of the most important actors in global politics. As such, its work is greatly shaping states' behavior in international politics and international justice. Hence, this framework also theorizes a predictive behavior of states, stemming from the prosecutor's signaling future cases. States in this case preemptively react to such signals. This behavior is not limited to the state that may be targeted by the investigation, or as it applies also to nonparty states (Table 2.2).

A UN Security Resolution examination or vote to refer a situation to the ICC brings out preemptive actions from states, especially the P5, but also nonpermanent members. The United States, China, and Russia have especially used their P5 status to veto or otherwise signal their intent to do so in an effort to shield their allies from the ICC reach. On the other hand, in the cases of the prosecutor signaling an intent to use his or her *proprio motu* powers to open a preliminary examination in a state party to the ICC, withdrawal or threats of withdrawal from such states and their allies are the expected preemptive action, as the cases of Burundi, the Gambia, and the Philippines show.

TABLE 2.2. *Preemptive actions*

Triggers	State preemptive actions	Examples
State referrals	N/A	N/A
UNSC referrals	P5 member vetoes resolution or signals its intent to do so to shield allies	United States, China, and Russia
Proprio motu	Withdrawal or threats of withdrawal from the ICC; threats against court and court officials	Burundi, the Gambia, the Philippines, United States, Israel, and Myanmar

CONCLUSION

This chapter has presented a novel theoretical framework that points to the ways in which weaker states in the international system use norms and the international justice regime instrumentally. The subsequent empirical chapters show that, while interacting with international organizations, states rearrange those values to retrofit them with their interests derived from political calculations and cost-benefit analyses. This study contends that African states that have so far engaged with the ICC did not refer cases or cooperate with the court because they believed in advancing the norms of individual criminal responsibility in the face of mass atrocities. Rather, they have strategically used the international justice system to advance their political and security interests.

Using this analytical framework, the following chapters illustrate patterns of state behavior in relation to the ICC that revolve around (1) the strategic use of self-referrals, (2) complementarity between national and international justice systems, (3) limits of state compliance with international courts, and (4) the strategic use of international courts in domestic politics. In fact, states that appear weaker in the international system actively engage with the ICC through one or a combination of the three trigger mechanisms: state referral, UNSC referral, *proprio motu*. From that point, the relationship between the court and the state is dynamic, as the latter adopts a pattern of behavior that seeks at any time to advance its political and security interests. Ultimately, this framework is generalizable and useful to examine the behavior of other states in and outside of the African continent. Hence, this framework also theorizes a predictive behavior of states, stemming from the prosecutor's signaling future cases.

3

Outsourcing Justice

INTRODUCTION

This chapter explores the ways in which states subvert international legal norms and use the international justice regime in the pursuit of their own political and security interests. Specifically, the chapter argues that the use of self-referrals to the International Criminal Court (ICC) stems from political calculations that allow state leaders to advance their own domestic and international agendas at the expense of furthering the goals of the international justice regime that, with the creation of the ICC, had vowed to work to end impunity for the preparators of the most serious crimes of concern to the international community.[1] The argument that actors, whether they are state agents, ICC officials, community leaders, or nongovernmental organizations (NGOs) use tools at their disposal – such as self-referrals, cooperation, or the complementarity principle – selectively with the ICC for the advancement of their political goals is a given. After all, as Nouwen (2014, xvi) notes, it is obvious that "African states have engaged in political calculations to avoid the costs and maximize the benefits of cooperation with the ICC." But what is less evident – and is the contribution of this chapter – is how states do so; what is also less evident are the effects of such calculations on the norms and regimes of international criminal justice. Hence, this chapter is a story of political calculations, political power, and security interests; the agency of African states; and the convergence and clashes of interests between these states and international legal institutions.

It is clear that Uganda and the Democratic Republic of Congo (DRC), the Central African Republic (CAR), and Mali have been able to use the ICC for their own political and legal gains. Gabon has also tried a self-referral of its

---

[1] See the preamble of the Rome Statute: www.icc-cpi.int/nr/rdonlyres/ea9aeff7-5752-4f84-be94-0a655eb30e16/0/rome_statute_english.pdf.

own, albeit unsuccessfully. These actions illustrate the need to explore further the agency of states in creating and shaping the delivery of international justice (Clark 2011, 1182). Such agency is even more crucial to understand when coming from African states, which are often viewed as weak links in shaping global norms. The focus here is on the use of self-referral, and the examples are driven mostly from Uganda's use of self-referral to the ICC. The selection of the Uganda case is dictated by the fact that Uganda was the first case before the ICC, but it is also the first instance of self-referral. The other instances of self-referral are briefly analyzed in the final chapter of the book.

In late 2003, the ICC prosecutor Luis Moreno-Ocampo announced that Uganda, a state party to the ICC, had referred a "situation concerning the Lord's Resistance Army (LRA)" to him. On 28 June 2004, Ocampo announced that there was "a reasonable basis to proceed with an investigation."[2] Ocampo said, "There was credible evidence that widespread and systematic attacks had been committed against the civilian population since July 2002, including the abduction of thousands of girls and boys" (Schabas 2011a, 39). The report indicated that rape, torture, child conscription, and forced displacement continued to take place. The prosecutor submitted applications for five arrest warrants on 6 May 2005. In the application, the prosecutor indicated that the LRA was conducting attacks against the Ugandan army and local militias as well as civilian populations. The warrants were unsealed and made public in October 2005, which led the LRA commanders to seek peace negotiations. Hostilities between the LRA and the Ugandan government subsequently halted in August 2006, and peace negotiations were held in Juba from 2006 to 2008.

The focus on self-referrals as a point of entry for the study of the ways in which states strategically use international courts to advance their political and security interests is compelling because this specific trigger mechanism spurred the first cases that came under ICC jurisdiction. In fact, the ICC prosecutor took up three self-referral cases during his first eighteen months in office: Uganda, DRC, and CAR. The use of self-referrals results from a peculiar reading of Article 14 of the Rome Statute that stipulates that state parties to the ICC may refer a situation to the Court. The focus of this argument is on state leaders and how they use the international criminal justice regime to further their own interests, and how they switch their strategy when the demands for their political interests warrants such action. Such political calculations and instrumentalization of the referral trigger mechanism came with a cost on the legitimacy of the Court, particularly because, as

---

[2] ICC: "Prosecutor of the International Criminal Court opens an investigation into Northern Uganda," Press Release, ICC-OTP-20040729-65, 29 July 2004.

Clark (2011, 1181) writes, "[The ICC] has failed to mitigate the ability of domestic governments to use international justice to their advantage, especially in insulating themselves from prosecution for serious crimes committed against their own civilians."[3]

Much in the literature on the ICC intervention in Uganda has focused on its consequences on the conflict in northern Uganda. It is often argued that the ICC prosecutor jumped into the opportunity to show the Court's usefulness and to build its legitimacy. Yet, the implication of the ICC has also made the conflict more difficult to settle, which prolonged the plight of the local populations and victims of the conflict (Gaeta 2004; Akhavan 2005, 2010, 2011; Branch 2007; Allen 2010; Clark 2011; Nouwen 2011, 2014; Wierda and Otim 2011).

If the warrants for the arrest of the LRA leaders triggered the cessation of hostilities and the initiation of peace negotiations, they also prevented the completion of the peace accords because the LRA commanders insisted that the arrest warrants be annulled before they sign the peace settlements. Facing the impasse, President Museveni, who had triggered the ICC prosecution when he used the self-referral, asked the prosecutor to withdraw the arrest warrants and promised immunity to the LRA commanders (Schabas 2011a, 42). This move by the Ugandan president clearly shows that the self-referral to the ICC was destined to further the president's own interests, mainly to guarantee his political survival, and when the situation had changed, he did not hesitate to withdraw his support for a legal solution to end the conflict in northern Uganda.

This process of criticizing the ICC's intervention in Uganda and highlighting the ways in which it may have been an impediment to achieving peace coincided with a process of delegitimization of the Court, which found many favorable echoes in Africa. This effort at delegitimization occurred merely a decade after the Rome Statute was adopted with big fanfare. The delegitimization of international norms is also often a project of legitimization of new norms (Hurd 2007, 196).[4] Although the delegitimization of the ICC may be prevalent among many circles in the African continent, this study shows that some African states have used the Court strategically to advance their interests.

---

[3] And as Peskin (2008) argues, governments in the former Yugoslavia and Rwanda also have been able to manipulate international justice for their own benefit. Subotic (2009) also makes a similar augment for the Balkans.

[4] For example, the African Union (AU) has amended the Protocol of the African Court of Human and People's Rights to give it jurisdiction over international crimes such as genocide, war crimes, and crimes against humanity. For the implications of such action, see Du Plessis (2012).

The first section of this chapter shows the processes through which the state referral trigger mechanism was transformed into a self-referral mechanism used by states to further their own political gains, which essentially amounts to outsourcing justice. But to contextualize Uganda's self-referral to the ICC and its consequences, a brief summary of Uganda's history of political violence and the conflict with the LRA that precipitated the ICC's involvement is necessary. The chapter then shows the agency of the government of Uganda in using self-referral, which was also in the interests of the ICC's Office of the Prosecutor (OTP). Finally, this chapter discusses the politics of self-referrals and how, while used strategically by states, they pervert international legal norms.

FROM STATE REFERRALS TO SELF-REFERRALS

All instances of state referral to the ICC have been self-referrals, except for the recent Venezuela situation.[5] This shows that states effectively used Article 14 of the Rome Statute not to refer other states but to refer *themselves* to the Court. Indeed, self-referrals to the ICC offered states new means to incapacitate or dispose of armed nonstate actors or even political adversaries. State referral therefore became the trigger mechanism for the first three cases before the Court: Uganda, DRC, and CAR. The Côte d'Ivoire's self-referral was a bit different; although it was not a party to the Rome Statute at the time, it had accepted ICC jurisdiction in 2003 by submitting an ad hoc declaration under Article 12(3), which in substance amounted to a self-referral (Akhavan 2010, 106). Mali also self-referred to the ICC in 2013 in relation to crimes that may have been committed in its northern regions during the 2012 jihadist takeover. Finally, Gabon also self-referred to the ICC following its 2016 postelectoral crisis, although the ICC prosecutor ultimately decided not to proceed with an investigation.

Although these situations are called self-referral cases (because the states themselves "invited" the ICC), the use of the term *self-referral* is misleading. In fact, while referring situations in their territory to the ICC, these states did not intend or anticipate having the ICC OTP investigate the cases or even all parties involved in the conflict. Instead, these states sought to have the OTP investigate and prosecute the rebel groups who were operating within their borders (Schabas 2011b, 160). For example, in its referral letter, the government of Uganda mentioned specifically "the situation concerning the Lord's

5 On 27 September 2018, a group of six states (Argentina, Canada, Colombia, Chile, Paraguay, and Peru) referred the situation in Venezuela to the ICC prosecutor, and it is currently under preliminary examination. See www.icc-cpi.int/venezuela.

Resistance Army." This specification clearly shows that the intention of the government of Uganda was to make the ICC direct its investigation and prosecution against the LRA.

However, self-referrals come with their own pitfalls for the prosecutor's office because states may be willing to cooperate with the ICC as long as the investigations are targeting their enemies, but the compliance may be withdrawn as soon as states' agents become the focus of the Court (Gaeta 2004, 952). Indeed, when the ICC prosecutor issued warrants for the arrest of five LRA leaders, both Amnesty International and Human Rights Watch (HRW) questioned the one-sided approach and called for the prosecution of the Ugandan military forces as well. However, a tacit, if not explicit, understanding between the Ugandan government and the ICC meant that that only the LRA would be investigated for war crimes and crimes against humanity. Schabas (2011a, 166) writes, "To the extent that the Prosecutor believed his strategy of encouraging self-referral was a productive one, he surely had to reassure States that those who referred the case were not threatened. Indeed, if he intended for the strategy to continue, and to solicit more self-referrals, he will need to show a track record of one-sided investigations…" Furthermore, the concept of self-referral has "the practical consequence of establishing a degree of complicity between the Office of the Prosecutor and the referring state" (Schabas 2008, 751). Therefore, self-referrals provide to states an avenue to gain immunity for their agents and military forces while at the same time having the ICC prosecute their political adversaries or the rebel leaders operating in their territory.

The next sections in this chapter use the example of the Ugandan situation at the ICC to make the following arguments: (1) Uganda used the self-referral mechanism because it aligned with its political calculations, (2) the use of self-referral served to isolate the LRA and make it an enemy of the international community, (3) self-referral was also in the interests of the ICC's OTP, and (4) self-referral is an example of perversion of international legal norms. It is first worthwhile, however, to retrace briefly the history of political violence in Uganda that led to the rise of the LRA and the conflict in northern Uganda.

UGANDA'S HISTORY OF POLITICAL VIOLENCE

Apollo Milton Obote, a Lwo-speaking Ugandan from the north of the country, became the first president of Uganda at independence, in 1962. By 1966, Obote had become increasingly dictatorial, relying heavily on the armed forces, until he was ousted in 1971 by Idi Amin. Amin, who hailed from the West Nile province, removed Lwo-speaking soldiers from the Langi and Acholi ethnic groups, many of whom fled and engaged in resistance against his troops. Some of those soldiers formed the Uganda National Liberation Army (UNLA). In 1979, with the support of the Tanzanian army, Yoweri Museveni's troops invaded Uganda to overthrow Amin (Allen 2006, 29). (Amin had previously invaded Tanzania.) Elections were subsequently organized, and Obote's Uganda People's Congress (UPC) won, which inaugurated the second Obote administration. Obote's second administration relied on the UNLA, which became the de facto national army, but it was composed mostly of northerners. However, in 1981, Museveni "went to the bush" with a small group of soldiers and founded the National Resistance Army (NRA). Museveni seized power in January 1986 at a time when, as Allen (2006, 31) aptly put it, "something really strange and unanticipated happened – spirit mediums emerged as military commanders."[6]

Although diviners and healers were common by the early 1980s, they were drawn into political processes by the mid-1980s. In 1985, in the northern Ugandan town of Gulu, Alice Auma established a remarkable healing cult (Allen 2006, 33). Alice claimed that she became involved in war on 20 August 1986 when NRA soldiers – the Museveni forces – kidnapped many young people of her age in Gulu. She then recruited 150 former UNLA soldiers and liberated them (Allen 2006, 34). This started a violent campaign against the Museveni forces, and her movement came to be known as the Holy Spirit Movement or the Holy Spirit Mobile Forces (HSMF).[7]

Alice's movement was very effective, with up to 18,000 "disciple-soldiers" by the end of 1986. As Allen (2006, 35) writes, the government soldiers were confronted by "scores of partly naked, glistening men and women marching towards them, some holding bibles, others throwing magical objects, and a few wielding guns. In several encounters, they seem to have been terrified or just did not know what to do. Initially, most ran away." Alice left Acholiland in October 1987 with about 10,000 followers and marched south. She was defeated eighty miles from Kampala and escaped to Kenya, where she lived in a refugee camp until her death in 2007. Although dozens of groups had resisted Museveni's rule over time, most of them had been defeated or gave up at some point. However, Joseph Kony's LRA, which combined remnants of previous national armed forces with the spiritual drive of Alice Auma's defeated movement, was still active twenty years later (Nouwen 2014, 125).

---

[6] These new leaders were called *ajwaki* (sing. *ajwaka*), which in Lwo means "diviner," "spirit medium," or "witch doctor" (Allen 2006, 32).

[7] But it is unclear that Alice Auma herself came up with that name; Allen (2006, 35) suggests that foreign media may have given her movement that name at first.

Kony was born in the early 1960s. He has asserted kinship with Alice, claiming to be her cousin. They both seem to have spent their early life near the town of Gulu. When Museveni signed a peace agreement with the Uganda People's Democratic Army – a rebel group that was operating in northern Uganda – in May 1988, one of its commanders, Odong Latek, refused to surrender and joined Kony, becoming the commander of the forces while Kony was most concerned with healing and divination. The group called itself Uganda People's Democratic Liberation Army (UPDLA). After Latek was killed in 1990, Kony changed the name of the group to the Lord's Resistance Army (LRA) and assumed its military leadership.

The LRA was estimated to have between 3,000 and 4,000 fighters in 1997. But large numbers have never been necessary for the LRA because, as Allen (2006, 40) argues, "[They] have rarely engaged in pitched battles with government forces but have used terror tactics to maximum effect." The often overlooked fact is that the LRA has also made political demands, such as an all-party national conference followed by elections, national unity, education for all, policies encouraging foreign investments, and so on (Allen 2006, 43).[8] Clearly, the LRA has often tried, when it has had the opportunity, to communicate to the civilian populations and the outside world and make its political demands known. One example of such an effort is the use of Radio Mega FM, a community radio based in Gulu. Kony and his lieutenant Vincent Otti called in during a live broadcast in December 2002, and the radio was subsequently prohibited by the Ugandan government from airing LRA communications (Dolan 2011, 85). LRA political demands have been ignored by both the Ugandan government and outside actors, who preferred to paint the movement as an evil organization that only commits unspeakable atrocities and against which only a military response is warranted.

Northern Uganda in the 1990s: Abductions, Internment, and Repression

Amid the conflict in northern Uganda in the 1990s, President Museveni appointed Betty Bigombe, a young Acholi woman, as Minister of State Pacification of Northern Uganda, based in Gulu, and she managed to engage with the LRA in peace talks. Thanks to Bigombe's efforts and her meetings

---

[8] The LRA is commonly characterized in Uganda and by the international media as a "barbaric cult," with no political agenda (Allen 2006, 25). Akhavan – who advised the Ugandan government on the self-referral – writes, "From its inception until the present, the LRA has had no coherent ideology, rational political agenda, or popular support" and that up to 85 percent of LRA's base is made of abducted or forcibly conscripted children (2005, 407).

with Kony in late 1993 and early 1994, a ceasefire was implemented to allow further negotiations between the Ugandan government and the LRA. Yet, in February 1994, Museveni abruptly gave Kony an ultimatum of seven days to surrender, which pushed the LRA to "return to the bush," and the conflict escalated again (Cakaj 2016, 61). In many ways, Museveni saw the continued fight against the LRA as beneficial to his presidency. In fact, the strange spirituality and the horrendous acts that the LRA engaged in allowed Museveni to present northern Uganda as a kind of "barbaric periphery" (Allen 2006, 49). The war in the north kept the Ugandan army busy, allowing senior officers to become wealthy and soldiers to engage in cattle raiding. As Lokwiya Francis, the executive coordinator of the Acholi Religious Leaders Peace Initiative (ARLPI) said,

> during the LRA war, there were no political will to stop it. We lost our cattle, and these cattle were later on discovered in Central Uganda, in Western Uganda…so you cannot say the war was just something not being used by the government [for other purposes.] And the government also wanted to justify its long stay in power. They would say 'I still have work to do in northern Uganda. The war is still there; we need to finish this war'.[9]

Indeed, in addition to the military assistance that Museveni garnered during the twenty-year conflict, the war in northern Uganda also became a "money-making venture" for senior military officers (Wierda and Otim 2011, 1159; Epstein 2017).

LRA raids and Ugandan government responses were catastrophic to the people in Acholiland, whom the Ugandan forces interned in camps. A study of the UN Office of the High Commissioner for Human Rights shows the widespread view among northern Ugandans that both the LRA and the Ugandan government were responsible for their suffering during the conflict (OHCHR 2007). Not only were the local populations at risk of being abducted by LRA fighters, they also suffered under the encampment policy of the government of Uganda, which drove the Acholi off their land. At the conflict's peak, 1.84 million people (about 90 to 95 percent of the population in the three Acholi districts) lived in camps for internally displaced persons (IDPs) in appalling humanitarian conditions (Nouwen 2014, 126).[10] In some cases, people who refused to move to the camps were forcibly displaced. People who wandered

---

[9] Author's interview with Lokwiya Francis, Executive Coordinator of ARLPI, in Gulu, March 2016.

[10] The Acholi were told that anyone found outside the camps would be considered a rebel and killed. And more people died due to the living conditions in the camps than from direct attacks (Nouwen 2014, 126).

outside the camps were at risk of being accused of collaborating with the LRA. By the time the ICC intervened in Uganda in 2004, the population in the camps encompassed nearly the entire rural population of Acholiland (Branch 2007, 181). The Ugandan government euphemistically calls the internment camps "protected villages," but they were effectively "internment or concentration camps" because the populations in them were forcefully displaced, and the government used violence to prevent them from leaving (Branch 2007, 181). There were over 250 of such squalid camps in northern Uganda (Clark 2018, 13), and mortality rates in them exceeded 1,000 per week, producing a humanitarian catastrophe (Branch 2007, 181). When asked about the dire humanitarian conditions in the internment camps, President Museveni replied,

> I am not able to understand why there should be a problem about the humanitarian situation. I have not been active in that area myself because we had sort of divided jobs. I was dealing with the army and fighting the terrorists, and I was leaving the government departments, aid [organizations] and UN agencies to deal with the humanitarian issues. I therefore do not know why the humanitarian situation should be a problem (The New Humanitarian 2005).

Northern Ugandans, including member of Kony's own Acholi community, have also suffered the consequences of this prolonged conflict at the hands of the LRA who would accuse them, of collaborating with Museveni's forces, and thus, punish them with "indiscriminate killings, torture, mutilation, looting, arson, enslavement and forced recruitment" (Nouwen 2014, 125). Nonetheless, significant resentment arose from the Acholi populations toward the Ugandan military forces and the Ugandan government because of the failure of the latter to end the conflict and their suffering, the internment, and stringent curfews that the Acholi perceived as an attack on their self-worth (Wierda and Otim 2011, 1159). This resentment toward the government was also due to the fact that it was largely composed of kidnapped relatives and children from local communities (Wierda and Otim 2011, 1159). Many Acholi people ascribe some collective Acholi responsibility for the crimes committed by the LRA, especially when discussing the young combatants. As one resident in a camp near Kitgum said, "All of the LRA are our children … If they behave badly, if they kill people, this is because of us. We didn't raise them well" (cited in Clark 2018, 108).

As northern Ugandans often point out, however, it seems that the wheels of international justice turn only toward the LRA and fail to consider the extent to which the Ugandan government contributed to the atrocities in northern Uganda, both through its actions and through its failure to fulfill its mission of protecting the citizens. For instance, Lokwiya Francis says,

So, if the LRA comes and abducts 200 people in this community, then it means the government failed in its role to provide security, to provide protection. And for the huts that were burned, and others that were looted, those are properties of the people, which falls within the mandate of the government to [protect]. And also, when the war was going on, other than failing to provide that protection, the army also conducted a lot of kind of bandit work, inhuman treatment to people. There were women who were raped. There were men also who were raped. But these people [the ICC] want to put it all on the LRA and say it was done by the LRA.[11]

Although abduction has become synonymous with the LRA modus operandi, it is also true that the numbers of abductees, especially children, are exaggerated by media reports. Allen (2006, 53) points out that he "[has] not been able to find evidence that over 85 percent of recruitment to the LRA is made up of abducted children – a figure that appeared in many reports and articles and is even repeated in the ICC press release of January 2004 on the situation in Uganda."[12]

Northern Uganda in the 2000s: Amnesty, Peace Talks, and ICC Prosecution

By the end of 2004, after eighteen years of fighting, changes in the international political context seemed to usher in a new era in northern Uganda. Those changes included the addition of the LRA to the US list of terrorist organizations after the 11 September 2001 (US State Department 2001) attacks. This also translated into US assistance to Operation Iron Fist, which Museveni launched against the LRA in 2002. The LRA responded with renewed attacks that accentuated the pressure on Museveni – whose prestige suffered – to engage in peace talks. By 2003, the European Union had expressed "reservations about the military option" (Allen 2006, 73). In January 2004, pressure deepened when the US Congress passed the Northern Uganda Crisis Response Act[13] (Allen 2006, 73).

In Uganda, the changes in the context of the conflict stemmed from the activism of civil society groups and NGOs, an offer of amnesty to the rebels[14] (all of them, not only LRA fighters), and efforts for renewed peace talks and a ceasefire. First enacted on 21 January 2000, the Amnesty Act stipulates, "An amnesty

---

[11] Author's interview with Lokwiya Francis, Gulu, March 2016.

[12] Allen (2006) interviewed many former LRA abductees and LRA fighters who recounted their personal experiences (see pp. 66–71).

[13] See US Congress, "Northern Uganda Crisis Response Act," www.gpo.gov/fdsys/pkg/PLAW-108publ283/pdf/PLAW-108publ283.pdf.

[14] Amnesty Act, Uganda Legal Information Institute, www.ulii.org/ug/legislation/consolidated-act/294.

is declared in respect of any Ugandan who has at any time since the 26th day of January 1986, engaged in or is engaging in war or armed rebellion against the government of the Republic of Uganda." An amnesty shall be granted to such person if he or she "reports to the nearest army or police unit, a chief, a member of the executive committee of a local government unit, a magistrate or a religious leader within the locality; renounces and abandons involvement in the war or armed rebellion; surrenders at any such place or to any such authority or person any weapons in his or her possession" (Amnesty Act 2000).

The Amnesty Act was set to expire within six months of its enactment, although the minister of internal affairs had the authority to extend it (Amnesty Act 2000). It did indeed lapse and has been restored a few times.[15] About 26,000 members of armed groups have been granted amnesty since 2000 (The New Humanitarian 2013), including over 5,000 former LRA fighters (Allen 2006, 75).

However, Museveni's referral to the ICC seemed to hinder the peace talks and ceasefire negotiations. In fact, over the years, Museveni had favored the military option as a means to end the conflict against the LRA. Proponents of peace talks won a battle in December 1999 when the Ugandan Parliament adopted the Amnesty Act, although Kony rejected the amnesty because it did not meet LRA's demands and implied defeat (Nouwen 2014, 128). In this context of failed peace talks and the inability of the government forces to defeat the LRA militarily, the government of Uganda referred the situation in northern Uganda to the ICC in 2004 (Clark 2011).

UGANDA'S SELF-REFERRAL TO THE ICC

A Ugandan official flew to the Netherlands in December 2003 with a briefcase containing a twenty-seven-page letter: the first ever referral to the ICC (Nouwen 2014, 111). Three months earlier, the focus of the ICC prosecutor had instead been on the DRC, which Ocampo had indicated he was monitoring closely and called on states to refer the situation to the ICC.[16] At the same time, the International Court of Justice (ICJ) was adjudicating a legal case from the DRC against Uganda for the latter's involvement in the war in DRC.[17] Whereas Phil Clark (2011, 1198–1199) writes that

---

[15] For example, in the 2013 version of the Amnesty Act, senior commanders of the LRA were not eligible (The New Humanitarian 2013).

[16] The ICC as well as the international community believed that the ICC cases would come from states referring to situations occurring in other states, not self-referrals.

[17] ICJ (1999): Armed Activities on the Territory of the Congo (*Democratic Republic of Congo v. Uganda*), www.icj-cij.org/en/case/116.

the ICC Prosecutor Ocampo approached Museveni in 2003 and persuaded him to use the self-referral trigger mechanism, Nouwen (2014) argues that her Ugandan interviewees and ICC officials denied that there were talks between the ICC and Uganda prior to the referral. According to Nouwen (2014, 113), the informal communications between the ICC and Uganda prior to the referral were at the initiative of the government of Uganda's foreign lawyers – not the ICC. It is worthwhile to note that the OTP has not made the Uganda referral letter public, unlike all other referral letters, possibly because the ICC was involved in the drafting of the DRC referral letter (Nouwen 2014, 113). In any case, the ICC's involvement in Uganda through self-referral was a joint enterprise between the government of Uganda and the OTP.

THE ICC IN UGANDA: A JOINT VENTURE

The ICC intervention in Uganda can be described as a joint venture between the government of Uganda and the ICC's OTP. The government of Uganda referred the "situation concerning the Lord's Resistance Army" to the ICC in December 2003, but it was not announced until a month later, on 29 January 2004, at a joint press conference in London of ICC Prosecutor Ocampo and President Museveni (ICC 2004c). The press statement that followed noted that "President Museveni has indicated to the Prosecutor his intention to amend [the amnesty law] so as to exclude the leadership of the LRA" (Allen 2006, 82). This clearly shows that the government of Uganda offered guarantees to the OTP that it will not impede any attempts by the ICC to prosecute LRA leaders by making them eligible for amnesty within Ugandan domestic law.

In the referral letter, Uganda accuses the LRA of crimes against humanity, but not war crimes, which probably means that the government of Uganda was trying to avoid implying that the LRA could be seen as a legitimate belligerent entity entitled to the lawful conduct of armed hostility (Nouwen 2014, 114). The referral letter was also silent on the possible commission of crimes by the Ugandan People's Defense Forces (UPDF). Human rights organizations immediately called for a correction of that omission, reminding the OTP to ensure that the investigation covered acts committed by the UPDF as well. Noting that it appears that the Ugandan government sought to limit the referral to crimes committed by one party to the conflict, Amnesty International (2004) wrote that the ICC investigation must be part of "a comprehensive plan to end impunity for all such crimes, regardless of which side committed them and of the level of the perpetrator." Human Rights Watch (2004) also reported "violations committed by the UPDF [that] include extra-judicial killings, rape and sexual assault, forcible displacement of over one million civilians, and the recruitment of children under the age of 15 into government militias" and called on the ICC to investigate all parties in the conflict.

The ICC prosecutor seemed to have been responsive to the calls to investigate both sides – or at least he expressed that intent at the time. Six months after the referral was made, Ocampo addressed a letter to the president of the Court in which he said that his office "has informed the Ugandan authorities that we must interpret the scope of the referral consistently with the principles of the Rome Statute, and hence we are analyzing crimes within the situation of northern Uganda by whomever committed" (ICC 2004b). Therefore, it seems that, in 2004, the OTP had intended to investigate both the LRA and the Ugandan security forces or, at the very least, they had voiced such intention. However, to date, sixteen years later, the ICC investigations have focused only on the LRA, and the prosecutor has issued warrants for the arrest of only LRA members. On 8 July 2005, the ICC unsealed the warrants for the arrest of Joseph Kony, Vincent Otti, Raska Lukwiya, Okot Odhiambo, and Dominic Ongwen. Even though the ICC is saying officially that analysis of information concerning the UPDF is ongoing, it is unlikely that the OTP will investigate the UPDF at all because it has reassigned its investigative staff in Uganda to other situations (Nouwen 2014, 116).

THE POLITICS OF SELF-REFERRAL

Self-referrals are the product of a thoughtful process from the state that intends to make them, but it is also very likely that the ICC is involved – at least informally – in the process leading to a self-referral. Phil Clark (2011, 1198) argues that "for nearly a year before President Museveni referred the situation in Uganda to the ICC Prosecutor, there were substantial negotiations between The Hague and Kampala over the nature and ramifications of a state referral." Payam Akhavan – who also advised the Ugandan government on the matter of the referral – contends that, by making the self-referral, "Uganda acted to ensure that justice would be achieved in a way that would avoid the politicization of any trials involving the LRA" (2005, 404).[18] As the Uganda situation at the ICC shows, however, a self-referral itself is, first and foremost,

---

[18] Akhavan (2005, 404) also argues that the self-referral was guided by "security considerations in Acholiland and by the consequent need to isolate and arrest the LRA leadership, operating from bases in southern Sudan."

a political act that cannot be dissociated from its legal meaning. Uganda's referral to the ICC was indeed a marriage of convenience between the state and the prosecutor's office. As Branch (2007, 180) contends,

> The Ugandan government cynically referred the ongoing conflict to the ICC, expecting to restrict the ICC's prosecution to the rebels in order to obtain international support for its militarization and to entrench, not resolve, the war…[And the ICC] chose to pursue a politically pragmatic case, despite that doing so contravened its own mandate and the interests of peace, justice, and the rule of law.

By seeking and accepting the Uganda referral, the ICC had made itself a political instrument at the hands of the Ugandan government.

In Uganda's Interests

The self-referral of Uganda to the ICC was in the interest of both parties. It had the potential of negatively affecting the reputation of the LRA while at the same time improving the reputation of the government of Uganda. It also served to improve international support for the militarized approach, especially in the aftermath of the *Kony 2012* saga.[19] At the time of the referral, the government of Uganda had already labeled the LRA as an irrational, religious fundamentalist cult and a terrorist organization, all part of a list of unflattering terms to which now the label of international wanted criminals could be added, thanks to the ICC arrest warrants.

Prior to the referral, however, Uganda had adopted a nonlegal strategy concerning the LRA, having opted to deal with the rebel group "through military defeat, [and] de facto or de jure amnesties…rather than through criminal justice" (Nouwen 2011, 1121). As Nouwen (2011, 1122) contends, the ICC referral was also part of this nonlegal tradition because it fit the government's *military* strategy to defeat the LRA, essentially by hoping that the ICC involvement would end Sudan's support for the LRA and help spur an international attempt to arrest Kony and his commanders. In fact, Payam Akhavan, has said that the referral was conceived as "a strategy for engaging the international community by committing the

---

[19] In October 2011, President Obama sent 100 US troops to central Africa to serve as "advisers" in efforts to hunt down Kony. Colonel Felix Kulayigye, the Uganda's military spokesperson, said of Obama's decision, "We are happy about it. We look forward to working with them and eliminating Kony and his fighters" (Associated Press, 2011). By early 2015, the Pentagon had spent a reported $500 million on counter-LRA operations (Cakaj 2016, 382).

ICC proponents to the arrest and prosecution of top LRA leaders" (cited in Kastner 2012, 45).

Indeed, international criminalization is an effective strategy for states that want to rally forces behind them to neutralize or delegitimize political adversaries or military enemies (Branch 2007, 183). By making the self-referral to the ICC, the government of Uganda adopted a strategy of international criminalization of the LRA. However, the ICC intervention and the involvement of the international community in the conflict in northern Uganda could not bring it to an end, especially given the wrong assumption that the government of Uganda was genuinely interested in ending the conflict (Branch 2007). But one may ask, why would the government of Uganda want a prolongation of a contained war in Acholiland? According to Branch (2007), a war against the "terrorists" allows the government of Uganda to silence political dissidents and opponents.[20] It also justifies maintaining a military presence in the north while garnering strong political support of the south by emphasizing the potential danger coming from the northern enemy. The prolonged conflict has also allowed President Museveni to reinvent himself as a key US ally after 9/11 and thus receive military aid (Epstein 2017).

In addition, for the government of Uganda, self-referral served the purpose of bringing another international institution to bear on an armed conflict over which it had failed to achieve a decisive military victory for more than a decade (Schabas 2011a, 160). In June 2005, President Museveni said in a state of the union address that the ICC was a good ally to the government of Uganda because it makes Kony isolated as long as he is indicted; "anybody who touches him will have problems with the International Criminal Court, therefore, that is the advantage," he said (cited in Nouwen 2014, 117). In 2007, Museveni said, "If [the LRA leaders] go through the peace process then we can use alternative justice, traditional justice, which is a bit of a soft landing for them. But if they persist, and stay in exile, then they will end up in The Hague for their crimes" (Reuters 2007). He also said, "If the [peace] talks succeed then it will be a soft landing for the terrorists," referring to the LRA leaders, adding that dropping the ICC warrants beforehand "would not be a good signal because that ICC indictment is actually a good pressure on Kony, it's an incentive on him to behave sensibly. Removing it without getting peace in exchange would be a mistake" (Sudan Tribune 2006).

---

[20] For example, Museveni's main challenger Kizza Besigye was arrested and charged with treason, allegedly for his links with the LRA (Branch 2007, 185).

Regarding the offer of amnesty, Museveni offered that Kony would be granted amnesty if he surrendered (The New Humanitarian 2005).

The issuance of the ICC arrest warrants against Kony and the top LRA commanders in 2005 seemed to reinforce the Ugandan government's strategy to pursue its military campaign against the LRA, claiming to do so in an attempt to enforce the warrants (Kastner 2012, 47). Referring to his preference for a military option in dealing with the LRA, Museveni said,

> There are those who believe in the magic of the peace talks – which I do not believe in. However, I do not want to be obstructive to those who wish to pursue this avenue – if you believe that you can convince evil to stop being evil, go ahead. But in the meantime, I do not want to give up my option [the military option]. That is why we have a dual track (The New Humanitarian 2005).

In addition to making the LRA commanders international criminals, the self-referral also made the Ugandan state "an ally of the ICC, a champion for international justice, and a friend of mankind" (Nouwen 2014, 116). When asked whether the ICC would also investigate misconduct of government soldiers, Museveni replied, "There are no atrocities committed by our soldiers. If there are atrocities committed, we punish them ourselves – the evidence of that is plenty. We have executed soldiers for killing people. But I would not mind if the ICC wanted to investigate [the Ugandan army]. They are more than welcome" (The New Humanitarian 2005). But in the public and official discourse, atrocities committed by the Ugandan government have been downplayed, and the focus has been on the atrocities committed by the LRA, which is portrayed as a bizarre group whose brutality defies understanding. As Branch (2007, 182) aptly notes, "It is concluded that the LRA, embodied in Joseph Kony, is simply insane, the latest manifestation of incomprehensible African violence."

Self-Referrals as ICC's Safe Bets

Compared to other ICC jurisdiction trigger mechanisms, namely, a UN Security Council (UNSC) referral and the prosecutor's own initiative or even (a third-party) state referral, self-referral has the potential to ease the fears of the ICC trampling on state sovereignty, which was very important, especially in the early years of the Court where it faced a lot of suspicion or outright opposition. For the OTP, self-referral also eases the fear of the absence of state cooperation. In fact, the ICC needs state cooperation at all stages of the prosecution, from the preliminary investigations to the incarceration of those convicted. For example, state cooperation is needed for issuance of visas to investigators, for executing arrest warrants, for the transfer of suspects, and so on. Cases of self-referral, such as the one from Uganda, are also advantageous to the OTP because, unlike *proprio motu* investigations, they do not require the approval of the Pre-Trial Chamber.[21]

In addition, the Uganda situation was attractive to the ICC because, unlike the DRC and CAR cases, the conflict in Uganda involved fewer parties, the territory was smaller, and few would come out and support the LRA (Nouwen 2014, 119). The LRA was already on the US terrorist list, and the United States could support the ICC investigation in Uganda because the government of Uganda had already signed a bilateral immunity agreement (BIA).[22] This plays especially in the ICC's favor because the Court needed a good case where state cooperation was ensured and one that would not antagonize the United States, given its opposition to the Court. Uganda's self-referral was also perfect for the ICC and the United States because it targeted the LRA, which was Sudan's ally (Nouwen 2014, 186). If the initial strategy of the OTP was to encourage self-referrals in order to make a caseload for the Court, the strategy appears to have succeeded because soon after the Uganda self-referral, DRC and CAR followed suit, and later on, CAR again, Mali, and Gabon. Indeed, ICC officials often cite these self-referrals from African states as evidence of African support for the Court and the fact that "the ICC has typically intervened by invitation" (Clark 2018, 54).

In strict legal terms, however, a voluntary referral such as the one by Uganda appears to fail to satisfy the threshold for admissibility set out in Article 17 of the Rome Statute, especially because the Ugandan judiciary system had not collapsed or even been affected by the insecurity in its northern territory (Arsanjani and Reisman 2005, 395). The Ugandan government instead made the claim in its referral letter that it was incapable of capturing Joseph Kony, which is essentially a matter of policing, and as Arsanjani and Reisman (2005, 395) assert, "An ineffective police force in the northern region does not meet the requirement set out in Article 17." Indeed, the Ugandan state decided to refer the LRA to the ICC as part of a military strategy and in an

---

[21] Pursuant to the Rome Statute, in the case of the prosecutor using his or her own prerogative to open a preliminary examination, Pre-Trial Chamber approval is needed before the opening of a full investigation.

[22] In an effort to shield American officials, military personnel, and citizens, the US government has signed BIAs with over 100 countries whereby those countries agree that they will never surrender a US citizen to the ICC.

attempt to stir an international campaign against the LRA rather than out of a concern for the rule of law and justice. The fact that the referral was initiated by the Ugandan Ministry of Defense – not the Ministry of Justice – speaks to this strategy (Nouwen and Werner 2010). By referring the LRA to the ICC, Uganda internationalized the conflict in its northern region in order to use the international criminal justice system strategically to defeat its enemy. With the help of the ICC, the LRA would become an enemy of the international community (Nouwen and Werner 2010).

MAKING FRIENDS AND ENEMIES OF MANKIND

By internationalizing the conflict in northern Uganda and referring the LRA to the ICC, the Ugandan state branded the LRA as "humanity's enemy" while portraying itself as a "defender and friend of mankind" (Nouwen and Werner 2010, 950). Not only has the OTP refrained from investigating Ugandan military forces for atrocity crimes, it has indeed nourished a team spirit with Ugandan authorities, conducting joint investigations and enjoying leisurely activities with senior Ugandan officials (Nouwen and Werner 2010, 952).[23] The OTP had already branded the LRA leaders as criminals when it received the referral and before conducting an official investigation. In fact, at the press briefing announcing the referral, the prosecutor had already mentioned that "locating and arresting the LRA leadership "was a key issue" (cited in Nouwen and Werner 2010, 952). This statement from Moreno-Ocampo effectively leaves out potential crimes committed by the Ugandan security forces.

Indeed, the internment of over a million people without adequate protection and assistance constitutes a grave violation of the laws of war and therefore falls within the ICC's jurisdiction (Branch 2007, 181). In addition, Olara Otunnu, the former UN Undersecretary-General and Special Representative for Children and Armed Conflict, himself a Ugandan, has argued, "[G]iven that internment is an explicit government policy that targets the Acholi as a group and has led to tens, or even hundreds of thousands of deaths and to the slow destruction of an entire ethnic group, it in fact amounts to genocide" (cited in Branch 2007, 181–182). This shows that there is clearly a legal basis for the OTP to investigate the government of Uganda and its military forces

---

[23] The Ugandan defense minister Mbabazi and his lawyers were pictured sitting with officials of the OTP's Jurisdiction, Complementarity and Cooperation Division (JCCD) on a boat in the Dutch canals, with the prosecutor himself, at the helm (Nouwen and Werner 2010, 952).

for actions that fall under the ICC's jurisdiction. The ICC investigations in Uganda also betray the prosecutor's own strategy because the ICC involvement is not based on the inability or unwillingness of the government of Uganda to prosecute the LRA leaders. Rather, it is based on the inability of the government of Uganda to arrest the LRA leaders: "The Ugandan judiciary – one of the most proficient and robust in Africa – is unquestionably able and willing to prosecute serious cases such as those involving the LRA" (Clark 2011, 1202).

UGANDA'S SELF-REFERRAL AND DOMESTIC PERCEPTIONS

In Uganda, the self-referral was not warmly received. Indeed, the self-referral and ICC intervention threatened to undermine local efforts at reaching peace. The vice president of ARLPI, Bishop Baker Ochola said, "This kind of approach is going to destroy all efforts for peace." ARLPI activist Father Carlos Rodriguez said, "[T]he issuing of … international arrest warrants would practically close once and for all the path to peaceful negotiation as a means to end this long war, crushing whatever little progress has been made during these years" (cited in Allen 2006, 85). James Otto, head of Gulu-based HRW said in March 2005, "We have our own traditional justice system. The international system despises it, but it works. There is a balance in the community that cannot be found in the briefcase of the white man … The ICC see [sic] Uganda as a soft target … We are forced to kneel" (cited in Allen 2006, 87).

At the time of the ICC referral, there were also in Uganda a deep misunderstanding and ignorance of how the ICC operates, even among Ugandan officials.[24] It seems that even Museveni was not aware of the workings of the ICC. As Allen (2006, 94) argues, Museveni said at the time that if the efforts for peace talks succeeded, he would ask the ICC to stop the investigations, which clearly denotes a lack of understanding of ICC proceedings. In fact, the best the government of Uganda could do in that scenario would be to persuade the OTP to make a case before the ICC's Pre-Trial Chamber that proceeding with the investigations would not be "in the interests of justice." However, one could also make the case that Museveni knew well what he was getting into given that, as Nouwen (2014) has shown, the Uganda self-referral

---

[24] For example, senior UPDF officers confused the International Criminal Court (ICC) with the International Court of Justice (ICJ), and thought the Court would deal with the border dispute between Uganda and Sudan (Allen 2006, 88).

was prepared by international lawyers hired by the Ugandan government. Therefore, it may well be the case that Museveni in fact knew the ICC procedures but was merely pursuing a political strategy to have the upper hand in the ICC involvement in the case and for the negotiations with the LRA.

Other concerns among the Ugandans about the ICC's intervention included the view that the Court is biased toward the Ugandan government; the fact that the referral was announced by Ocampo and Museveni at a joint conference accentuated that perception. An official with the Justice and Reconciliation Project (JRP), a local NGO based in Gulu, said, "That Ocampo press conference was really bizarre...It was such an inaccurate representation of the war. That's a huge problem. People always talk about this."[25] As Clark (2018, 124) argues, in the early years of the ICC intervention in Uganda, "the two dominant and mutually reinforcing views of the ICC among northern Ugandan interviewees were distrust of the close relationship between the Court and Museveni's government and insufficient information about the workings of the ICC." Following news of the Ocampo and Museveni joint conference in London, a victim of the LRA in an IDP camp in Uganda said, "If the ICC and Museveni are working together, there can't be justice" (cited in Clark 2018, 125). Other concerns about the ICC in Uganda are related to the fact that the Court could exacerbate the violence and make the peace process more volatile by undermining the amnesty offer and ignoring local justice initiatives. In fact, leaders of the communities in northern Uganda visited the ICC in The Hague in April 2005 to voice their opinions (ICC – OTP 2005). Finally, some northern Ugandans questioned the legitimacy of the ICC to be involved in the conflict given that they had never heard about the Court, not even when Uganda ratified the Rome Statute in 2002 (Wierda and Otim 2011, 1161).

THE ICC WARRANTS: UGANDA'S WINNING STRATEGY AND THE ROAD TO JUBA

Uganda's self-referral, because it aligned with the interests of both the Ugandan government and the ICC's OTP, followed an initial trajectory that was beneficial for both parties and obviously detrimental to the LRA's leadership. On 7 October 2005, after the ICC had issued the warrants for the arrest of Kony and his top lieutenants, Uganda's defense minister Amama Mbabazi announced, "The [ICC] investigation is complete and the court has taken a decision"

---

[25] Author's interview with JRP official, Gulu, 30 March 2016.

(Allen 2006, 182).[26] But, of course, the investigation was not supposed to be complete given that only one side of the conflict had been investigated and that there were credible reports of war crimes committed by the government forces. For the ICC, however, a nascent institution, the issuance of the warrants for the arrest of Kony and the top LRA commanders was a milestone because the court was eager to make its mark on international justice and politics.

The aftermath of the warrants for the arrests proved to be much more complicated than both the ICC and the Ugandan government had anticipated because the interests of the two partners started to diverge in 2006, when the OTP pursued the legal proceedings while the Ugandan state began exploring multiple routes, including those that would bypass the Court. As the ICC proved unable to accomplish the task for which it was invited – namely, arresting the LRA leaders, the Ugandan government started incurring domestic political costs (Nouwen 2014, 124). As the subchief in the Pabbo IDP camp said, "Until the LRA leaders are captured, the ICC means nothing to us" (cited in Clark (2018, 127). While the northern populations lingered in the refugee camps long after the ICC issued the warrants for the arrest of the LRA leadership, the disillusionment and resentment toward the ICC grew, especially given that the earlier support for the ICC among the local populations, as Clark (2018, 126) writes, was due to the perception that "the ICC had a military and police force capable of arresting the LRA commanders. When respondents were informed that this was not the case, the vast majority questioned the virtues of the ICC operations." At that point, most northern Ugandans started viewing the Court's involvement as an obstacle to peace.

With the arrest warrants, the Ugandan state had in effect instrumentalized the Court by having it criminalize the LRA. This allowed the state to boost its international legitimacy and aura and to pursue its military campaigns. Ugandan internal affairs minister Dr. Ruhakana Rugunda – who was also the leader of the government's negotiating team in the Juba peace talks – said that for the government of Uganda, "the ICC indictments [of the LRA commanders]

---

[26] As Allen (2006, 182) points out, Minister Mbabazi jumped the gun, releasing information that was technically still sealed by the ICC. The OTP applied for the arrest warrants in May 2005 but had requested that the proceedings be under seal. Pre-Trial Chamber II accepted the request and issued the warrants on 8 July 2005, which too was kept secret. However, some people who knew of the warrants divulgated the information. The initial leak appears to have come from the UN system at the end of September 2005. The UN undersecretary general for political affairs Ibrahim Gambari told a news conference in Nairobi that the ICC had issued an arrest warrant for Kony (Allen 2006, 183). Although Gambari said later that he "misspoke," the damage was done. The OTP then applied for the unsealing of the warrants before the Pre-Trial Chamber on 9 September 2005. The chamber finally unsealed the warrants on 13 October 2005 (Allen 2006, 183).

are not a hindrance to the peace process" (Sudan Tribune 2007). In other words, the Ugandan government viewed the ICC indictment as a sword of Damocles hanging over the head of the LRA, which would eventually lead them to follow through with the peace process, at the end of which, amnesty could be eventually granted. This strategy is made clear in the words of Stephen Kagoda, a member of the government team for the Juba peace talks, who said,

> The warrants would not be withdrawn unless the rebels fulfill some obligations. These include signing the final peace agreement with the government, abandoning rebellion, observing total cease-fire, disarming and integrating into the Acholi community … That is when Uganda will tell the United States, the ICC and the world that the LRA have met all the required conditions and should be removed from the terrorist list [and then we will have] the cancellation of the ICC warrants. (New Vision 2007)

This means that, during the Juba peace talks between the Ugandan government and the LRA, the warrants for the arrest of the LRA leaders were a bargaining chip in the hands of Kampala. Soon after his indictment by the ICC, the elusive Kony appeared on a video with the Sudan People's Liberation Army (SPLA)'s vice president Riek Machar and appealed for peace.[27] In the video, Kony says, "Most people do not know me … I am not a terrorist … I am a human being. I want peace also … I want you to know that we, the LRA, want peace … That is why I was in the bush … I am fighting for peace" (Reuters 2006). Under the auspices of the SPLA, the Juba peace talks went on from 2006 to 2008, between the Ugandan government and the LRA, with the ICC arrest warrants still hanging over the heads of the rebel leaders. The Ugandan state played well with its bargaining chips, opening the possibility of withdrawing the warrants while at the same time reassuring the ICC that it would not infringe on its jurisdiction.

When asked about the ICC indictment of Kony and his commanders, the Ugandan minister of information Ali Kirunda Kivejinj said,

> Kony and his commanders have not been fighting in Uganda. He has never set foot in Uganda and right now he is not in Uganda … It is up to the DR Congo, where Kony is hiding, and the United Nations to arrest and hand him over to the ICC. We have been the victims of his long war, but we cannot do anything about the arrest (The New Vision 2006a, 2006b).

Such a statement clearly makes the attempt to arrest Kony someone else's responsibility because the Ugandan state appears to distance itself from the

---

[27] The video also showed Machar handing to Kony an envelope stuffed with cash and telling him: "Twenty-thousand dollars, okay? Buy food with it, not ammunition" (Reuters 2006).

project. In the meantime, the ICC stayed clear from the Juba talks, reiterating the fact that the arrest warrants still stood and complaining that the talks were allowing the LRA to rearm and regroup (Wierda and Otim 2011, 1167).

In the end, the government of Uganda and the LRA signed the Agreement on Accountability and Reconciliation (AAR) in Juba on 29 June 2007, following the Cessation of Hostility Agreement that was reached the previous year. The AAR and its Annexure stipulate that "[t]raditional justice mechanisms, such as Culo Kwor, Mato Oput, Kayo Cuk, Ailuc and Tonu ci Koka and others as practiced in the communities affected by the conflict, shall be promoted, with necessary modifications, as a central part of the framework for accountability and reconciliation (Uganda, 2007)." The parties also affirmed that "Uganda has institutions and mechanisms, customs and usages as provided for and recognized under national laws, capable of addressing the crimes and human rights violations committed during the conflict."[28] Furthermore, the government of Uganda agreed to

> [a]ddress conscientiously the question of the ICC arrest warrants relating to the leaders of the LRA/M …, [r]emove the LRA/M from the list of Terrorist Organisations under the Anti-Terrorism Act of Uganda upon the LRA/M abandoning rebellion, ceasing fire, and submitting its members to the process of Disarmament, Demobilisation, and Reintegration, [and] [m]ake representations to any state or institution which has proscribed the LRA/M to take steps to remove the LRA/M or its members from such list.

The Annexure to the AAR, on 19 February 2008, decided that a special division of the High Court of Uganda shall be established "to try individuals who are alleged to have committed serious crimes during the conflict," which essentially meant that Uganda could bypass the ICC. A "Disarmament, Demobilisation and Reintegration" deal was signed on 29 February 2008, and it was believed that Kony himself would come out to sign the peace treaty on 28 March 2008 in Juba, but this was delayed to April 2008. However, and quite ironically, if the ICC warrant for the arrest of the LRA leaders triggered the cessation of hostilities and the initiation of the Juba peace talks, they also prevented the completion of the peace accords because the LRA commanders insisted that the arrest warrants be annulled before they sign the peace settlements. In the end, Kony and his commanders never travelled to Juba to sign the treaty.

---

[28] For instance, the International Crimes Division (ICD) was created within the Ugandan judiciary potentially to try cases domestically that could fall under ICC jurisdiction. This decision, however, appears to result from Museveni's pragmatic calculations, as a backup plan in case the ICC would investigate UPDF forces (Clark 2018, 156–157).

More than a decade after the Juba peace process, there is yet to be a full accounting and accountability of the decades of conflict in northern Uganda. Civil society organizations, such as the Refugee Law Project (RLP), pushed for the implementation of the Juba accords, despite the fact that the LRA did not ultimately sign it, and the adoption of the Beyond Juba program.[29] As Chris Dolan, the director of RLP said, "The government [of Uganda] does not want the truth to be told … Acknowledgement is a critical part of the transitional justice process. And you can't have it without a truth seeking and truth telling process. The government is not ready for that."[30]

CONCLUSION

This chapter argued that self-referrals served the advancement of political and military gains for the states that have used them to trigger ICC jurisdiction. The five African cases of the use of self-referrals – Uganda, DRC, CAR, and later Mali and Gabon – tell a story of agency of these states in shaping and reformulating the process and delivery of international criminal justice. Self-referrals are an effective strategy for governments in volatile political or security situations to use the ICC as a tool to assert their legitimacy and grip on power while weakening their enemies or political adversaries. Because the use of norms and international justice regimes in ways other than for which they were originally intended is not necessarily in violation of them, this chapter argued that strategic and instrumental use of self-referrals is an example of perversion of the "Referral of a situation by a State Party" as outlined in Article 14 of the Rome Statute.

Even if the use of the self-referral mechanism shows the convergence of interests between the state and the ICC – namely, the OTP – that does not diminish the fact that the states that have used the self-referral trigger mechanism resorted to political calculations and weighted the domestic and international costs and benefits of such action. With Uganda as the main empirical case (because Uganda was the first country to use the self-referral mechanism), this chapter outlined the ways in which Uganda used the self-referral mechanism because it aligned with its political calculations. Indeed, the use of self-referral isolated the LRA and made it an enemy of the international community.

---

[29] Author's interview with Lyandro Komakech, senior researcher for RLP, Kampala, 22 March 2016.
[30] Author's interview, Dolan, Kampala, 22 March 2016.

This chapter also showed the ways in which the interests of the government of Uganda were aligned with those of the ICC – namely, the OTP – at the start of the process (they diverged later) and concluded that the Ugandan government perverted the legal system for its political gains. In fact, self-referral in Uganda had the effects of hindering the peace talks, justifying the amendment of the Amnesty Act of 2000, while at the same time legitimizing further the military approach and potentially prolonging the conflict in northern Uganda. And this may be in fact what the government of Uganda had in mind in late 2003 when it decided to draft the referral letter to be delivered to the ICC.

4

The International Politics of Justice

The tragedy of the ICC is its incapacity to exercise political jurisdiction over great powers, thus, creating a permanent two-tier justice system in which strong states use global institutions to discipline the weak

Stephen Hopgood[1]

INTRODUCTION

International justice is inherently political. Throughout history, political will created international courts, special tribunals, and commissions of inquiry. Two decades ago, political compromise between states resulted in the creation of the first permanent international criminal court. And perhaps the compromise that exemplifies the intricacy between international politics and international justice is the relationship between the UN Security Council (UNSC) and the International Criminal Court (ICC). Yet, as Aloisi (2013, 159) argues, the working relationship between the two institutions is a "political-judicial paradox" in the sense that there is an assumption that "in order for international justice to be legitimate, independence from political will is a necessary requirement" (Aloisi 2013, 159). However, efforts to demarcate law and politics are untenable, and they render an analysis of the politics of law impossible (Clarke and Koulen 2014). Even more so, the ICC is inherently and inextricably political (Nouwen and Werner 2010).

In the realm of domestic political institutions and courts, a distinction is often made between legal and political institutions. Courts are perceived to be divorced from and above politics, which is the domain of political institutions. This distinction offers law a foundation upon which to legitimate itself

---

[1] Hopgood (2013).

as a system of neutral rules that is above the partisan processes (Clarke and Koulen 2014, 301). The same distinction has been translated to international law and international politics, re-creating the play between "the law" and "politics," where in the international realm, the ICC would embody the legal, and the UN Security Council would exemplify the political. This chapter argues, however, that such a distinction is problematic and does not reflect the reality of the workings of these institutions. In fact, the UNSC and the ICC do not occupy, respectively, the realms of the political and legal. The relationship between these institutions, as shown through the debates that animated the Rome Conference negotiations, the drafting of the Rome Statute, and the use of Security Council referrals, all show that international justice is inherently political.

This chapter first explores the institutional relations between the ICC and the Security Council, as set by the Rome Statute, before arguing that the ways in which the Security Council has selectively referred Sudan and Libya to the ICC while failing to refer Syria, for instance, exemplify the political dimension of the workings of international justice. Given that the Security Council is the institution that allows the ICC to gain jurisdiction over states that have not ratified the Rome Statute, this chapter also explores the application of international treaties such as the Rome Statute over states that are not signatories. During the early days of the uprisings, defectors from the Gaddafi regime at the UN pushed for the Security Council to take up the Libya case and adopt the resolutions that ultimately referred the situation to the ICC. Finally, an analysis of the complementarity principle also highlights the international dimension of the politics of the ICC. The example of Libya shows the ways in which, after the fall of the Gaddafi regime, a state that is not a member of the ICC chose to engage the Court through an admissibility challenge, in pursuit of its security and political interests. Despite the ICC rulings, however, the Libyan authorities have repeatedly refused to surrender Saif Gaddafi to the Court.

THE UNSC AND THE ICC

Unlike other international or hybrid ad hoc tribunals, such as the International Criminal Tribunal for the Former Yugoslavia (ICTY), the International Criminal Tribunal for Rwanda (ICTR), and others, the ICC was not created by the United Nations and therefore is not a UN organ. This means that the Court has a distinct international legal personality, independent from the UN system. However, the Rome Statute provided that the Court "shall be brought into relationship with the United Nations through an agreement."[2] As paragraph 4 of the Rome Statute reflects, the ICC was established with the consideration that prosecuting atrocity crimes of concern to the international community would enhance peace and security around the world. The UNSC, as the international body par excellence that is tasked with ensuring peace and security through its Chapter VII powers, would then work in tandem with the Court when necessary. To that end, the Rome Statute included a provision – namely, Article 13(b) – by which the Security Council could authorize the ICC to investigate and prosecute situations that arise in states that are not members of the Court. This gives the ICC a *virtual* universal jurisdiction, regardless of the number of states that opt not to join the Court. Also, Article 16 of the Rome Statute gives the UNSC the power to defer any prosecution or investigations for a period of twelve months.

During the Rome conference, permanent members of the Security Council sought to place ICC jurisdiction under the supervision and control of the Security Council and thus make the Court's jurisdiction subject to its approval. In the end, the so-called Singaporean Compromise was reached, taking into consideration both the desires of those who sought to place the ICC under the supervision of the Security Council and the desires of those who wanted an independent court: the compromise gave the Security Council the power to refer non-state members to the ICC – Article 13(b) – and the power to defer cases before the ICC, using Article 16 of the Rome Statute (Glasius 2006; Scheffer 2013; Clarke and Koulen 2014). This gives the Security Council effective control over the ICC, the irony being, of course, that three of the five permanent members of the UNSC – the United States, Russia, and China – are not ICC members. It also effectively merges a political agenda into one that *prima facie* claimed to be first and foremost a legalistic approach to ending impunity for atrocity crimes around the world. As Louise Arbour (2011), the former chief prosecutor at the ICTY and ICTR, argues, "[I]nternational criminal justice cannot be sheltered from political considerations when they are administered by the quintessential political body: the Security Council. I have long advocated a separation of the justice and the political agendas and would prefer to see an ICC that had no connection to the Security Council. But this is neither the case nor the trend."

The relationship between the ICC and the Security Council is certainly a conundrum for the Court. In the absence of universal jurisdiction, the ICC can receive cases only from states that have willingly joined the Court or have

---

[2] Article 22 of the Rome Statute. www.icc-cpi.int/resource-library/documents/rs-eng.pdf.

accepted its jurisdiction on an ad hoc basis. The ICC prosecutor can use his or her own initiative but only for crimes committed in states that have ratified the Rome Statute or by citizens of such states.[3] Hence, UNSC referrals are the only way by which the ICC may have jurisdiction over nonconsenting, nonparty states.[4] But Article 16 had the potential of trapping the vision of an independent and impartial court into the political calculations of the UNSC members and power politics.

THE ARTICLE 16 TRAP

Soon after the Rome Statute went into effect, on 12 July 2002 the UNSC adopted Resolution 1422, in which it requested that the ICC not start or proceed in any investigation arising from an operation established or authorized under Chapter VII of the UN Charter that involves officials or persons from states that are not party to the Rome Statute.[5] The Security Council reasoned that this resolution was in accordance with Article 16 of the Rome Statute (Elias and Quast 2003). Although the ICC is not exactly an organ of the UN, members of the Security Council have sought to control the Court since its inception (Clarke and Koulen 2014, 298). During the Rome Conference, it became clear that most delegations supported the inclusion of a provision where the Security Council would be able to have a trigger mechanism for the Court jurisdiction. For instance, the US delegation was primarily concerned with finding ways to protect its military personnel from prosecution by the Court. As David Scheffer, the head of the US delegation at the Rome Conference writes,

> I struggled to avoid the train wreck at Rome only to embrace certain defeat. I would have risked my own removal from the negotiations if I had pressed too openly or too hard on the Pentagon or on Senator Jesse Helms, so I had to maneuver in ways that steadily built broader circles of support for the policies that stood any chance of adoption at Rome ... The stubbornness of various Washington agencies and officials in seeking full immunity from prosecution for American soldiers and other citizens, regardless of whether the United States joined the International Criminal Court, seemed at times to be forged in Alice's Wonderlands (Scheffer 2013, 413).

---

[3] Again, states can still accept the ICC's ad hoc jurisdiction without ratifying the Rome Statute.
[4] See for instance the debates about referring the civil war in Syria to the ICC. Syria being a nonparty state to the ICC, the only way the Court can gain jurisdiction is through a UNSC referral. Such attempts have been defeated at the UNSC because of the reluctance of some of the P5 members (notably Russia and China) to support such resolution.
[5] UN Security Council Resolution 1422 (2002), S/RES 1422(2002). https://documents-dds-ny.un.org/doc/UNDOC/GEN/N02/477/61/PDF/N0247761.pdf.

David Scheffer and the US delegation went to the Rome conference, obligated to defend the position of the Pentagon that required full immunity of US personnel – which, by the way, was not the position of the State and Justice departments. The United States was also opposed to an independent prosecutor for the Court and sought to give the Security Council exclusive power of referral. This position held by the United States and a few other delegations was untenable because the majority of the conference attendees sought to create a court that would allow prosecutorial independence from the Security Council.[6] The compromise thus became the possibility for the Security Council to refer "situations," which are wider in concept – than "cases" or "matters" (Arbour 2014, 197).

Article 16 of the Rome Statute, titled "Deferral of investigation or prosecution," provides the following: "No investigation or prosecution may be commenced or proceeded with under this Statute for a period of 12 months after the Security Council, in a resolution adopted under Chapter VII of the Charter of the United Nations, has requested the Court to that effect; that request may be renewed by the Council under the same conditions." Its provisions were more contentious among the delegations and the non-governmental organizations (NGOs) because it opened the possibility of political interference once ICC proceedings were underway. It is because the International Law Commission's draft had previously suggested that the Court seeks permission from the Security Council for proceedings, and the Singaporean Compromise replaced that provision by making the Court defer proceedings rather than the Court asking for permission (Scheffer 2013). The Canadian delegation added a twelve-month expiration for any deferral. Although the criticism against Article 16 has been more vocal than that of Article 13(b),[7] in essence, both present the risk of politicization of ICC proceedings (Arbour 2014). It is important to note that Article 16 deferrals do not prevent the Court from exercising jurisdiction indefinitely – they are issued for periods of twelve months, renewable. Interestingly though, UNSC Resolution 1422 (2002) was adopted less than two weeks after the entry into force of the Rome Statute, a resolution that was inspired by the staunch opposition of the United States to the ICC at the time

---

[6] After what had become a fiasco for the American delegation at the negotiations in Rome, Scheffer (2013, 230) writes that upon his return, his bosses did not acknowledge his efforts and that his relationship with Secretary of State Albright became distant. He notes that Albright omits any reference to the ICC in her memoirs.

[7] Article 13(b) is related to the Court exercising its jurisdiction over situations referred to it by the UNSC under Chapter VII of the UN Charter. Article 16 relates to the ability of the UNSC to defer cases already in the hands of the ICC. See the Rome Statute www.icc-cpi.int/nr/rdonlyres/ea9aeff7-5752-4f84-be94-0a655eb30e16/0/rome_statute_english.pdf.

(Elias and Quast 2003, 170), and it would later inspire the UNSC referral resolutions of Darfur and Libya, in relation to not extending the ICC jurisdiction over service members from states who are not party to the Rome Statute.

Could the UNSC use the leverage conferred upon it by the Rome Statute in a way that would be devoid of politics? The UNSC has in fact acted just as a quintessential political body, for example, using its power to refer Sudan and Libya to the ICC which contrasts with its failure to act in Sri Lanka and Syria. The Security Council has also refused to grant Article 16 deferral for Sudan and Kenya, while recalling the provisions of Article 16 in the resolution that referred Libya. UNSC Resolution 1970 also excluded nationals from states that were not party to the Rome Statute from ICC jurisdiction in the situations of Sudan and Libya. All these examples point to international politics within the UNSC that tainted its actions, or failures to act, in relation to cases that may have been within the ICC mandate.

But perhaps none of these actions exemplifies the politics that guide the UNSC in regard to its relationship with the ICC and in the domain of international criminal law better than UNSC Resolution 1970 that referred the situation in Libya to the ICC (UN Security Council 2011c). As Stahn (2012) writes, "The language of [Security Council Resolution] 1970 stands as an unfortunate precedent for future practice." Stahn (2012) shows that UNSC referrals come to the ICC with their own pitfalls and problems and pose challenges to the idea of "shared responsibility" as outlined in the Responsibility to Protect (R2P) doctrine and the Rome Statute. Following the two UNSC Libya resolutions, the mandate of the ICC coexisted with an authorization of the use of force to protect Libyan citizens, which falls within the purview of R2P, and provided the legal rationale for the North Atlantic Treaty Organization (NATO) intervention in Libya. The referral was initially applauded by the international community and human rights organizations as a victory of justice. But as Stahn (2012, 326–327) writes, "[with] emerging criticism regarding NATO's wide interpretation of the enforcement mandate under Resolution 1973, the controversial circumstances of…Gaddafi's death, allegations of crimes relating to the conduct of all sides, including abuses by opposition forces and NATO, the role of the ICC has become a bone of contention."

Although the Security Council has done little to support the ICC in its investigations in Sudan, the Libyan case shows a quick reaction of the Security Council, which adopted a referral resolution that copied the same flaws of the Sudan referral, namely, excluding citizens of nonparty states – except for Libyans – from the ICC jurisdiction, and making the ICC bear the cost of the investigations and prosecution (Stahn 2012, 328). The ICC reacted to UNSC Resolution 1970 with lightning speed: the Office of the Prosecutor opened the investigation only a couple of days after the referral, on 2 March 2011. Soon after the referral, Prosecutor Ocampo requested that arrest warrants be issued for the "Tripoli Three" – Muammar Gaddafi, Saif Gaddafi, and Abdullah Al-Senussi, and the Pre-Trial Chamber issued all three warrants on 27 June 2011. By moving swiftly, the ICC clearly wanted to have a say in mitigating the ongoing violence in Libya, but it also raised concerns over the prospects of a negotiated political solution. For instance, the African Union (AU) argued that "[the warrant] concerning Colonel Qadhafi seriously complicates the efforts aimed at finding a negotiated political solution to the crisis in Libya" (African Union 2011, para. 6). The AU also urged its members not to cooperate with the ICC for the execution of the arrest warrant against Muammar Gaddafi; similar to the call regarding the warrant for the arrest of President Bashir.

THE POLITICS OF UNSC REFERRALS AND NONPARTY STATES

Do international treaties apply to nonsignatories? Part 9 of the Rome Statute addresses state cooperation with the ICC and sets out the obligations of state parties to assist the Court in its mission. Particularly, Article 86 says that "States Parties shall, in accordance with the provisions of the Statute, cooperate fully with the Court in its investigations and prosecutions of crimes within the jurisdiction of the Court" (Rome Statute, 1998). But the ICC is a treaty-based court, and states willingly choose to join the institution, which also means that many states have opted not to sign or ratify the Rome Statute.[8] Therefore, UNSC referrals are made under Article 13(b) of the Rome Statute, whose purpose is to extend jurisdiction of the Court to states that have not ratified the Rome Statute. Therefore, states that fall under the UNSC referral – to date, only Sudan and Libya – are likely to be non-ICC members. As nonparties to the ICC, those states do not have any preexisting obligations set out in Part 9 of Rome Statute (Akande 2012, 301). Contrary to state parties to the Rome Statute, they do not have any obligation to cooperate with or assist the Court. The contending question among legal scholars then becomes, Does the Rome Statute apply to a state that has become the subject of a UNSC referral? In other words, does a UNSC resolution makes a state bound to a treaty that it has not joined? This raises a broader question on how treaties apply to nonsignatories. For instance, Article 27 asserts the irrelevance of official capacity, which essentially removes head-of-state immunity for crimes that fall under the Court's jurisdiction. Does that rule apply to nonsignatories

---

[8] As of June 2019, there are only 122 states that are parties to the Rome Statute of the International Criminal Court. For an overview of the ICC and its relations with nonparty states, see Cryer (2015).

of the Rome Statute, or more precisely, does the UN Security referral strip President Bashir of Sudan of his immunity while in office?[9]

It is well established under customary international law that incumbent heads of states enjoy immunity from prosecution in foreign courts. The drafters of the Rome Statute had that in mind when they sought to make sure that such immunity does not apply in the case of the core crimes that fall under the ICC's jurisdiction. Article 27 of the Rome Statute, in its first paragraph, provides that "[t]his Statute shall apply equally to all persons without any distinction based on official capacity. In particular, official capacity as a Head of State or Government, a member of a Government or parliament, an elected representative or a government official shall in no case exempt a person from criminal responsibility under this Statute…"[10] The question of head-of-state immunity is however more complex in cases of states that are not signatories of the Rome Statute given that the ICC is a treaty-based institution.

Obviously, any state that has ratified the Rome Statute has accepted the fact that its head of state and other government officials would not be immune from the Court's investigation or prosecution. But does the UNSC, through an ICC referral, have the power to lift head-of-state immunity of nonsignatories of the Rome Statute? For the first time, the ICC issued a warrant for the arrest of a sitting head of state, namely, President Bashir of Sudan, on 4 March 2009 (ICC Pre-Trial Chamber I 2009). Although the customary international law of immunity for high-level state officials was confirmed by a decision of the International Court of Justice in the case of the *Democratic Republic of Congo* v. *Belgium*,[11] the ICC Pre-Trial Chamber found that Bashir has no immunity before the ICC, in accordance with Article 27(2) of the Rome Statute, even though Sudan is not a signatory of the treaty. The ruling also extends an obligation for the states to cooperate with the Court or use the Court's legal proceedings to challenge admissibility of the cases (Akande 2012). This argument posits that a nonsignatory state is still obligated to cooperate with the Court in case of a UNSC referral. Such a state may introduce an admissibility challenge to the ICC – which is what Libya did – and while the challenge is still pending, the state may postpone its requirement to assist the Court in its investigation and prosecution.

---

[9] The case of Libyan president Gadaffi is moot because he died soon after the UNSC referral.
[10] Rome Statute, Article 27.
[11] A Belgian judge had issued a warrant for the arrest of the Democratic Republic of Congo's (DRC) incumbent minister of foreign affairs. The International Court of Justice ruled for the immunity of the Congolese minister from criminal jurisdiction in another state. See Arrest Warrant of 11 April 2000, *Democratic Republic of the Congo* v. *Belgium*, International Court of Justice, 14 February 2002, ICJ Reports (2002), 3. www.icj-cij.org/docket/files/121/8126.pdf.

For its part, the ICC has made the case that Security Council resolutions under Chapter VII of the UN Charter are compulsory (ICC Pre-Trial Chamber II 2014b). In fact, UNSC ICC referrals under Article 13(b) are done under Chapter VII of the UN Charter provisions, to restore peace and security, which then necessarily engage all states. Following this reasoning, Papillon (2010) contends that the Security Council implicitly removes head-of-state immunity when referring a case to the ICC, even when the said state is not an ICC member. This question would have been resolved if Sudan had waived Bashir's immunity, for instance, by ratifying the Rome Statute.

On the other hand, Jacobs (2015) maintains that the UNSC does not have the power to lift head-of-state immunity of a nonsignatory to the ICC. In this case, the UNSC referral of Sudan to the ICC cannot override President Bashir's immunity as a head of state. As Jacobs (2015) argues, the removal of head-of-state immunity originates first from the Rome Statute, specifically in its Article 27. It follows from this argument then that a UNSC ICC referral of the situation in Darfur, even when invoking Chapter VII powers from the UN Charter, is still limited by the fact that Sudan has not acceded to the Rome Statute and therefore has not accepted the removal of the immunity of its head of state. Gaeta (2009) argues along the same lines, albeit with nuance. Whereas she argues that the ICC can lawfully issue a warrant for the arrest of Bashir, despite the fact that Sudan is not an ICC member, she also contends that the ICC's request for states to execute that warrant is not permitted under international law.

Probably the most intriguing ICC proceeding on this question relates to Jordan's failure to arrest Bashir and surrender him to the Court. The ICC Pre-Trial Chamber II had decided that Jordan, as a state party to the Rome Statute, had failed to comply with its obligation to arrest President Bashir and surrender him to the Court while Bashir was in Jordanian territory in March 2017 during an Arab League summit. The Pre-Trial Chamber had also decided to refer Jordan's noncompliance to the Assembly of States Parties and the UNSC. Surprisingly, the Appeals Chamber subsequently ruled that there is no head-of-state immunity vis-à-vis an international court and therefore upheld the first Pre-Trial Chamber's decision, although it found that the chamber had erred in referring Jordan's noncompliance to the Assembly of States Parties and the Security Council.[12] In any case, the ruling by the Appeals Chamber has been met with confusion by legal scholars, who have pointed out its many flaws.[13]

---

[12] See "Al-Bashir Case: ICC Appeals Chamber confirms Jordan's non-cooperation but reverses the decision referring it to the ASP and UNSC." Press Release, ICC-CPI-20190506-PR1452.

[13] At the time of writing, no peer-reviewed articles have been published on this ruling. However, there have been many publications in international law blogs. See, for instance, Kiyani (2019), Heller (2019a), Akande (2019), and Jacobs (2019b).

THE POLITICS OF UNSC ICC NONREFERRALS: THE CASE OF SYRIA

The political calculations that underpin the relations between the UNSC and the ICC in relation to nonparty states are also exemplified in the cases in which the Security Council fails to adopt a resolution that grants the Court jurisdiction over a situation. The civil war in Syria provides an interesting example of the ways in which political considerations and patronage at the UNSC play into the deployment of the Security Council's power to refer or defer cases to the ICC. The conflict in Syria has escalated since it started in 2011 in the wake of the so-called Arab Spring. The government forces loyal to President Assad and its militias have deliberately targeted civilian areas while the armed opposition groups have attacked civilians, used child soldiers, kidnappings and torture (Human Rights Watch 2016b). Extremist groups such as the Islamic State and Al Qaeda affiliates in Syria are also responsible for targeting civilians, kidnappings, and summary executions. By 2017, more than 400,000 had died in the Syria conflict while 5 million sought refuge abroad and over 6 million Syrians were internally displaced (Human Rights Watch 2018). Various human rights organizations have documented, in the context of the conflict, instances of targeting civilians; indiscriminate attacks; and use of cluster munitions, chemical weapons, and nerve agents (Human Rights Watch 2018). Alleged acts that fall within the material jurisdiction of the ICC – war crimes and crimes against humanity – may have been committed in Syria, as preliminary evidence shows, which warrant further investigation by the ICC prosecutor. The ICC would also have temporal jurisdiction over the situation in Syria because these events occurred after the entry in force of the Rome Statute in 2002. Given that Syria is not an ICC member, however, the Court could have territorial jurisdiction in Syria only through a UNSC resolution.[14]

Indeed, various resolutions that would have referred Syria to the ICC have been introduced before the Security Council, but they all were vetoed, which prompts questions regarding the play of politics in the Security Council–ICC dynamic (Clarke and Koulen 2014). A UNSC referral would give the ICC prosecutor the green light to investigate and prosecutes all crimes against humanity and war crimes committed in Syria by all parties to the conflict, including the government forces, the Syrian opposition militias, and the Islamist groups. By September 2013, when major human rights organizations were pushing for

---

[14] Another way the ICC prosecutor could gain jurisdiction to investigate and prosecute in Syria is if the Syrian government accepted the Court's jurisdiction through an ad hoc declaration. But that is unlikely to happen, for obvious reasons. The only viable way for the ICC to gain jurisdiction then is through a UNSC referral.

the UNSC to refer Syria to the ICC, Security Council members were divided in the support for such referral. Whereas six members – France, the United Kingdom, Luxembourg, Argentina, Australia, and South Korea – supported a referral, the United States, China, and Russia were not in favor (Human Rights Watch 2013). In January 2013, Switzerland sent a letter to the Security Council on behalf of fifty-eight countries that called for a resolution referring Syria to the ICC (Gurber 2013).[15]

But in May 2014, Russia and China vetoed a UNSC resolution introduced by France that would have referred Syria to the ICC, although it was supported by the other thirteen members of the Security Council (UNSC 2014).[16] In his statement, the Russian representative said that, when the Security Council referred Libya to the ICC in 2011, that referral had only resulted in "throwing oil on the fire," and the Court has evaded "the matter of the bombardment by North Atlantic Treaty Organization (NATO) forces against civilians" (UNSC 2014). Russia also recalled that the United States was pushing for the referral, despite not being a member of the ICC, and the United Kingdom, while a party to the Rome Statute, "was reluctant to try its own nationals who were fighting as members of armed groups in Syria" (UNSC 2014). As in the case of previous resolutions for ICC referrals, this draft resolution also included a provision to exclude any citizen of a state that was not an ICC member from prosecution – except for Syrians, of course – at The Hague.

In a surprising move at the time, the Obama administration decided to support the draft resolution that France had introduced. As another example of the high-stakes politics of UNSC referrals to the ICC, the United States indicated, however, that it could support the draft resolution "only after seeking assurances that the ICC prosecutor … would have no authority to investigate any possible war crimes by Israel, which has occupied the Golan Heights since the Six-Day War in 1967" (Lynch 2014). This caveat is noteworthy because with the ICC gaining jurisdiction in Syria, Israel's occupation of the Golan Heights could fall within the jurisdiction of the Court. The exclusion of citizens from states that are not members of the ICC from prosecution reassures Israel in the case of a Syria referral, but also US military personnel who may be involved in the Syrian conflict one way or the other.

The provision to shield non-Syrian nationals from ICC prosecution, which is copied from the Sudan and Libya referrals, has become de facto part of UN proposals to refer states that are not signatories to the Rome

---

[15] See the letter addressed to the Security Council. www.news.admin.ch/NSBSubscriber/message/attachments/29293.pdf.

[16] See the minutes of the UNSC meeting. www.un.org/press/en/2014/sc11407.doc.htm.

Statute to the Court. Had the Syria ICC referral passed, except for Syrian nationals, any citizens of a non-ICC member state would be safe from investigation and prosecution by the ICC in relation to the conflict. Both the previous resolutions on Darfur and Libya were written with a similar language. As Cryer (2006) noted regarding the Sudan referral (UNSC Resolution 1593), this not only limits the independence of the prosecutor but also defies the idea of equality before law. It raises concerns about exclusionary and selective justice but also a hierarchy of crimes based on the nationality of the individuals who perpetrated them (Aloisi 2013, 153). Argentina and Brazil voiced their disapproval of this limitation of jurisdiction within Resolution 1593 (Sudan) (UN Security Council 2005), and Brazil did the same for Resolution 1970 (Libya).

In any case, while the narrative on the failure of the UNSC to act in the case of Syria is construed around the images of Russia and China being responsible for the ongoing impunity, the story is indeed more complex. During the Obama administration, the United States shifted its position on the matter, moving toward the states that proclaim to be on the right side of history, to refer Syria to the ICC, which, according to this narrative, works toward accountability for atrocity crimes and acts toward putting an end to the civil war. But the text of the draft resolution that would have referred Syria to the ICC contains caveats that can barely pass the ending-impunity test. With the precedents of the Libya resolution in 2011 and its aftermath, one can see why using the UNSC to refer a state to the ICC does not necessarily end an ongoing conflict or provide an avenue for accountability for war crimes and crimes against humanity. In the end, politics and strategic interests among UNSC members and their allies and protégés are what guides both action and failure to act to grant the ICC jurisdiction over conflicts in states that are not members of the Court.

Beyond the Syria case, the UNSC has also failed to take action in situations that bore similar characteristics to Libya and Darfur, to some extent. For instance, a UN report had documented that tens of thousands of civilians had lost their lives in Sri Lanka between January and May 2009 as a result of the fighting between the Sri Lankan forces and Tamil rebels and that it was likely that both sides had committed war crimes.[17] China's support to the Sri Lankan government and Russia's opposition to consider the case have meant that the issue of referring Sri Lanka to the ICC has never been seriously contemplated. In the wake of the Arab Spring, the civil war in Yemen and human rights abuse and repression in Bahrain are also examples of instances where the UNSC has

---

[17] See Report of the Secretary General's Panel of Experts on Accountability in Sri Lanka, 31 March 2011. www.securitycouncilreport.org/atf/cf/%7B65BFCF9B-6D27-4E9C-8CD3-CF6E4FF96FF9%7D/POC%20Rep%20on%20Account%20in%20Sri%20Lanka.pdf.

not seriously considered an ICC referral (Aloisi 2013, 165). The details of the Libya referral show the long shadow of power politics in the deliberations that led the UNSC to grant jurisdiction to the ICC during the 2011 uprisings.

THE LIBYA REFERRAL: R2P WHOM?

As a nonparty state to the Rome Statute, the trigger mechanisms through which the ICC could obtain jurisdiction over events that occurred in Libya were limited.[18] The UNSC Resolution 1970, passed on 26 February 2011, during the uprisings in Libya, included a battery of sanctions against the embattled Gaddafi regime. It also referred the situation in Libya to the ICC, without much dissent or concern from the Security Council members, unlike the first Security Council ICC referral related to Darfur.[19] But it was clear from the beginning that the Libya ICC referral was politicized – after all, the UNSC, which is the international lawmaking body par excellence, is a quintessential political institution (Kersten 2015a). First, the referral excluded citizens from nonmember states of the ICC – except for Libyans – thus, granting them *de facto* amnesty.[20] Without a doubt, this was a move to shield US soldiers and other NATO service members from the ICC jurisdiction in connection to the events in Libya. Brazil was the only UNSC member that openly criticized the exclusion of nonparty states from the jurisdiction of the ICC referral in Libya.[21]

---

[18] The only way the ICC can have jurisdiction over non-state parties without their consent is through a UN Security Council resolution. Note that nonparty states can still accept ICC jurisdiction by submitting an ad hoc declaration to the Court, pursuant to Article 12(3) of the Rome Statute. The ICC could also obtain jurisdiction in the case of a citizen of a state-party who commits core crimes in a nonparty state.

[19] UNSC Resolution 1970 was unanimously adopted under Article 41, Chapter VII of the UN Charter. Resolution 1973 imposing the no-fly zone was passed three weeks later. Even the United States, despite having previously abstained for the Sudan referral, voted in favor of the Libya referral.

[20] The wording of the resolution leaves no doubt about that. It "[decides] that nationals, current or former officials or personnel from a State outside the Libyan Arab Jamahiriya which is not a state party to the Rome Statute of the International Criminal Court shall be subject to the exclusive jurisdiction of that State for alleged acts or omissions arising out of or related to operations in the Libyan Arab Jamahiriya established or authorized by the Council, unless such exclusive jurisdiction has been expressly waived by the State" (UNSC Resolution 1970 [2011]).

[21] Brazil's representative "expressed strong reservations to the provision in the resolution allowing for exemptions from jurisdiction of nationals from non-States Parties, saying those were not helpful to advance the cause of justice and accountability." The representative also noted that five members of the Security Council were not state parties to the ICC (UN 2011c). The five members of the Security Council that were not members of the ICC at the time of the referral were the United States, Russia, China, India, and Lebanon.

Second, Article 16 of the Rome Statute about UNSC deferrals was recalled in the resolution, which was meant to reassure the NATO allies that, should the ICC become an impediment to the intervention or the political transition, the Security Council could always suspend the Court's involvement.[22] The resolution therefore reiterates the fact that the Security Council still exercises control over the ICC judicial process in Libya as well. Finally, the temporal limitation of the referral to events that occurred only on or after 15 February 2011, may have been meant to shield Western powers from the Court's investigation of potentially damaging dealings with the Gaddafi regime, in the context of the warm-up between Libya and the West in the years immediately preceding the 2011 Libyan crisis.[23] The UNSC stated that it "[recognizes] that none of the expenses incurred in connection with the referral, including expenses related to investigations or prosecutions in connection with that referral, shall be borne by the United Nations," leaving it up to the ICC to finance the investigations and the prosecutions.[24]

However, the Responsibility to Protect (R2P) doctrine that UNSC Resolution 1970 (2011b) invoked appeared at first sight to be concerned only with the lives of Libyans, who were facing calamity at the hands of the Gaddafi regime. In the language of the resolution, the Security Council "[expresses] concern at the plight of refugees forced to flee the violence in the Libyan Arab Jamahiriya, [and recalls] the Libyan authorities' responsibility to protect its population." The Libyan conflict was the first instance in which the UNSC explicitly invoked the R2P doctrine within a Chapter VII resolution,

---

[22] The Resolution "[recalls] article 16 of the Rome Statute under which no investigation or prosecution may be commenced or proceeded with by the International Criminal Court for a period of 12 months after a Security Council request to that effect," acted under Chapter VII of the UN Charter.

[23] It is important to note that the Libyan crisis occurred following a few years of Western powers engaging the Gaddafi regime, after decades of sanctions against Libya.

[24] Article 115 of the Rome Statute notes that Court expenses "shall be provided" not only by the state parties but also "by the United Nations, subject to the approval of the General Assembly, in particular in relation to the expenses incurred due to referrals by the Security Council." This explains why many were disappointed that the UNSC failed to authorize UN funding in the Sudan and Libya situations (Kaye 2013, 4). The funding of referrals, or costs incurred by UNSC referrals, is a major point of contention. Although the Rome Statute provides for the possibility of the ICC receiving funding from the UN, all the cases of investigation and prosecutions, including those referred by the UNSC, have been paid for by the state parties. This has to do with the US position toward the Court. From the early days of the US opposition to the ICC, the US Congress passed the consolidated Appropriation Public Law of 2000, which prohibits any funds from being used by or in support of the ICC. See Title 22, Chapter 7401 (b) www.govinfo.gov/content/pkg/USCODE-2013-title22/pdf/USCODE-2013-title22-chap81-subchapI-sec7401.pdf.

which imposed arms embargo, travel bans, and assets freezes on Libya and also referred the situation to the ICC. It is clear that, as far as the ICC referral is concerned, the Security Council went to great lengths to ensure that NATO personnel and citizens of other countries who would intervene in Libya would be protected from the ICC prosecutor's reach. This brings the high politics of the UNSC and international criminal justice back into focus. However, the Libyan authorities, both in Tripoli and New York, were also major players in the political machinations of the ICC referral.

LIBYA'S POLITICAL MANEUVERING AT THE UN

The UNSC referral of Libya occurred at a time of political upheaval in the country: in the wake of the Arab Spring. The political maneuvering of the diplomatic mission at the UN, which played a crucial role in the lead-up to the referral, begs questions about its legitimacy. The *chargé d'affaires* of the Permanent Mission of Libya to the UN, Ibrahim Dabbashi, had sent a letter to the UNSC requesting an urgent meeting of the Security Council "to discuss the grave situation in Libya and to take the appropriate actions" (UNSC 2011a).[25] This means that the UNSC process that led to the referral was initiated by a party whose legitimacy may be questioned. In fact, Dabbashi, who had been until then the deputy ambassador for Libya to the UN, had announced that he had defected from the Libyan government on 21 February 2011, the same day he sent the letter to the UNSC. That defection did not lead, however, to his resignation or removal as a Libyan diplomat. In fact, he held the press conference at the Libyan mission to the UN and had requested an emergency meeting of the UNSC about the situation in Libya.[26]

Dabbashi's letter to the Security Council reads in part, "In accordance with rule 3 of the provisional rules of procedure of the Security Council, I have the honour to request an urgent meeting of the Council, to discuss the grave situation in Libya and to take the appropriate actions."[27] In fact, rule 3 refers to the possibility of a member nation to the UN requesting a meeting; thus, Dabbashi, as a defector, should not have been able to request a meeting

---

[25] See UNSC document S/2011/102, dated 22 February 2011. www.securitycouncilreport.org/atf/cf/%7B65BFCF9B-6D27-4E9C-8CD3-CF6E4FF96FF9%7D/Libya%20S%202011%20102.pdf.

[26] Shalgham too, the head of the Libyan mission at the UN, defected by 25 February 2011, and denounced the Libyan government at the Security Council meeting that same day.

[27] See UNSC document S/2011/102, dated 22 February 2011. www.securitycouncilreport.org/atf/cf/%7B65BFCF9B-6D27-4E9C-8CD3-CF6E4FF96FF9%7D/Libya%20S%202011%20102.pdf.

because he was no longer a representative of the Libyan state.[28] And as one would expect, the Libyan government had sent a letter to the UN Secretary General revoking the credentials of Dabbashi and Shalgham, the head of the Libyan mission at the UN, yet they continued to speak in the name of Libya at the UN meetings.[29] This process calls into question not only the political maneuverings that led to the Libya referral to the ICC but also the extent to which the Council was willing to play along.

ADMISSIBILITY CHALLENGES: LIBYA LOSES AND WINS

After the UNSC decided unanimously to refer the situation in Libya to the ICC, the prosecutor concluded on 3 March 2011, that there were reasonable grounds to believe that crimes under ICC jurisdiction were committed and decided to open an investigation. Then, on 16 March 2011, the prosecutor requested issuance of warrants for the arrest of Muammar Gaddafi, Saif Al-Islam Gaddafi, and Abdullah Al-Senussi "for their alleged criminal responsibility for the commission of murder and persecution as crimes against humanity from 15 February 2011 onward throughout Libya in, inter alia, Tripoli, Benghazi, and Misrata, through the Libyan State apparatus and Security Forces" (ICC PTC I 2011). The Pre-Trial Chamber I issued the warrant for the arrest of Saif Al-Islam Gaddafi on 27 June 2011, considering, under Article 25(3)(a) of the Rome Statute, that there were reasonable grounds to believe that he was criminally responsible as indirect co-perpetrator for two counts of crimes against humanity: murder and persecution (ICC PTC I 2011). The warrant for the arrest of Muammar Gaddafi was withdrawn and his case terminated following his death on 22 November 2011. The proceedings against Al-Senussi before the ICC ended on 24 July 2014, when the Appeals Chamber confirmed a decision by the Pre-Trial Chamber I declaring the case inadmissible before the ICC.

---

[28] Here are the Rules of Procedure for Termination of Service at Permanent/Observer Missions: "Before relinquishing his/her post, a Permanent Representative/Observer should inform the Secretary-General in writing and, at the same time, communicate the name of the member of the mission who will act as Chargé d'Affaires a.i. pending the arrival of the new Permanent Representative/Observer. It is of special importance to note that a Chargé d'Affaires a.i. cannot appoint himself and can hold this function only after being appointed by the Permanent Representative/Observer or by the Ministry of Foreign Affairs of the State concerned" (Section XII).

[29] https://www.npr.org/sections/thetwo-way/2011/02/25/134069630/libyan-ambassador-denounces-gadhafi-at-u-n.

Article 19 of the Rome Statute, which establishes the grounds on which a state may challenge the admissibility of a case to the ICC, is ambiguous regarding complementarity and UNSC referrals (Fairlie and Powderly 2011, 661). For situations of state referral or *proprio motu* trigger mechanisms, Article 18 applies to the possibility of mounting an admissibility challenge. However, in the first UNSC ICC referral, which came from the UNSC resolution on Darfur, the government of Sudan chose not to challenge the admissibility of the ICC cases, preferring to adopt a defiant stance that did not recognize the legitimacy or legality of the Court to investigate or prosecute its state officials. Following the fall of the Gaddafi regime, the Libyan authorities adopted a different strategy: they did not question the legality of the UN Security referral, but they tried to find legal mechanisms to be in control of the cases against Saif Gaddafi and Al-Senussi. What explains these two different attitudes toward UNSC ICC referrals has to do with the fact that the prosecution in Sudan targeted incumbent government officials whereas in Libya, the fall of the Gaddafi regime prompted the rise of the National Transitional Council – the Libyan transitional government – to power. And given that the ICC prosecutor was trying to prosecute former officials of the Gaddafi regime, the new authorities in Libya had no reason to stonewall the ICC. However, they introduced an admissibility challenge before the Court, arguing that they were willing and able to prosecute Saif Gaddafi and Al-Senussi before Libyan national courts.

The transitional government of Libya challenged the admissibility of the Saif Gaddafi case before the ICC on 1 May 2012. The admissibility challenge was based on the principle of complementarity, as outlined in Article 17 of the Rome Statute. In its admissibility challenge, Libya had held that the domestic investigation in relation to Saif Gaddafi was initially conducted with respect to financial crimes and corruption but later extended to "all crimes committed by Mr Gaddafi during the revolution…starting from 17 February 2011" (Admissibility Challenge, para. 44). Libya also explained the investigative steps that had taken place so far and that it was already investigating the alleged crimes for which the ICC wanted to prosecute Saif Gaddafi (ICC Appeals Chamber 2014a, para. 52). Libya further argued that its domestic investigation was "much broader than the ICC's investigation, both in its temporal and geographical scope" (ICC Appeals Chamber 2014a, para. 52).

However, Pre-Trial Chamber I rejected the admissibility challenge of the Saif Gaddafi case on 31 May 2013, "[and reminded] Libya of its obligation to surrender [him] to the Court" (ICC-PTC I 2013b, 91). Having determined that Libya was unable to genuinely carry out the investigation or prosecution against Saif Gaddafi, the Pre-Trial Chamber did not find it necessary to address the issue raised by the defense about the impossibility of a fair trial in Libya (ICC PTC I 2013b, 89). Finding that it had not been presented with enough evidence to demonstrate that Libya was able genuinely to carry out an investigation against Saif Gaddafi, the chamber ruled that the case was admissible before the Court and recalled Libya's obligation to surrender him (ICC PTC I 2013b, 90). The Appeals Chamber confirmed the ruling from the Pre-Trial Chamber I on the admissibility of Saif Gaddafi's case before the Court on 21 May 2014 (ICC Appeals Chamber 2014a).[30]

The transitional government of Libya introduced another admissibility challenge in the case of Al-Senussi on 2 April 2013. Unlike in the case of Saif Gaddafi, where the ICC chamber ruled that Libya needed to surrender him to the Court, Pre-Trial Chamber I decided that the Al-Senussi case was inadmissible before the Court because it was currently subject to domestic proceedings, and Libya was willing and genuinely able to prosecute him. Al-Senussi's defense team appealed the ruling, showing its preference for their client to be taken to The Hague rather than have him face justice in Libya. The Appeals Chamber unanimously confirmed the Pre-Trial Chamber I's ruling on 24 July 2014, which ended the proceedings against Al-Senussi before the Court (ICC Appeals Chamber 2014b). The Appeals Chamber noted, in rejecting Al-Senussi's appeal, that its findings were not about whether the due process of the accused was violated (ICC Appeals Chamber 2014a, 3).[31] One is left to wonder why the ICC chambers ruled that Libya can try Al-Senussi but must surrender Saif Gaddafi to the ICC.

---

[30] The Appeals Chamber's decision was in majority, with Judge Ušacka (2014) dissenting, and Judge Song (2014) issuing a separate opinion. For a critique of the Pre-Trial Chamber's decision, see Pitts (2014).

[31] The Procedural history of the Al Senussi case, started with Libya filing an "Application on behalf of the Government of Libya relating to Abdullah Al-Senussi pursuant to Article 19 of the ICC Statute" ("Libya's admissibility challenge" on 2 April 2013 (ICC-01/11-01/11-309). On 24 April 2013, the prosecutor filed the "Prosecution's Response to 'Application on behalf of the government of Libya relating to Abdullah Al-Senussi pursuant to Article 19 of the ICC Statute'" (ICC-01/11-01/11-321-Conf.) After the Pre-Trial Chamber's invitation, the prosecutor, the defense counsel of Al Senussi, and the victims filed their responses to the Admissibility Challenge on 14 June 2013. And the Pre-Trial Chamber issued the "Decision on the admissibility of the case against Abdullah Al-Senussi" on 11 October 2013 (CC-01/11-01/11-466-Conf). The defense filed an appeal on the Pre-Trial Chamber's decision on 17 October 2013. The Appeals Chamber recalls that the Pre-Trial Chamber had found that the same proceedings against Al-Senussi brought before the ICC were being prosecuted before domestic jurisdictions and that Libya was neither unwilling nor unable to prosecute (para. 66, p. 23). The defense had requested the Appeals Chamber to consider new evidence of Al-Senussi being mistreated by Libyan authorities.

TWO ADMISSIBILITY CHALLENGES, TWO DIFFERENT OUTCOMES

According to the preamble of the Rome Statute, the ICC was established with the aim of ending impunity for "the most serious crimes of concern to the international community as a whole." The preamble of the Rome Statute stresses the "duty of every state to exercise its criminal jurisdiction over those responsible for international crimes" and that ICC's jurisdiction "shall be complementary to national jurisdictions." The ICC is thus meant to be complementary to national judicial institutions, which have primacy of jurisdiction. To that extent, a case shall be inadmissible before the ICC if a state is able and willing to investigate and prosecute it, according to Article 17 of the Rome Statute.

When the ICC decides to prosecute a case, it is up to the state to challenge that decision by arguing that the case is inadmissible to the ICC, pursuant Article 17 of the Rome Statute. Therefore, the state has the burden to show that it is investigating the same case (same person and same conduct) and is willing and able to bring the accused to justice.

The Trial Chamber arrived at two different conclusions when it ruled on the admissibility challenges introduced by the government of Libya regarding the cases against Saif Gaddafi and Al-Senussi. It declared that the Al-Senussi case was inadmissible before the ICC, thus granting the Libyan state the possibility of investigating and prosecuting him. But it declared the case against Saif Gaddafi admissible before the ICC, requesting the Libyan state to transfer him to ICC custody. The Appeals Chamber accepted that "distinctions between the two cases permitted the Pre-Trial Chamber to arrive at different conclusions" (ICC Appeals Chamber 2014a, 35). Such distinctions between the two cases included the fact that the case against Saif Gaddafi concerned crimes allegedly committed throughout Libya, while the case against Al-Senussi was limited to crimes allegedly committed in Benghazi. Libya submitted substantially more evidence supporting its admissibility challenge for the Al-Senussi case that it did for the Gaddafi case (ICC Appeals Chamber 2014a, 35–36).[32]

The ICC rejected Libya's challenge to the admissibility of the Gaddafi case on 31 May 2013, by arguing that Libya failed to show enough evidence that its investigation covered the same case that the ICC's case did (ICC Pre-Trial Chamber, 2013). The Appeals Chamber rejected Libya's appeal

---

[32] Although Al-Senussi's defense argued that Libya at that time had not a law allowing it to prosecute Al-Senussi for the international crime of persecution, the Appeals Chamber (2014a, 45) "observes that Libya envisages charging Mr Al-Senussi with domestic offences that include civil war, assault[ing] the political rights of the citizen, stirring up hatred between the classes and 'other crimes associated with fomenting sedition and civil war'" and these crimes are included in the Libyan Criminal Code (ICC Appeals Chamber 2014, footnotes 253, 254, and 255).

on 21 May 2014, and found that Libya was not investigating the same case, which led the chamber to not consider the arguments about Libya's inability to carry out the domestic proceedings. In a separate opinion appended to the judgment, Judge Song argued that Libya was investigating the same case, but the case was still inadmissible before the ICC because Libya was unable to exercise custody over Gaddafi. For the Al-Senussi case, however, the Pre-Trial Chamber decided on 11 October 2013, that the case was inadmissible before the ICC because the case in Libya was the same case as the one before the ICC. Although the ICC Pre-Trial Chamber acknowledged that Al-Senussi lacked legal representation before Libyan courts and that the Libyan national authorities did not have effective control over certain detention facilities, it nonetheless concluded that Libya was not unwilling or unable to genuinely carry out its investigations against Al-Senussi (Ferstman et al. 2014, 3).

In a nutshell, the ICC decided that Gaddafi must be tried in The Hague but Al-Senussi may be tried in Libya. In any case, the ICC has been inconsistent in matters of complementarity. For the self-referral situations, such as Uganda, DRC, and the Central African Republic (CAR), complementarity challenges have not been raised by the states. With the first UNSC referral of Darfur, however, the ICC has stressed its jurisdiction in the absence of domestic investigations and prosecutions. The Court stressed also on the duty of state parties to help enforce the warrants for arrest. In Kenya, the Court agreed to prioritize domestic proceedings, subject to conditions specified in the Agreed Minutes, which set out clear benchmarks and timelines for investigation and prosecutions (ICC OTP 2009a, 1; Stahn 2012, 332).[33] Unlike in Darfur, in Libya, the Office of the Prosecutor proposed several options such as priority of domestic proceedings, a sequencing of proceedings, and the possibility of holding ICC proceedings in Libya (Stahn 2012, 355). Complementarity is however one of the main points of contention regarding ICC proceedings, and is readily invoked by states who want to challenge the admissibility of some cases before the Court by arguing that they are genuinely willing and able to investigate those cases. The Libyan situation also highlights the issue of a state's genuine willingness and ability to guarantee fair domestic trials that uphold the rights of the accused. The ICC is not a human rights court, however, which is a blind spot in the principle of complementarity.

---

[33] See the Agreed Minutes of the meeting. www.legal-tools.org/doc/27d6b9/pdf/.

THE ICC IS NOT A HUMAN RIGHTS COURT

The creation of the ICC may be hailed as a great achievement for the global human rights agenda, yet, at its core, the Court is not a human rights court. Its material jurisdiction, as defined in the Rome Statute, are the core crimes (genocide, war crimes, crimes against humanity, and the crime of aggression), which must meet a certain gravity threshold. The defense team for Al-Senussi argued before the ICC that a trial in Libya would not guarantee the rights of their client to due process. Therefore, in their view, the ICC case against their client should be admissible and his trial conducted in The Hague rather than before Libyan national courts. As Angela Walker (2014) contends, however, an analysis of the text, object, and purpose of Article 17 on complementarity shows that the ICC lacks authority to rule on the presence or not of due process when determining admissibility. It is certainly paradoxical that an international tribunal that aims at ending impunity for crimes of concern to the international community does not take into consideration whether or not due process is guaranteed in national jurisdictions before deciding whether to defer to those courts.

On the other hand, Frédéric Mégret and Marika Giles Samson (2013) ask whether due process and its violation should be taken into consideration at all when the ICC is evaluating complementarity and admissibility. Mégret and Samson (2013) argue that the ICC is not a human rights court and should not behave like one. There is in fact a functional division of labor between international criminal and human rights courts. However, in instances where the violations of due process are so grave that the proceedings cannot be described as a trial or reveal an unwillingness to prosecute, the ICC may take that into consideration, but only at the end of the process, to allow the domestic judicial system to correct itself in the meantime (Mégret and Samson 2013). Along the same line of argument, the ICC prosecutor has also said, "[We] are not a human rights Court. We are not checking the fairness of the proceedings. We are checking the genuineness of the proceedings."[34] Responding to calls to investigate the Jammeh regime in The Gambia, Prosecutor Bensouda stated, "It has to be clear that the ICC is not a human rights court but a court that deals with specific crimes under the Rome Statute" (*Jollof News* 2016). In any case, and despite the ICC ruling on the admissibility challenges presented by the Libyan state, there are clear signs of violation of due process for Saif Gaddafi by Libyan authorities.[35] But Mégret and Samson (2013,

---

[34] Statement made by Ocampo during a visit to Libya to November 2011. The video is available at Aljazeera.com/news/Africa/2011/11/201111239582170909.html.

[35] For example, his ICC-appointed lawyer was arrested and held for one month during a visit to Libya in June 2012.

577–581) argue that the violation of the due process for Saif Gaddafi does not constitute grounds for the ICC to pass the admissibility test, and they make the case for "letting flawed trials be" because, among other things, the ICC is a treaty court; there is an inherent value in local trials, such as maximizing deterrence, creating a sense of ownership of the justice, and facilitating the administration of justice; and there is a tendency to exaggerate the distinction between "flawed" domestic proceedings and a "pristine" international criminal justice.

CONCLUSION

The UNSC is primarily tasked to maintain peace and security around the world, using specifically its Chapter VII powers under the UN Charter. Although the ICC is an international court that is not a UN organ, it aims at ending impunity by investigating and prosecuting those responsible for the most serious crimes of concern for the international community. The two institutions have a working relationship that is enshrined in the Rome Statute. The UNSC is the channel through which the ICC gains universal jurisdiction, given that many states have not ratified the Rome Statute. However, Security Council members may also use their veto power to stop the ICC from prosecuting crimes that would otherwise fall within its jurisdiction.

Therefore, it is insufficient to argue only that the relationship between the UNSC and the ICC is one concerned with the maintenance of peace and security. The ways in which the UNSC has deployed its power in using the ICC to intervene in Libya and Sudan but also rejecting Kenya's request for a deferral of the proceedings against President Kenyatta are examples of such power dynamics. The failed UNSC attempts to pass a resolution to refer Syria to the ICC are also symptomatic of the political plays between members of the Security Council. Such deployment of power in the use of Articles 13(b) and 16 of the Rome Statute undermine the judicial independence of the ICC. Even the drafting negotiations that underpin Article 16 show the powers at play and the "workings of the political origins of the law and the manner in which foundational inequalities were woven into the fabric of the Rome Statute" (Clarke and Koulen 2014, 297).

In addition to the imbalance in power relations that link the UNSC and the ICC, this chapter has also shown that the ICC itself is not immune from making decisions that take into consideration those political outcomes. The speed with which the ICC prosecutor moved from the preliminary observation to the investigation phase in the Libyan case in the midst of the uprisings shows that the Office of the Prosecutor sought to have an effect on the ongoing events by issuing warrants for the arrests of the Tripoli Three. The different outcomes of the two admissibility challenges that the National Transitional Council (NTC) introduced also reflect such political influence. After the fall of the Gaddafi regime, the Libyan state also deployed its strategies to retain control of the fates of the ICC suspects.

5

The Limits of State Cooperation

Why should the Kenyan flag be dragged into the court? ... If the president goes to the ICC it's like the whole country is being prosecuted.

James Gakuya, Kenyan member of parliament (2013)

INTRODUCTION

The need for state cooperation constrains the ability of the International Criminal Court (ICC) to accomplish its mission, which is "to put an end to impunity for the perpetrators of [atrocity] crimes and thus to contribute to the prevention of such crimes."[1] Compliance of state parties to the Rome Statute and state cooperation is needed at every step of the ICC's work, ranging from the Office of the Prosecutor's (OTP) investigations to providing jail facilities for those convicted of crimes.[2] However, compliance and cooperation of states with the ICC at any moment are not a given, although state parties to the Rome Statute are legally obliged to assist the Court. By ratifying the Rome Statute, states delegate their power and privileges to an international institution, whose main purpose is to limit the sovereignty of said states, which in turn raises questions about why states choose to delegate those powers. This chapter empirically tests the actions of states that, after willingly delegating some of their powers and privileges to the ICC, discover that some of their officials or nationals have become the target of an investigation. Whether the actions of state parties to the Rome Statute are consistent with their avowed

[1] Preamble of Rome Statute of the International Criminal Court, www.icc-cpi.int/nr/rdonlyres/ea9aeff7-5752-4f84-be94-0a655eb30e16/0/rome_statute_english.pdf.
[2] It is important to note that states that are parties to the Rome Statute are legally bound to comply and cooperate with the Court, whereas states that are signatories to the Rome Statute without having ratified it are only bound not to impede the work of the Court.

compliance and cooperation with the ICC is the focus of this chapter, which outlines the limits of state cooperation in the area of international criminal justice by studying the Kenyan example.

DELEGATION TO INTERNATIONAL INSTITUTIONS

The literature about international organizations has addressed extensively the reasons why and the conditions under which states delegate authority to international institutions (Pollack 1997; Hurd 1999; Moravcsik 2000; Nielson and Tierney 2003; Lake and McCubbins 2006; Koremenos 2008). States, acting as *principals*, choose to delegate some powers to international organizations, which in this case are the *agents*. From a rational design perspective, the issues of agency and delegation involve a cost-benefit analysis, with states choosing the delegation option when the benefits of such delegation exceed its costs (Koremenos 2008; Koremenos et al. 2001). Although external delegation involves sovereignty costs, it still remains a viable option for states, especially in the areas of human rights and international criminal justice, where states aim at increasing their credibility. This would explain why states choose to ratify the Rome Statute and join the ICC, delegating some of their powers and prerogatives to an international tribunal. However, the ICC and other international institutions are also created by states, which discuss beforehand how much power they are willing to delegate, and such deliberations make their way into the framework or organizational structure of the international institutions. For instance, the Rome Statute stipulates that states' domestic judicial systems have supremacy over ICC's jurisdiction, which shows that states want to reserve to themselves the power of adjudicating judicial matters on their own if they wish to.[3] This framework contrasts with that of the UN-created ad hoc tribunals for Rwanda and the former Yugoslavia, for example, which had given those courts the primacy of jurisdiction over domestic courts.[4]

Koremenos (2008) suggests that the autonomy of agents (i.e., international organizations) is restricted and confined within the design that the principals (i.e., states) have set, while Lake and McCubbins (2006) give much more leeway and independence to international institutions. But in any case, international organizations have a tendency to acquire their own identity in which

---

[3] For a thorough discussion of the Rome Statute, see Schabas (2010a). For an insider's account of the negotiations during the Rome Conference that led to the creation of the ICC, see Scheffer (2013).

[4] One main difference between the ICC and these ad hoc tribunals is that the former is treaty-based, with states deciding to join the institution by ratifying the Rome Statute.

agents gradually increase their autonomy and act against the interests of the principals, which Barnett and Finnemore (1999) have termed a "pathology." Barnett and Finnemore (1999) argue that, as bureaucracies, international organizations are also creators of social knowledge; they create new interests for actors and, as such, they tend to become unresponsive to their environments and obsessed with their own rules. It is also the case that international institutions are prone to taking on a life of their own. States may step in and take action to influence the international agents, but that occurrence is rare due to legal restrictions and high information costs (Vaubel 2006). This is particularly true in the case of the ICC, given that the Court is a judicial body that operates within a legal culture, pursuant to the Rome Statute. It is not always clear whether states have full knowledge of the Court's procedures when they opt to relinquish their jurisdiction to the ICC. In fact, the Kenyan state may not have had knowledge of the full extent of their action when the members of its parliament were chanting "Don't be vague. Let's go to The Hague," instead of passing the bill that would have created a domestic tribunal, as recommended by the Waki Commission.[5]

Human rights regimes challenge the Westphalian order to the extent that they empower citizens against their own governments. One may ask then, Why do states create those international human rights regimes in the first place because they are designed to hold the states accountable (Moravcsik 2000)? Whereas realists may argue that states join human rights regimes because they are coerced by great powers, liberal scholars retort that states join the regimes because of norms and as a response to pressure from interest groups and civil society organizations. Focusing on the European Convention on Human Rights (ECHR) of 1953, the most elaborate and effective human rights regime in the world, Moravcsik (2000) shows that the realist argument does not hold up well because well-established democracies did not push anyone into joining the ECHR; they in fact opposed it. The decision of newly established democracies to join ECHR is not a result of civil society pressure either, which refutes the liberal argument as well. In fact, the accession to the regime is based on domestic political self-interest, with governments trying to reduce political uncertainty by constraining future governments, which Moravcsik (2000) calls a republican liberal explanation.

---

[5] Following the inquiry into the 2007–2008 postelection violence, the Waki Commission recommended the creation of a domestic court that would investigate and prosecute the crimes committed during the violent episode. But the Kenyan Parliament failed to establish that court and many members of parliament (MPs) voiced their preference to have the ICC investigate instead.

One may also add that socialization theory helps shed some light on the reasons why states choose to join international organizations such as the ICC. As Johnston (2001) argues, socialization theory has not been fully incorporated in the cooperation scholarship and focuses on persuasion and social influence. Most international relations scholars would agree that states join international institutions due to the incentives to be gained by doing so and because of pressures from domestic interest groups (Towns 2010).[6] Constructivists would add to that the idea that a socialization process through the involvement in international institutions could change a state's behavior. As Johnston (2001, 488) presumes, "actors who enter into a social interaction rarely emerge the same." Neorealist scholars would agree with this statement insofar as the change in behavior is driven by exogenous forces in an anarchic world, whereas constructivists would argue that the change in behavior of the actors in a social interaction is due to socialization (Kratochwil and Ruggie 1986).[7]

STATES' SUPPORT OF THE ICC AND THE EROSION OF SOVEREIGNTY

Why would states support international courts that clearly erode their sovereignty? Classical realism portrays international judicial institutions as idealist wishful thinking, whereas others may view international courts as part of an order established by a hegemon (Keohane 1984). Powell (2013) contends that states support international courts because they agree with the values of those institutions, and international courts also provide avenues for states to make credible commitments (Simmons and Danner 2010). However, legitimacy, which can be defined as "the normative belief by an actor that a rule or institution ought to be obeyed" (Hurd 1999, 381), also may ultimately lead to support for an international court such as the ICC. In addition, the court institutional design and its performance are key factors that shape states' perception of its legitimacy (Powell 2013, 351).

As Simmons and Danner (2010, 225) contend, however, the creation of the ICC is a puzzle unto itself given that the Court represents "a serious intrusion into a traditional arena of state sovereignty: the right to administer justice to one's own nationals." Drawing on credible commitment theory, Simmons and Danner (2010, 225) argue that "the states that are the least and the most vulnerable to the possibility of an ICC case affecting

---

[6] Noting that most states around the world have now recognized equal voting rights for women and have national policies for the advancement of women and/or gender quotas, Towns (2010) argues that the adoption of these norms establishes a social hierarchy of states.

[7] For instance, Kratochwil and Ruggie (1986) propose treating international organizations as social institutions "around which actor expectations converge."

their citizens have committed most readily to the ICC, while potentially vulnerable states with credible alternative means to hold leaders accountable do not." Knowing that the ICC will likely focus on the prosecution of high-level officials, it was clearly not in the interest of states to join the Court. In opposition to views that portray the Court as merely symbolic, or detrimental to peace and stability, Simmons and Danner (2010) show that the Court is indeed useful for some governments to tie their own hands credibly and to foreswear certain modes of violent conflict. In other words, the theory of credible commitment "predicts that states that are at risk for committing the kinds of atrocities governed by the Court but that lack a dependable domestic mechanism for holding government agents accountable are likely to be among the Court's earliest and most avid subscribers" (Simmons and Danner 2010, 252). This would explain the early enthusiasm of African states about joining the Court. However, one must dissociate the commitment to join the ICC and that of cooperating with the Court when the stakes are high.

THE LIMITS OF STATE COOPERATION

For the ICC to be operational, it must rely on the willingness of states to comply with the Rome Statute and to assist the Court in its investigations and prosecutions. As Peskin (2009) shows, after the first few years of operation, the ICC OTP's strategy shifted from a cautionary stance to a confrontational one, which is due to the lack of cooperation from states in the case of Sudan and Uganda. In both instances, the ICC has failed to persuade states to arrest and hand over the suspects, and the lack of international support for the arrest warrants has been noticeable.[8] Prosecutor Ocampo's early sole focus on rebels instead of state officials showed his cautionary approach in seeking state cooperation. By courting state referrals instead of using his *proprio motu* powers, Ocampo was assured of state cooperation in the first situations that he was investigating. Indeed, because the first cases before the ICC (Uganda, Democratic Republic of Congo [DRC], and Central African Republic [CAR]) resulted from self-referrals, Ocampo was assured of the cooperation of those states, who had willingly invited an ICC investigation. Even after the UN Security Council (UNSC) referral of the situation in

---

[8] Since the ICC has issued a warrant for his arrest, President Bashir of Sudan has traveled to the following ICC member states: Chad, DRC, Djibouti, Kenya, Malawi, Nigeria, and South Africa. All these states are in fact required by the Rome Statute to arrest Bashir and surrender him to the Court.

Darfur, Ocampo was cautious, trying not to antagonize the Sudanese government and seeking its cooperation (Peskin 2009). Ocampo later changed course from his diplomatic caution and took an adversarial turn in mid-2007, especially with his approach to Sudan. He was openly critical of Sudan's noncompliance and criticized the international community for its failure to pressure Khartoum. Ocampo also later antagonized the government of Uganda by refusing to drop the bid for the arrest of the Lord's Resistance Army (LRA) leaders.

Unlike the International Criminal Tribunal for Rwanda (ICTR) and the International Criminal Tribunal for the Former Yugoslavia (ICTY), the ICC cannot count on crucial international backing – especially from the UNSC – to press reluctant states to cooperate with its investigations or to enforce its arrest warrants. For instance, ICC Prosecutor Bensouda has criticized the UNSC for its lack of support in the Darfur situation. Bensouda said,

> Given this [UNSC's] lack of foresight on what should happen in Darfur, I am left with no choice but to hibernate investigative activities in Darfur as I shift resources to other urgent cases, especially those in which trial is approaching. It should thus be clear to this Council that unless there is a change of attitude and approach to Darfur in the near future, there shall continue to be little or nothing to report to you for the foreseeable future. (UN News Centre, 2014)

Indeed, the current relationship between the two institutions is one defined by friction (Verduzco 2015). The lack of support from the UNSC is symptomatic of a wider participation problem that the ICC faces regarding states (Chapman and Chaudoin 2012). Ultimately, states for whom compliance with the ICC is the easiest, such as democracies with little internal violence, are the most likely to ratify the Rome Statute. Alternatively, states that have the most to fear from ICC prosecutions, such as "non-democracies with weak legal systems and a history of domestic political violence" tend not to ratify the Rome Statute (Chapman and Chaudoin 2012, 400). These findings also lend support to the notion that states act strategically when deciding whether or not to join supranational judicial agreements. For instance, out of the twenty-two member states of the Arab League, only Tunisia and Jordan have ratified the Rome Statute. However, sub-Saharan Africa constitutes an exception in the ratification pattern because many nondemocracies that experienced recent civil wars have acceded to the Rome Statute. This lends itself to the fact that, in the current prosecutions in Africa, the target is nonstate actors, except for Kenya, where the prosecutor used his own initiative, and Libya and Sudan, which are nonparty states referred to the ICC by the UNSC. Kenya is thus the only case to date of an ICC *member state* where the target for prosecution were state officials.[9]

THE SITUATION IN THE REPUBLIC OF KENYA

At the onset, the Kenya situation at the ICC presents two defining features: it is the first instance of the ICC intervening in a situation that is not the result of a civil conflict, and the number of victims was relatively low compared to other ICC cases at the time. The Kenya situation before the ICC is rather one of political violence in the aftermath of contested elections. For the first time since the entry in force of the Rome Statute, the ICC prosecutor had targeted suspects from both sides of the contention. Following a *proprio motu* trigger mechanism, the Pre-Trial Chamber II had authorized the ICC prosecutor to open an investigation in the Kenyan postelection violence on 3 March 2010 and had ruled that, since the Kenyan government was not investigating, the cases would be admissible before the Court (ICC Pre-Trial Chamber II 2010).[10] After the Pre-Trial Chamber gave the ICC prosecutor the authorization to open a full investigation, the Kenyan government introduced a challenge of admissibility before the Appeals Chamber, which subsequently was rejected under Article 19(2)(b) by a majority vote of 4–1, on 30 August 2011 (ICC Appeals Chamber 2011).[11]

In its admissibility challenge, and recalling that a situation is admissible before the ICC only in case of the state's failure or unwillingness to investigate and prosecute, the Kenyan state had argued that it was investigating the alleged offense. The Appeals Chamber contended that Kenya bears the burden of demonstrating that it was investigating the case – a burden that Kenya had simply failed to discharge (Jalloh 2012, 120–121). However, Judge Ušacka strongly dissented, arguing that she would have reversed the Pre-Trial Chamber's decision because, in her view, the Court did not properly account for Kenya's arguments and it applies "an unduly high burden" in

---

[9] The recent opening of an investigation in Burundi is likely to target current state officials, but Burundi has withdrawn from the Rome Statute.

[10] See ICC Pre-Trial Chamber II: "Decision Pursuant to Article 15 of the Rome Statute on the Authorization of an Investigation into the Situation in the Republic of Kenya, 31 March 2010, www.icc-cpi.int/iccdocs/doc/doc854562.pdf.

[11] See ICC Appeals Chamber: "Judgment on the Appeal of the Republic of Kenya Against the Decision of Pre-trial Chamber II of 30 May 2011" entitled "Decision on the Application by the Government of Kenya Challenging the Admissibility of the Case Pursuant to Article 19(2)(b) of the Statute," 30 August 2011, www.icc-cpi.int/iccdocs/doc/doc1223134.pdf. See also Judge Ušacka's dissenting opinion, www.icc-cpi.int/iccdocs/doc/doc1234872.pdf .

its definitions of "investigation" and "case" (Jalloh 2012, 121). In the end, the Appeals Chamber ruling effectively gave primacy to the international court, pursuant to its interpretation of Article 17 of the Rome Statute defining the rules of admissibility. That ruling cleared the path for the ICC prosecutor to open a full investigation in Kenya and, later on, issue accusations against six key figures in the state's political landscape.

GOING AFTER THE OCAMPO SIX

The situation in the Republic of Kenya before the ICC involved the indictment of six individuals for crimes against humanity. In 2011, at the request of the prosecutor, the Pre-Trial Chamber judges summoned the Ocampo Six, who at the time were high-ranking officials in the Kenyan administration, to appear before the Court, in The Hague: Uhuru Kenyatta (deputy prime minister and minister of finance), Francis Muthaura (head of the public service and secretary to the cabinet), Mohammed Hussein Ali (former chief of police), William Ruto (minister of higher education, science, and technology), Henry Kosgey (member of parliament), and finally Joshua Arap Sang (head of the private radio station Kass FM).[12] At the time, Kenyatta, Muthaura, and Ali belonged to one side of the postelectoral conflict, while Ruto, Kosgey, and Sang supported the opposing side. The fact that the ICC investigation targeted high-level officials in the Kenyan state from both sides of the conflict played a major role in the ways in which the state refused to comply with its obligations to the Court. By adopting various strategies of noncompliance and noncooperation, the Kenyan state was ultimately able to impede on the prosecutor's ability to investigate and prosecute the cases successfully.

HIGH POLITICAL RISKS AND LOW COMPLIANCE

While facing ICC charges of crimes against humanity, Uhuru Kenyatta and William Ruto joined forces and launched a presidential bid for the 2013 elections, which was effectively a strategy to deflect the ICC and shield themselves once they won (Kendall 2014; Lynch 2014; Mueller 2014; Wolf 2015). Their strategy included delaying tactics and pressures aimed at making sure

---

[12] See Situation in the Republic of Kenya, No. ICC-01/09-01/11, Decision on the Prosecutor's Application for Summons to Appear for William Samoei Ruto, Henry Kiprono Kosgey, and Joshua Arap Sang (8 March 2011); and No. ICC-01/09-02/11, Decision on the Prosecutor's Application for Summonses to Appear for Francis Kirimi Muthaura, Uhuru Muigai Kenyatta, and Mohammed Hussein Ali (8 March 2011).

the ICC trials would not take place until after the elections, when their executive power would give them an extra layer of protection and a greater ability to undermine the ICC's prosecution. The tactics also included mobilizing international organizations such as the African Union (AU) against the ICC. While delaying the ICC proceedings by mounting numerous legal challenges, Kenyatta and Ruto's allies would also engage in intimidation of potential witnesses. Finally, through the demonization of opponents, the politicization of ethnicity, and portraying the ICC as a Western tool for African subjugation, Kenyatta and Ruto mounted a successful presidential campaign that led them to victory in 2013 (Mueller 2014).

After their 2013 presidential victory, Kenyatta and Ruto adopted another series of tactics aimed at shielding them from the ICC. Their tactics were based on their political power, and they claimed that their physical presence at the trials in The Hague would be impossible given their mandates as president and deputy president of Kenya. While they have always expressed their cooperation with the ICC, their efforts to undermine the Court never waned, as ICC Prosecutor Bensouda "has [accused] Kenya of spying on its staff, not honoring promises for documents and interviews, interfering with witnesses, politicizing the law, and using frivolous delaying tactics to postpone trial" (Mueller 2014, 26).

Why did Kenya join the ICC and then attempt to undermine the Court once the investigation into the 2007–2008 postelection violence started? As Mueller (2014, 25) contends, this phenomenon is better explained with changes in political risk, particularly in states where institutions are weak and malleable, and the rule of law index is low. For states, an increase in postratification political risks decreases the likelihood of compliance. Indeed, Kenya signed the Rome Statute in 1999 under President Moi, a period marked by authoritarian rule, and ratified it in 2005 under President Kibaki.[13] Although human rights treaties limit sovereignty, states – including those under authoritarian rule – may adhere to them anyway because the treaties typically do not have enforcing power. For instance, authoritarian states may ratify the Torture Convention because they do not need to use torture (Vreeland 2008), and new democracies at the end of World War II – such as Italy, France, and Germany – signed the ECHR to avoid reverting to fascism (Moravcsik 2000). Unlike those

---

[13] Kenya's Polity IV scores ranged from −6 to −2 (autocracies) during President Moi's tenure (1978–2002). The opposition united behind Kibaki in 2002 to defeat Moi's chosen successor, Uhuru Kenyatta, which raised prospects of major shifts in Kenyan politics, but it wasn't until 2005 that the state moved from an anocracy to a democracy. See "Authority Trends, 1963–2013: Kenya," Polity IV, www.systemicpeace.org/polity/ken2.htm. See also Mutua (2008).

human rights treaties, however, the Rome Statute has teeth because there is no head-of-state immunity. Those found guilty of core crimes by the ICC can be imprisoned for up to thirty years, or a life sentence, and state parties to the Rome Statute are required to cooperate with the Court. This raises the stakes and makes the cost of joining the ICC high.

Simmons and Danner (2010) argue that states that ratify the Rome Statute tend to be peaceful democracies or autocracies with recent histories of conflict, whereas the states that refuse to join the ICC are democracies engaged in wars (the United States, Israel) or unaccountable autocracies (China, Russia, Sudan). Violent autocracies sign the Rome Statute as a form of "credible commitment" (Simmons and Danner 2010). Chapman and Chaudoin (2012) find "credible commitment" to be problematic, however, because states with poor indices of rule of law and governance, and high indices of violence, are less likely to ratify the Rome Statute. In any case, Kenya would be an outlier in both Simmons and Danner's (2010) and Chapman and Chaudoin's (2012) theories. In fact, Kenya would have not been expected to join the ICC when it did because Kenya had a history of violence in the 1990s and mixed democratic credentials, and it lacked an independent judiciary; but Kenya was not a violent autocracy engaged in civil war either (Mueller 2014, 29). Actually, Kenya ratified the Rome Statute because, at the time, the ratification carried little political risk for the state. When compliance with the ICC requests started carrying political risk, however, the Kenyan state and the ICC suspects were tempted to defy the Court rather than cooperate. States with poor governance scores and low rule of law indices such as Kenya "are prone to halt compliance when the political context changes" (Mueller 2014, 29). Consequently, when political risks and cost of compliance increased, Kenya's response to the ICC shifted.

POSTELECTION VIOLENCE AND NATIONAL RECKONING

In the wake of the postelection violence, the parties to the conflict signed the Kenya National Dialogue and Reconciliation (KNDR) Accord on 28 February 2018.[14] The accord established the Commission of Inquiry into the

---

[14] After postelection violence broke out in December 2007, the AU mandated a Panel of Eminent African Personalities chaired by Kofi Annan to mediate a political solution to the crisis. The panel brought together the two main political parties – the Party of National Unity (PNU) and the Orange Democratic Movement (ODM) – into the Kenya National Dialogue and Reconciliation (KNDR) process, which led to the establishment of a coalition government with power sharing between the leaders of both parties and the creation of the Commission of Inquiry into the Post-Election Violence (CIPEV).

Post-Election Violence (CIPEV), also known as the Waki Commission,[15] which, in addition to its chair Judge Philip Waki, included two foreigners – Gavin McFayden of New Zealand and Pascal Kambale of DRC. Two Kenyans, David Majanja and George Kegoro, were appointed as counsel assisting and commission secretary, respectively. The CIPEV mandate included the following: (1) to investigate the facts and circumstances related to the violence that followed the 2007 presidential election; (2) to investigate the actions and state security agencies during the period of violence and make recommendations; and (3) to make recommendations on legal, political, and administrative measures, including bringing to justice the persons responsible for criminal acts.[16] After four months of investigations, the Waki Commission published a 539-page report on 15 October 2008, which recorded 3,561 injuries, 117,216 instances of property destruction, and 1,133 deaths resulting from the post-electoral violence (Waki Commission 2008). The report suggested that the Kenyan police were responsible for 405 deaths and found evidence of massive failures by state security agencies to anticipate and contain the violence. It also identified land grievances, the centralization of power in the presidency, and the deliberate weakening of public institutions as root causes of the violence.

Confronted with the decision on whether or not to name the individuals most responsible for the postelectoral violence, the Waki Commission (2008, 8) took the middle ground, and explained that

> [it] has decided against publishing the names of alleged perpetrators in its report. Instead, these names will be placed in a sealed envelope, together with its supporting evidence. Both will be kept in the custody of the Panel of African Eminent Personalities pending the establishment of a special tribunal to be set up in accordance with our recommendations. In default of setting up the Tribunal, consideration will be given by the Panel to forwarding the names of alleged perpetrators to the special prosecutor of the International Criminal Court (ICC) in The Hague to conduct further investigations in accordance with the ICC statutes.

In its report, the Waki Commission recommended that the government of Kenya establish a Special Tribunal to seek accountability from the persons responsible for the crimes. The Special Tribunal shall be composed of six judges, three in the trial chamber and three in the appeals chamber, with the presiding judge of each chamber being a Kenyan while the other four judges

---

[15] The commission was colloquially named after its chair Justice Philip Waki of the Kenya's Court of Appeals.

[16] Waki Commission Final Report, https://reliefweb.int/sites/reliefweb.int/files/resources/15A0 oF569813F4D549257607001F459D-Full_Report.pdf.

would be non-Kenyans (Waki Commission 2008, 474). The jurisdiction of the tribunal would include serious crimes committed during the postelectoral violence, particularly crimes against humanity (Waki Commission 2008, 475). As a precautionary measure, Judge Waki handed to Kofi Annan – the head of the Panel of African Eminent Personalities – a sealed envelope containing the names of key persons believed to have orchestrated the violence and specified that the list would be forwarded to the ICC if an agreement establishing the special tribunal was not signed within sixty days. The commission also recommended that "[a]ll persons holding public office and public servants charged with criminal offences related to the post-election violence be suspended from duty until the matter is fully adjudicated upon" (Waki Commission 2008, 476). The commission noted that violence related to elections has erupted in Kenya in five-year cycles since the establishment of multiparty politics in 1992, and the government has systematically failed to investigate and prosecute the perpetrators of such events adequately. In addition, lack of political will and fear of the political establishment have hindered any serious investigation and prosecution of political violence. Soon thereafter, however, the Kenyan political class started undermining the findings and recommendations of the Waki Commission.

UNDERMINING THE WAKI COMMISSION

The Waki Commission had received early support from Kenyan politicians on all sides who felt they had nothing to fear. In its final report, the commission called for the Kenyan state to put in place a hybrid special tribunal comprised of both domestic and international judges. The Kenyan parliament was expected to pass the bill establishing the hybrid tribunal by January 2009, but the bill was defeated on 12 February 2009. Two later attempts at passing the bill failed as well (Mueller 2014, 30). At that point, Kofi Annan, as the lead of the Panel of Eminent African Personalities, which had brokered the accord that had ended the postelectoral violence, allowed two extensions to the parliament to establish the special tribunal, but to no avail. Annan later handed to the ICC prosecutor the materials from the Waki Commission, consisting of "six boxes of documents . . . and an envelope with a list of possible suspects" (ICC OTP 2009b).

Prosecutor Ocampo subsequently came to Kenya in November 2009 and requested a self-referral. The Kenyan state refused because any investigation was likely to target the political elite on both coalitions in the postelection violence. With the preliminary evidence available to him, Ocampo proceeded then to use his *proprio motu* powers and request from the Pre-Trial Chamber an authorization to open a full investigation in Kenya, an authorization that was

granted on 31 March 2010. It is important to note that the suspects identified by
the Waki Commission and sealed in Annan's envelope were never made public.
It would be fair to assume, however, that the Kenyan government and parliament failed to take concrete steps to follow through on the Waki Commission's
recommendation to establish the hybrid tribunal because such prosecutions
would primarily target high-level officials and their political allies. The prosecution dossier landed on Ocampo's desk because "the big fish [wouldn't]
fry themselves" (Brown and Sriram 2012). Consequently, international justice
became the only means through which criminal accountability could be delivered in the wake of Kenya's postelection violence. The delivery of such justice,
however, faces noncooperation from the Kenyan state and political elite.

KENYA'S DELAYING TACTICS AND OUTREACH AGAINST THE ICC

As Mueller (2014, 31) writes, "Once the ICC began to investigate the Kenya
situation, the political risk factor increased dramatically. Thereafter, Kenya
responded by demonizing the ICC, mobilizing support against it both
domestically and internationally, and arguing for trials to be held in Kenya."
The ICC intervention in Kenya also recalibrated the political field in the
country, bringing together former rival factions as a unified front against
the Court, to the dismay of civil society organizations and human rights
groups (Kendall 2014, 405). The Kenyan strategy succeeded in mobilizing
domestic political support against the Court ahead of the 2013 presidential
elections, and the candidates Kenyatta and Ruto capitalized on their indictment for crimes against humanity during their political campaign to win
the elections. The indictment of Kenyatta and Ruto, which was at first a
liability, was turned into a political gain and became a vital asset for their
winning presidential ticket (Wolf 2015). Kenyatta and Ruto came together
to form the Jubilee Alliance as a new political platform that would launch
their presidential bid. The Jubilee Alliance was an opportunistic alliance of
convenience, put in place to gain political power, and would in turn be used
as a shield against the ICC (Mueller 2014; Wolf 2015). It also targeted the
Kenyan opposition and civil society groups as responsible for the predica-
ment of the ICC suspects. As Wolf (2015, 164) notes, it is clear that, after they
were indicted by the ICC, Kenyatta and Ruto knew that their fate hinged on
the outcome of the 2013 elections; they recognized that running as a team
was their safest bet, and they mobilized their ethnopolitical constituencies
to ensure victory for their ticket (Mueller 2014). And as the electoral data
showed, Kenyatta and Ruto in fact obtained the vast majority of the votes
from their "fellow-ethnics" (Wolf 2015, 165).

Kenya's concerted campaign against the ICC started as soon as Ocampo named the six defendants – the "Ocampo Six" – on 15 December 2010. A week later, members of the Kenyan parliament passed a motion to withdraw from the ICC while the government started lobbying African countries and the AU for support against the Court. When charges against the defendants were confirmed by the ICC Pre-Trial Chamber in February 2012, the political risk increased even more for the Kenyan elites because it meant that the Pre-Trial Chamber agreed that the prosecutor had enough preliminary evidence to warrant moving the cases to the trial phase. Kenya's diplomatic offense against the ICC resulted in the East African Legislative Assembly and the East African Community requesting that the ICC cases be transferred to the East African Court of Justice (EACJ), whose mandate, ironically, did not include crimes against humanity (Mueller 2014, 31).[17] The defendants had also asked for their trials to be moved from The Hague to either Kenya or Arusha, Tanzania.[18] The ICC Assembly of States Parties left it up to the judges to determine the feasibility of relocating the trials to Kenya or Tanzania. But many factors influenced the reluctance of the judges to grant such requests, including the fact that the judges were also working on other cases located in The Hague, the lack of logistical support away from The Hague, and safety concerns for the witnesses.

Within Kenya, the campaign against the ICC had largely been success-ful by the time the 2013 presidential elections were held; at which point, the remaining ICC cases were seen as part of a Western-driven conspiracy of the "three O's" (i.e., Ocampo, Obama, and Odinga) (Lynch 2014, 106).[19] Ironically, Kenyatta and Ruto's anti-Western campaign was devised by a prominent British public relations firm that successfully turned them "from suspected perpe-trators into victims" (Wolf 2015, 180). After they had won the 2013 elections, Kenyatta and Ruto used the Kenyan state to enlist the AU to help their case against the ICC. At the May 2013 AU summit, which coincided with the fiftieth

---

[17] The East African Court of Justice, based in Arusha, Tanzania, is an organ of the East African Community, which is comprised of Kenya, Uganda, Tanzania, Rwanda, and Burundi.

[18] At the time, the Arusha International Conference Center had been the seat for the International Criminal Tribunal for Rwanda (ICTR) since its creation in 1994, but all of the remaining work of the ICTR had been transferred to a UN judicial body called the Mechanism for International Criminal Tribunals. It thus raised questions about whether Arusha had adequate facilities to host the Kenya trials at that point.

[19] Raila Odinga, as the leader of the Orange Democratic Movement, was the main challenger to the incumbent president Kibaki in the 2007 elections. The author's interviews in Kenya show that those who were critical of the ICC were quick to point out that none of the ICC suspects belonged to Odinga's Luo ethnic group.

anniversary of the AU, Kenya pushed for its cause to be taken up by the organization. Subsequently, the African Union Commission (AUC) asked the UNSC to
defer the Kenya cases based on Article 16 of the Rome Statute.[20] On 2 May 2013,
the Kenyan ambassador to the UN, Macharia Kamau, wrote a letter to the UNSC
asking for a termination of the Kenya cases, arguing that "the ICC continues to
be a hindrance and a stumbling block for the aspiration of the Kenyan people."[21]
The AU also sent a delegation to The Hague in August 2013 to ask that the cases
be transferred back to Kenya, and it convened a special summit in October 2013
to discuss a mass withdrawal of African states from the ICC (Mueller 2014, 32).

Incidentally, the Al Shabaab terrorist attack on the Westgate Mall in Nairobi
had given Kenyatta and Ruto more ammunition for their calls to have the ICC
drop the charges against them or, at the very least, have the UNSC defer the
cases pursuant to Article 16 of the Rome Statute.[22] Arguing that Kenya faced
terrorist attacks and needed its head executive to devote all of his time to the
fight against terrorism, Kenya claimed that it could not afford to be dragged
through interminable legal proceedings before the ICC, which would violate
the mandate that the Kenyan citizens bestowed upon their leaders. Deputy
President Ruto was in The Hague during the Westgate Mall attacks, and his
statement leaves no doubt that he suggested that the ICC proceedings against
him and President Kenyatta impeded their work as Kenyan leaders:

> It's really unfortunate that these terrorist attacks were timed to coincide
> with my presence here at The Hague and the visit by His Excellency the
> president of Kenya to New York for the UN General Assembly. Meaning that
> both the president and myself would not have been in the country…We
> hope that some people will begin to contextualize what is going on and
> begin to appreciate the challenges that Kenya is going through, the region
> is going through, and the complications that are brought by what is going on
> here. We believe in justice, we believe in fair play and we have as a country,
> both the president and myself as individuals, we've committed ourselves to
> be present here in court so that we can clear our names but we have to coun-
> ter balance our individual responsibilities or responsibilities as individuals
> and legitimate constitutional requirements by 40 million Kenyans.[23]

---

[20] Article 16 of the Rome Statute allows the UN Security Council to defer cases before the ICC
for twelve months, renewable.

[21] See the letter here: www.jfjustice.net/the-icc-is-a-hindrance-and-a-stumbling-block-for-the-
aspiration-of-kenyan-people-amb-kamau-macharia/.

[22] In September 2013, the Somali militant group Al Shabab launched a terrorist attack in
Nairobi's Westgate Mall, which resulted in sixty-seven deaths.

[23] "Shock: Ruto Claims West Gate Mall Attack was Arranged to Fix Him and President
Kenyatta," *Kenya Today*, 23 September 2013, www.kenya-today.com/news/shock-ruto-claims-
west-gate-mall-attack-pre-planned-occur-country.

Kenya's buying time with the ICC also included two strategies adopted by the defendants: the first one was the use of all legal means available, with multiple processes and appeals, to get the cases dismissed under the Rome Statute's admissibility and jurisdiction rules (Mueller 2014, 32). That strategy had the advantage of buying time to make sure that, if the cases went to trial, it would be after the 2013 presidential elections, in which Kenyatta and Ruto were contenders. The second strategy was to engage the Kenyan state itself in the legal challenges, although the ICC prosecution targeted individuals in their personal capacity, not the state. The admissibility challenges started on 31 March 2011 and lasted until 31 August 2012, when the Appeals Chamber rejected them. Following the rejection of their admissibility challenge, the defendants raised jurisdiction challenges, questioning whether the Kenya situation met the threshold of crimes against humanity. In doing so, the Kenyan defendants invoked Judge Kaul's dissenting opinion. Indeed, Judge Kaul had issued a dissenting opinion that differed from his colleagues of Pre-Trial Chamber II in which he argued that there was no evidence of an "organizational policy" of the postelection violence and, because the violence was not attributable to a state-like organization, it did not meet the threshold of crimes against humanity. This meant that the ICC would not have material jurisdiction over the Kenya cases.[24] This strategy worked in favor of Kenya because successive delaying tactics ensured that the trials would not take place until after the 2013 elections. As Mueller (2014, 33) writes,

> Having initially been postponed from April until May and July 2013, additional defense appeals were successful in getting Ruto and Sang's trial delayed until September 2013, and Kenyatta's until November 2013 and then until January 2014, and once again until February 2014. Each delay was in part the result of witness intimidation. This occasioned the need for new witnesses, opening up the prospect of more witness intimidation and more delays.

In its filing request for a postponement of the trial until after the 2013 Kenyan presidential elections, Ruto's defense had argued that the elections are "a significant step and important for both the democratic process and the Kenyan people … [It] provides an important and further opportunity for Mr Ruto to advance the process of reconciliation in that country and to help ensure the pacific nature of the election."[25] Thus, it shows that Ruto had used the upcoming 2013 presidential elections and the need to avert potential violence as

---

[24] See Judge Kaul's dissenting opinion at www.haguejusticeportal.net/Docs/ICC/Kenya/Justice%20Kaul%20Dissent%2015%20March%202011.pdf.

[25] ICC Defense of Mr. William Samoei Ruto: "Written Submission in Response to 'Order Scheduling a Status Conference,'" 28 May 2012, www.icc-cpi.int/iccdocs/doc/doc1418881.pdf.

leverage in his strategy to delay the proceedings against him before the ICC. If anything, Ruto would be in a better position defending himself before the ICC as an elected deputy president, which would ensure him the backing of the Kenyan state. While running for office in the 2013 elections, Kenyatta and Ruto resorted to ethnic polarization, joining Kikuyus and Kalenjin – the two groups that targeted each other in the 2007–2008 postelection violence – against Odinga's Luo ethnic group.[26]

Kenyatta and Ruto's political rhetoric also included attacking the ICC as a Western, anti-African, and colonial institution. Their strategy to enlist other voices across the African continent to portray the ICC as a political tool against African leaders was also successful. For instance, Ugandan President Museveni used the opportunity of Kenyatta's swear-in ceremony to criticize the ICC. He said,

> I want to salute the Kenyan voters for the rejection of the blackmail by the International Criminal Court (ICC)…I was one of those that supported the ICC because I abhor impunity. However, the usual opinionated and arrogant actors using their careless analysis have distorted the purpose of that institution. They are now using it to install leaders of their choice in Africa and eliminate the ones they do not like. (The New Vision 2013)

And sure enough, Kenyatta and Ruto became president and deputy president, respectively, of Kenya in 2013, which gave them even more leverage to amplify their strategy against the ICC, now to include intimidation, bribery, and witnesses disappearing. As the trial neared, more witnesses dropped out, which led the ICC prosecution to seek more time to review the new evidence and search for more witnesses. For instance, the ICC prosecutor was able to submit to the Court 288 pages of evidence of witness interference by Kenyan authorities.[27]

As the Kenya cases show, prosecuting senior state officials before the ICC presents its own challenges, ranging from the AU siding with the Kenyan government to questions of immunity, jurisdiction, and physical presence at the Court, which hindered the ability of the Court to bring the Kenya cases to trial successfully (Hobbs 2015). This difficulty arose despite the fact that Kenya has also sought to reassure the ICC that Kenyatta and Ruto will be cooperative and follow the rules and respond to their summons. The Kenyan

---

[26] Odinga was Ruto's ally during the 2007 elections, but the latter entered into a new alliance with Kenyatta after both were indicted by the ICC. Ruto and Kenyatta formed the Jubilee Alliance Party, which subsequently won the 2013 elections.

[27] ICC Trial Chamber V(A), Decision on Defense Application for Judgment of Acquittal. No ICC-01/09 01/11, 5 Avril 2016. Note 341, p. 114.

authorities also had assured the ICC that they would be cooperative and would submit to the Court all requested documents. On 8 April 2013, Kenya Attorney General Githu Muigai assured Trial Chamber V that, as a member state to the ICC, Kenya would meet its obligations. However, the ICC's OTP had very little room for maneuvering in the face of Kenya's stonewalling and refusal to cooperate with the Court, which ultimately would lead to the case against Kenyatta being dropped before it reached the trial phase, and charges against Ruto and Sang being vacated after the prosecution finished presenting its case. This ultimately leads to the issue of the limited power of the ICC to address political violence, especially in situations in which the main suspects are at the heart of the state apparatus.

THE KENYA CASES: PROSECUTION FAILED

The ICC's OTP failed to prosecute any of the Kenyan suspects in the 2007 postelection violence successfully. Ultimately, the strategy of the Kenyan state paid off because it was able to shield its agents from being convicted for crimes against humanity at The Hague. The argument in this chapter is not one about the delivery of justice and whether or not the ICC ultimately rendered fair and just judgments in the cases. Instead, the analysis here focuses on the failure of the ICC prosecutor – not necessarily the Court writ-large – to pursue any of the trials of the "Ocampo Six" to its completion. No one has been convicted for crimes against humanity in the Kenyan cases, which were also the first instance of the prosecutor using his *proprio motu* powers to open an investigation. Such failures result from the challenges of prosecuting state officials, especially in instances where the state has adopted multiple tactics to impede the investigation. Charges against Henry Kosgey and Muhammed Hussein Ali were not confirmed by Pre-Trial Chamber II on 23 January 2012 because the chamber found that the prosecutor had not provided sufficient preliminary evidence and had relied on a single anonymous witness in the case of Kosgey. The chamber declined also to confirm charges against Ali, the former commissioner of the Kenya police, because of insufficient evidence connecting the Kenya police force to the attacks carried out by the Party of National Unity (PNU) supporters.

With two suspects out of the Ocampo Six, the remaining four were merged into two cases. One involved the two members of the Orange Democratic Movement (ODM) led by Raila Odinga: Ruto and Sang. As members of the PNU, which was the incumbent party during the 2007 elections, Kenyatta and Muthaura made up the second case. In March 2013, however, the ICC prosecutor announced that she was dropping all charges against Muthaura because she lacked evidence for his probable conviction due to the loss of a key witness who had recanted testimony, the death of potential witnesses, and lack of cooperation from the Kenyan government (ICC Trial Chamber V 2013). The case against President Kenyatta had collapsed in December 2014 before reaching the trial phase. In fact, the Pre-Trial Chamber had requested that the OTP either proceed to trial or drop the charges against Kenyatta. The prosecutor has cited lack of cooperation from the Kenyan state as a reason for the failure to obtain enough evidence to move the case against Kenyatta to the trial phase. Kenyatta was charged as an indirect co-perpetrator of the crimes against humanity of murder, forcible transfer, rape, persecution, and other inhumane acts.

Ultimately, the investigations in the Kenyan situation led to one trial at the ICC: the joint case against Deputy President Ruto and former journalist Sang – who were on trial from September 2013 to April 2016. Ruto was charged as an indirect co-perpetrator of crimes against humanity of murder, forcible transfer, and persecution. Sang was charged for having contributed to the commission of those crimes.

The Kenyatta Case: Witnesses' Conundrum and Case Collapse

The collapse of the case against Uhuru Kenyatta that ended with the prosecutor dropping the charges exemplifies the difficulty of prosecuting state officials at the ICC. It showed that state compliance and cooperation for a fruitful investigation are difficult to obtain if the suspects are state officials, even more so when the suspect is the sitting head of state. The Kenya situation showed the degree to which noncooperation of a state party to the Rome Statute and hostile action taken by the state against the Court resulted in the impossibility of gathering satisfactory evidence to go to trial. By early 2014, the prosecutor's office had withdrawn at least seven witnesses because they had either recanted their earlier testimonies, or they feared testifying in the Kenyatta case (Maliti 2014a). Because the prosecutor's case relied heavily on testimonies rather than physical evidence, failure to secure the willingness of the witnesses to testify in court basically meant the unraveling of the prosecutor's case.

In a letter dated December 2013, Prosecutor Bensouda requested an adjournment of the trial, arguing that she needed more time because the withdrawal of witnesses meant that the case against Kenyatta could not meet the threshold needed to secure conviction (ICC OTP 2013). In fact, a prosecutor witness had admitted that "he provided false evidence regarding the event at the heart of the Prosecution's case against [Kenyatta]," and another witness had informed the prosecution that he was no longer willing to testify at trial (ICC OTP 2013).

Facing what was viewed as the state's obstruction and refusal to submit requested documents for the investigation, the prosecutor referred the matter to Trial Chamber V (B) in the Kenyatta case (ICC 2015). The chamber then requested that the Kenyan state provide to the prosecutor eight categories of records related to Uhuru Kenyatta that she had requested.[28] The documents that the prosecutor had requested from the Kenyan attorney general covered company records, land ownership and transfers, tax returns, vehicle registrations, bank records, foreign exchange records, telephone records, and intelligence records. The prosecutor hoped to be able to use such records for evidence to link Kenyatta to the postelection violence of 2007–2008. But Kenya's attorney general Githu Muigai had argued that the prosecutor's request was a "fishing expedition" because it lacked specificity, a result of the prosecutor requesting documents covering the period between June 2007 and December 2010. Attorney General Muigai contended also that conducting such searches was difficult because the registry of Kenyan companies was paper-based before 2009.

Facing obstruction from the Kenyan state and witnesses withdrawing or recanting their testimonies, the ICC prosecutor finally came to the conclusion that she did not have enough evidence to proceed to a trial.[29] Before deciding to drop the charges, however, Prosecutor Bensouda had asked the judges for an indefinite adjournment of the case, until the circumstances changed to the point of making the Kenyan state more willing to cooperate with the prosecution. But the chamber requested that either the prosecutor move to the trial phase or dismiss the case against Kenyatta. In a unanimous decision, judges of Trial Chamber V (B) terminated the charges against Kenyatta on 13 March 2015.[30] With the charges against Kenyatta dropped, there were only two suspects left on trial in relation to the 2007–2008 postelection violence: Deputy President Ruto and former journalist Sang. They, too, would later have the charges against them vacated.

The Collapse of the Ruto-Sang Case: Witness Problem Redux

The extent to which the ICC faces challenges when prosecuting state officials is evident not only in how the Kenyatta's case collapsed before going to trial but also in the trial proceedings of the Ruto-Sang case. Because the ICC

[28] ICC Trial Chamber V(b): Decision on the Prosecutor's Revised Cooperation Request, 29 July 2014, www.icc-cpi.int/iccdocs/doc/doc1801984.pdf.

[29] ICC Office of the Prosecutor: Notice of Withdrawal of the Charges against Uhuru Muigai Kenyatta, 5 December 2014, www.icc-cpi.int/iccdocs/doc/doc1879204.pdf.

[30] ICC Trial Chamber V(B): Decision on the Withdrawal of Charges against Mr Kenyatta, 13 March 2015, www.icc-cpi.int/iccdocs/doc/doc1936247.pdf.

prosecutor failed to gather enough material evidence against the accused, she relied mostly on witness testimonies that had been collected during the investigation. But by the time the trial had started, most of the witnesses had either ceased to cooperate with the prosecution or had recanted their testimonies to the point of being declared hostile witnesses. Declaring a witness hostile allows the prosecution to cross-examine its own witness to establish his or her incredibility, which would be based on the extent to which the witness has refuted his or her earlier testimony. For instance, Witness 727 was scheduled to testify via video link in the Ruto-Sang trial, but he failed to appear, and on 24 March 2015, his lawyers said that he was in hiding after a Dutch court issued an order compelling him to appear before the ICC. In fact, the witness and his family had been granted asylum in the Netherlands. His Dutch lawyer said that he had been in hiding – in the Netherlands – because he feared testifying before the Court (Maliti 2015b). He went into hiding after the Dutch court threatened to jail him if he did not testify before the ICC. The law firm that represented him said, "The witness … ha[s] received serious threats due to a potentially incriminating statement that [he] could make against Mr. Ruto before the International Criminal Court" (Maliti 2015b).

In another interesting twist of events, the prosecution called its own witness "thoroughly unreliable and incredible" (Maliti 2015a). The prosecutor had previously submitted an application for the chamber to declare Witness 743 hostile. Four other prosecution witnesses had also been declared hostile. Witness 800 expressed how frustrated he was with the prosecutor's office and the witness protection program that gave him insufficient allowance for him and his family (Maliti 2014c). Witness 637 also was declared hostile after he had said in court that three people had coached him to implicate Ruto and Sang (Maliti 2014e). Witness 516 was declared hostile as well, after having admitted that a promise of a good life induced him to give false claims (Maliti 2014d). Witness 495 said that he never made statements to the prosecution and that when he met OTP staff in November 2012, he was given two statements and asked to copy them in his own handwriting to make them look like his own statements (Maliti 2014b). Prosecutor Bensouda also said that eight prosecution witnesses were unwilling to testify in the Ruto-Sang trial: they were Witnesses 15, 16, 323, 336, 397, 495, 516, and 524.

All the above-mentioned instances of witnesses recanting their testimonies or simply refusing to testify weakened the prosecution case to the point that the accused filed a motion of "no case to answer," which calls for the judges to acquit them without them having to present their defense. In the end, the three judges ruled, by a majority of 2–1, to vacate the charges against Ruto and Sang (ICC 2016b). As Presiding Judge Eboe-Osuji wrote in his judgment, "eight witnesses who potentially possess evidence that the prosecution considered relevant to the case never appeared before the Court" (ICC 2016b, 128). He added that, even in the absence of proof that Ruto and Sang had personally engaged in meddling and witness intimidation, "It is enough that the atmosphere had been fostered – by persons and entities to have [Mr Ruto] and Mr Sang's best interests at heart – in a way reasonably likely to intimidate witnesses" (ICC 2016b, 128). Judge Fremr made a similar argument, stating, "Although it has not been shown, or argued, that the accused were involved in the interference of witnesses, they did profit from the interference, *inter alia*, by the falling away of several key witnesses that this Chamber found to have been interfered with" (ICC Trial Chamber V [A] 2016, 55). He added that "there was a disturbing level of interference with witnesses, as well as inappropriate attempts at the political level to meddle with the trial and to affect its outcome" (ICC Trial Chamber V [A] 2016, 55).[31]

It was clear to the judges that the witness intimidation and tampering was part of a collective effort on the part of the Kenyan state and its agents. Judge Eboe-Osuji noted also that the government of Kenya was not a party to this trial and that the Court had indeed accommodated Ruto so he could carry on his duties as deputy president during the trial, having granted him a continuous excusal from physically being present in The Hague. Therefore, Judge Eboe-Osuji found that "it is difficult to see where the good faith lay in the Government's involvement of itself in the campaign against the trial" (ICC 2016b, 125). The judge also noticed that there was an "openly aggressive campaign that the Government [of Kenya] and some opinion leaders in Kenya had mounted against the Court for the apparent purpose of ensuring that the case against the accused is peremptorily terminated" (ICC 2016b, 115). The legal proceedings against Kenyatta, Ruto, and Sang were indeed tainted by political meddling and interference orchestrated from Nairobi to ensure that the cases against the accused would collapse. The ICC may well wish to remove itself from political considerations, but it is nonetheless evident that the Court must operate in a political world in which states, even though not standing trial at The Hague, have nonetheless major stakes in ICC proceedings. This also raises questions regarding the ICC's posture as a court avowedly operating without political considerations – but in a world of politics.

---

[31] ICC Trial Chamber V(A), 2016, "Situation in the Republic of Kenya: Public Redacted Version of Decision on Defence Applications for Judgments of Acquittal," ICC-01/09-01/111, 5 April, www.icc-cpi.int/CourtRecords/CR2016_04384.pdf.

THE LIMITS OF A PROFESSED APOLITICAL COURT

The ICC's involvement in postelection violence in Kenya and Côte d'Ivoire indicated a venture into unchartered territory for the Court, which, until then, had only intervened in civil conflicts. The ICC involvement in Kenya had the effect of representing the 2007 electoral violence as exceptional when, in reality, electoral violence in Kenya is hardly exceptional (Kagwanja 1998; Höhn 2014; Ruteere and Wairuri 2015).[32] As Ruteere and Wairuri (2015, 120) argue,

> In countries like Kenya where electoral contests degenerate into ethnic conflict, it is much more than individual culpability that is at stake when individuals such as those indicted by the ICC in the Kenya case are brought to trial. Rather, such trials also serve to frame new narratives of victimhood – both individual and collective, which may reignite new cycles of violence.

Indeed, new narratives of victimhood were salient in the wake of the ICC's intervention. Whereas Kenyatta and Ruto were able to frame their indictment as an attempt by the Court to victimize Kenya as a nation, it was also clear that within Kenya, the ethnic communities to which the ICC suspects belong also embarked into victimhood narratives. Therefore, in addition to those who were victimized by the electoral violence, a new category of victims also emerged: those who were targeted by the ICC and the ethnic communities to which they belong. For instance, a victim of the postelection violence who, almost a decade later, still lived in the Nakuru Pipeline internally displaced persons (IDP) camp, said in 2016, "How it came to be that Uhuru [Kenyatta] was in the list [of ICC suspects] is something we can't understand. How come Raila [Odinga] was not in the list of suspects yet Uhuru and Ruto were suspects? Did you see any Luo in that list? Yet we had the Kikuyu and the Kalenjin [on the list of ICC suspects.] Where are the Luo?"[33] Indeed, the three remaining ICC suspects at the time of this interview all belonged to the Kikuyu and Kalenjin ethnic communities. Odinga, who was the main challenger in the 2007 and 2013 elections, belongs to the Luo ethnicity, and no Luo was included in the ICC indictment. This statement is from a victim of the violence, who in turn views the ICC as an institution that victimizes Kenyatta and Ruto and the communities to which they belong, and has failed to target any individual from the Luo community. Along the same lines,

---

[32] In fact, political violence has been a quasi-recurrent occurrence that accompanies Kenyan elections since the introduction of multiparty contests in 1991. Elections in 1992, 1997, 2002, and 2007 have all seen eruptions of political violence. See Ruteere and Wairuri (2015). See also Kagwanja (1998).

[33] Author's interview with resident of Nakuru Pipeline IDP camp, Kenya, February 2016.

another victim who lives in the Subukia IDP camp in Nakuru said, "My own son was pierced by an arrow by one of his classmates. So, saying that Uhuru and Ruto were the perpetrators is sheer nonsense."[34]

The ICC involvement in the prosecution of political violence in Kenya did not trigger positive complementarity (Jalloh 2013). Positive complementarity denotes instances in which an ICC intervention would lead the state to put in place domestic mechanisms to investigate and prosecute atrocity crimes, thereby strengthening the rule of law in the state. To the extent that positive complementarity may trigger the state to address atrocity crimes domestically rather than ignore them, it poses also a dilemma to local nongovernmental organizations (NGOs) because, if they insist on strengthening the local judiciary, they will not be able to make the case that the state is unwilling or unable to prosecute. During the preliminary examination in Kenya, local NGOs did not advocate for domestic prosecutions; they instead lobbied for the opening of a full investigation by the ICC (Bjork and Goebertus 2011). This in turn puts the local human rights NGOs in an uncomfortable situation because they were criticized for being the enablers of the ICC prosecutions (Mue and Gitau 2015). For instance, an IDP said, "[T]he ICC is a political court. Because they did not come to get information from the grassroots. They got their statements from the human rights commission and the civil society. They also paid people to give witness statements."[35] In the end, many factors contributed to the failure of the ICC to prosecute the Kenyan cases successfully.

Successful ICC investigations and prosecutions of state officials are also hindered by other factors besides the limits of state cooperation. The extent to which a state is willing to go to protect its officials always constitutes a potential roadblock, but the ICC's professed vow not to venture into politics is also a problem (Roach 2013). ICC officials have asserted that the Court is an impartial and apolitical institution. Unlike national courts that have stronger enforcement mechanisms, however, the ICC is compelled to negotiate with state officials in order to be effective at prosecuting cases, which requires the Court to develop a political and diplomatic capacity (Roach 2013, 508). Such venturing into politics and capacity creates a tricky situation for the Court, especially given the propensity of the ICC prosecutors to meet with "unsavory" leaders (Kersten 2019a; Labuda 2019; McDougall 2019). In any case, in a world of states, and where state cooperation is needed for the ICC to deliver justice, the Court faces increased challenges when the targets for investigation are the agents of the state.

---

[34] Author's interview with resident of Subukia IDP camp, Nakuru, February 2016.
[35] Author's interview, Nakuru, Kenya, February 2016.

CONCLUSION

In the wake of the ICC's OTP abandoning the charges against President Uhuru Kenyatta because its case was too weak to proceed, Mark Kersten (2015b) writes, "Kenyatta has written the political manual on how to win an election, stay in power and simultaneously quash an ICC case against a sitting head of state." A little over a year later, the ICC Trial Chamber V(A) would also dismiss the case against Ruto and Sang. It means that, from the list of six suspects that were at first accused of crimes against humanity in the wake of the 2007–2008 postelection violence, not one was convicted. In fact, none saw the proceedings against them unfold to its normal term. The collapse of the Kenya cases brings out questions about what it means for the ICC to investigate and prosecute state officials within a framework where state cooperation is needed and where state compliance is expected from state parties to the Rome Statute. In the Kenya cases, the ICC prosecutor had taken an unpreceded strategy in the short history of the Court: to investigate and prosecute both sides of the conflict simultaneously. Up to that point, the prosecutor had always targeted one side of the conflict – the rebels or political adversaries – and always claimed that what it calls the "sequencing" of investigations was a better strategy. Kenya was the first instance where the prosecutor had not used a sequencing approach to investigation, but it was also the first instance where the prosecution targeted state officials in the absence of a UNSC referral. Given the outcome of the Kenya cases, one wonders whether the ICC prosecutor can successfully prosecute state officials at all, even those from states that are parties to the Rome Statute.

    Despite making credible commitments by joining international institutions such as the ICC, states also exercise discretionary power in relation to the extent to which they comply with the rules and cooperate with the Court. Although norms diffusion is important here, it is mitigated by calculations of political risks, that, if low, ensure state compliance. But when the political risks are high for the state, for example, in instances where state officials are the main suspects at an international court, as was the case in Kenya, the state engages in acts that undermine the work of the Court to ensure that the prosecution would fail. Since it became operational in 2002, the ICC has gone to great lengths to portray itself as an institution that does not venture into the political and that is guided only by the rule of law. Prosecutors at the ICC have indeed repeatedly emphasized that they are "solely guided by the law" (Bensouda 2012); and Prosecutor Bensouda (2013) has said that "politics have no place and will play no part in the decisions I take." The reality, however, is that the Court operates in a political world and is shaped by political events. State compliance with the ICC also results from political calculations, especially when the stakes are high.

6

The Court Is the Political Arena

I won't send any more Ivoirians to the ICC.

President Alassane Ouattara (AFP 2016)

INTRODUCTION

The International Criminal Court (ICC) is a place of staged performance where various actors deploy their political narratives and pursue their political interests. The Court in The Hague becomes a transposed arena where domestic politics are enmeshed with the rule of law and legal procedures. As such, the situation in Côte d'Ivoire is a prime example of the ICC becoming involved in a highly politically charged crisis that was set off by contested electoral results in December 2010. However, the crisis in Côte d'Ivoire was also the result of over two decades of political intrigue in the midst of power struggles between powerful brokers in a climate where xenophobia and political exclusion had created the conditions for a rebellion that partitioned the country in half. After an attempted reunification and a presidential election organized in a bid to return to normal in late 2010, the demons of political division resurfaced in the aftermath of contested elections results, leading to a crisis that left over 3,000 people killed.

The ICC intervention in the Ivoirian political crisis hence becomes a stage of performative discourse where actors create, change, frame, make, and unmake their political narratives. In The Hague, the defendants Laurent Gbagbo and Charles Blé Goudé used their appearance before the Court not only to address the chamber but also to speak to their compatriots and to a global audience about their (his)stories, which fit in the larger frame of the (dis)placement of the Ivoirian crisis into an international criminal justice apparatus (Ba 2015b). The Court is therefore the domestic political arena for Ivoirian politics, where the Ouattara administration is as much a political actor as the Court itself.

To date, the situation in Côte d'Ivoire before the ICC involves the prosecution of three individuals for whom the ICC had issued an arrest warrant: former president Laurent Gbagbo; his wife, Simone Gbagbo; and Charles Blé Goudé, a former official in Gbagbo's administration. The prosecution of these individuals by the ICC comes on the heels of the political crisis that engulfed the country after the 2010 elections, which triggered six months of unrest and human rights abuses. Gbagbo had refused to leave power despite having been defeated by his opponent Alassane Ouattara. In the violence that followed the struggle for power, at least 3,000 people were killed by forces on both sides along political, ethnic, and religious lines (Human Rights Watch 2013). Although the ICC's Office of the Prosecutor (OTP) claims that the investigation is still ongoing, especially in the Ouattara side,[1] all the individuals who have been charged so far belong to the Gbagbo camp. Three years after the start of the trial, on 15 January 2019, the ICC Trial Chamber I acquitted Gbagbo and Blé Goudé of all charges and ordered their immediate release from prison (ICC 2019). This decision followed a motion for acquittal that the defense teams had introduced after the prosecutor had finished making its case. The acquittal of Gbagbo and Blé Goudé constituted a major setback for the prosecutor's office and raised questions about its strategy in the Côte d'Ivoire situation (Ba 2019).

In fact, the OTP argued that it adopted a "sequential approach" in the situation of Côte d'Ivoire, unlike in the case of Kenya, where the prosecution targeted both sides of the conflict simultaneously. Côte d'Ivoire and Kenya share the feature of political violence that led to the involvement of the ICC, unlike other situations where the Court's intervention followed a breakout of civil conflict. The prosecution of matters of political violence at the ICC comes with its own set of challenges, mainly domestic politics being transferred to the ICC, which I argue becomes a political arena where the actors deploy their own narratives in pursuit of their political interests.

Ultimately, this chapter shows the ways in which a state strategically called in the ICC prosecutor to investigate a political crisis as an attempt to incapacitate their political adversaries. Both the Gbagbo and Ouattara

---

[1] In 2015, Prosecutor Bensouda said, "My office has been very clear that all parties to the conflict, all sides to the conflict will not be spared … We couldn't start both sides at the same time, [but] hopefully, in the middle of this year [2015], we would start the investigations [into the Ouattara side]." See Perelman (2015).

administrations issued ad hoc declarations recognizing the Court's jurisdiction in 2003 and 2010, respectively, pursuing the same aims. The ICC prosecutor seized on the opportunity and focused on prosecuting crimes presumably committed by Gbagbo and his allies, adopting a selective policy in the name of expediency. Having outsourced justice to The Hague, the Ouattara administration ensured cooperation – selectively – to the ICC prosecutor, again in the pursuit of its own domestic political interests. As was the case with the removal of Bemba from the Congolese political scene, the arrest and transfer of Gbagbo to The Hague transformed the Ivoirian political landscape, allowing Ouattara to secure an easy victory in the 2015 presidential election, with over 85 percent of the votes (Clark 2018, 289). Gbagbo's trial in The Hague loomed over Ivoirian politics, however, with some opposition vowing to "bring Gbagbo home" as a political platform (Rosenberg 2017a).

This chapter first explores the roots of the Ivoirian crisis, before showing how, for almost a decade, successive Ivoirian administrations tried to use the ICC to settle political scores, before the Court finally intervened in the aftermath of the 2010 elections. The sequential approach adopted by the OTP played into the hands of the Ouattara administration, which essentially outsourced justice to The Hague despite flimsy evidence tying the suspects to the alleged crimes. The trial at The Hague ultimately resulted in the acquittal of Gbagbo and Blé Goudé.

ANATOMY OF THE IVOIRIAN CRISIS

The political turmoil that engulfed Côte d'Ivoire over the past three decades has its roots in the longevity of the Ivoirian postindependence regime. Félix Houphouët-Boigny established his political preeminence already as a cocoa farmer and doctor in the 1940s and 1950s within French colonial politics and became president of Côte d'Ivoire at independence in 1960 (McGovern 2011, 15–17).[2] He held onto the one-party state ruled by his Democratic Party of Côte d'Ivoire (Parti Démocratique de la Côte d'Ivoire [PDCI]), even when Laurent Gbagbo created his own opposition party, the Ivoirian Popular Front (Front Populaire Ivoirien [FPI]) in 1982, and went into exile in France. However, the end of the Cold War, which saw France calling on its former colonies to democratize, put Houphouët-Boigny's cult of personality and one-man

---

[2] This section was previously published in Ba (2015). Reproduced with permission of the publisher.

rule under pressure.[3] At the Ivoirian first multiparty election on 28 October 1990, opposition leader Laurent Gbagbo won 18 percent of the vote against Houphouët-Boigny's 82 percent and gained nine seats in the parliament against PDCI's 163 seats (McGovern 2011, 113).

In Côte d'Ivoire, the decades 1960 to 1980 were a period of economic growth, governed through what is referred to as the "Houphouëtist compromise". Under this system, political support was maintained through the economic opportunities afforded by the benevolent hand of Houphouët-Boigny's charismatic father figure (Akindès, Fofana, and Kouamé 2014). However, the economic hardships of the late 1980s eroded those foundations, plunging Côte d'Ivoire into a post-miracle period concomitant with the post-Cold War demands for democratic openness. Houphouët-Boigny, being a clever patriarch, had avoided having any of his heirs amass too much political power.[4] When he called on Alassane Ouattara in 1990 to be his prime minister, Houphouët-Boigny wanted to benefit from Ouattara's relations with international financial structures.[5] Henri Konan Bédié, his other potential heir and not very charismatic, was a member of the Baoulé group, which had ruled Côte d'Ivoire since independence (Banégas 2006). A brief succession struggle ensued between Bédié, then president of the National Assembly, and Ouattara, then prime minister at Houphouët-Boigny's death in 1993. Bédié prevailed, as provided by the Ivoirian constitution.

As the Ivoirian economy entered a difficult phase in the 1990s due to the fall of the price of cacao and the devaluation of the CFA currency that lost half its value, political tensions arose as well, and the concept of *Ivoirité* ("Ivoirianness") entered the debate when Bédié excluded Ouattara from the 1995 presidential elections. Ouattara's exclusion was enacted through the parliament passing a law that was meant to do just that. The law stated that only Ivoirian citizens by birth and of parents who were also born in Côte d'Ivoire would be allowed to run for the presidency. In Ivoirian political circles, it

---

[3] At the 1990 Franco-African Summit in La Baule, which saw the attendance of twenty-two African heads of state, France made clear that democratization must become part of the agenda for African states and will be tied to foreign aid. President Mitterrand declared, "Of course we must speak of democracy … France will link its entire contribution effort to efforts made to move in the direction of greater freedom … Aid will be more lukewarm toward regimes which conduct themselves in an authoritarian manner without accepting evolution toward democracy; it will be enthusiastic for those which take the step with courage." See Coleman and Paddack (1990).

[4] On Félix Houphouët-Boigny's life and presidency, see Grah Mel (2003, 2010).

[5] Prior to becoming prime minister of Côte d'Ivoire in 1990, Ouattara had been an economist at the International Monetary Fund (IMF) from 1968 to 1973, and later director of the African Department. He would eventually return to the IMF as deputy managing director in 1994.

was said that Ouattara's father was born in Upper Volta (now Burkina Faso). Although the French colony of Côte d'Ivoire – let alone the Ivoirian state – did not yet exist, the supreme court In Côte d'Ivoire ruled that Ouattara's father was not an autochthon, ultimately barring him from running for the 1995 presidential elections.

At its core, the *Ivoirité* concept gave "pseudo-intellectual justification to an instrumentalized xenophobia whose main object was keeping Ouattara and his [party] out of politics" (McGovern 2011, 17).[6] Indeed, *Ivoirité* was first used by Ivoirian intellectuals as a cultural idea in the 1970s, but it did not become popular until Bédié made it a political concept that redefined nationhood and citizenship (Förster 2013, 11). And in a country where 28 percent of the population were immigrants, mostly from Burkina Faso, Mali, and Guinea, *Ivoirité* redefined exclusionary citizenship and nationality that excluded not only the immigrants but also other Ivoirian citizens (McGovern 2011, 14). This was compounded by the fact that Côte d'Ivoire was never a melting pot but rather a cohabitation and division of labor between different communities (Banégas 2006, 540).

The Christmas Eve coup of 1999 put General Robert Guéï in power, and he promised to "sweep" the political scene and leave. General Guéï promised new elections, but in October 2000, the Constitutional Court once again rejected Ouattara's bid for the presidency on the grounds that he held a Burkinabé diplomatic passport during his career as an official of the International Monetary Fund (IMF). Indeed, the new Ivoirian constitution included a clause disqualifying any candidate who has held a nationality other than Ivoirian (Cutolo 2010, 528). General Guéï had also introduced in the new Ivoirian constitution the infamous Article 35, which required that both parents of any presidential candidate be Ivoirian citizens and the Ivoirian supreme court – whose members were appointed by Guéï – ruled that neither Bédié nor Ouattara were allowed to run for president. This ruling basically left only Gbagbo standing for the political opposition (McGovern 2011, 18). Naturally, Gbagbo won the election as Ivoirians were faced with few options, but Guéï declared himself the winner nonetheless, which led to popular uprisings, and Gbagbo was eventually sworn in as the president in 2000.

Nearly two years after President Gbagbo assumed power, another major event would rock Côte d'Ivoire. On 19 September 2002, an attempted coup and rebellion was launched from the north, initiated by soldiers and citizens that felt excluded by the *Ivoirité* policies of Bédié, Guéï, and Gbagbo, successively.

---

[6] On the concept of *Ivoirité*, see also Cutolo (2010). For a study of the ideological, political, and economic justifications of *Ivoirité*, see Akindès (2003) and Akindès and Fofana (2011).

Indeed, Gbagbo too had embraced the exclusionary politics of *Ivoirité* that sought to disenfranchise northerners who appeared to be Ouattara loyalists.[7] Although the pro-Ouattara rebel forces failed to capture Abidjan, they occupied the northern half of the country, centered around the city of Bouaké, from 2002 to 2010, while Guillaume Soro emerged as the political leader of the Forces Nouvelles, the rebellion movement (Soro 2005). The Ivoirian conflict between 2002 and 2010 was never a full-blown war but rather a situation that was perpetually tense and characterized by frequent instances of violence (McGovern 2011, xviii). The aftermath of the 2010 postelectoral crisis ushered in a level of violence that had not been reached before.

By January 2003, following the de facto partition of the country, the Economic Community of West African States (ECOWAS) had deployed an interposition force along the *zone de confiance* – a buffer zone that separated the Forces Nouvelles–controlled north and the south under Gbagbo's government control. The two sides held the Lina-Marcoussis talks outside Paris in January 2003 and agreed to a power-sharing mechanism. At the same time, however, pro-Gbagbo militants known as the Young Patriots were staging protests in Abidjan against France, stirring up a strong anti-France sentiment from Gbagbo loyalists (Chirot 2006; Bovcon 2009; Schumann 2013). Prime Minister Seydou Diarra was chosen to lead the coalition government, but the Forces Nouvelles ministers would later pull out, claiming obstruction from Gbagbo. As a new round of negotiations followed, the parties signed the Accra III accords in July 2003 and agreed to a timetable for legislative reforms, which the government failed to enact, while the Forces Nouvelles refused to disarm (McGovern 2011, 21). President Gbagbo's forces launched a military operation to reconquer the north in November 2004. While bombing the city of Bouaké, they hit the French peacekeepers barracks, killing nine French soldiers. France retaliated by bombing and destroying Gbagbo's military planes and helicopters. France's involvement in the conflict then reached a point of no return (Smith 2003; Carroll and Henley 2004; Marchall 2005).

As the Ivoirian crisis faced another deadlock, Thabo Mbeki, the African Union (AU) mediator, invited Soro, Bédié, Ouattara, and Gbagbo to Pretoria in March 2005 and "locked them in a conference room together for three straight days" (McGovern 2011, 23). Gbagbo subsequently signed a presidential decree under his exceptional powers to suspend Article 35 of the Ivoirian constitution,

---

[7] In his testimony before the ICC, Joel Kouadio N'Guessan, spokesperson of Ouattara's Rassemblement des Républicains (RDR) party, reaffirmed that *Ivoirité* had poisoned Ivoirian politics to the extent that Gbagbo himself had said in 2005 that he wanted to "disinfect" the voters' lists, which, according to N'Guessan, meant preventing northern Ivoirians from voting (Panaïté 2016b).

with the effect of allowing Ouattara to run for the October 2005 presidential elections. After some additional episodes of violence, Mbeki convened the parties to the Pretoria II round of negotiations in June 2005, and President Gbagbo promulgated revised versions of the law on nationality and naturalization and created an independent electoral commission. But it was clear that Côte d'Ivoire was not ready to hold elections in October 2005 because the disarmament of the Soro's Forces Nouvelles and the Gbagbo militias proved impossible (Banégas 2006; Toh and Banégas 2006; McGovern 2011). The AU and the UN then gave President Gbagbo a one-year grace period within which the presidential elections needed to be held. But the state was not ready to hold elections in October 2006 either. Gbagbo and Soro entered into direct dialogue in 2007; the Ouagadougou Accords put forward a new peace plan that made Soro the prime minister of a unity government and scheduled elections for 2008. However, the elections did not take place until November 2010, five years after Gbagbo had completed his legally elected presidential term.

THE 2010 PRESIDENTIAL ELECTIONS:
POLITICAL VIOLENCE UNLEASHED

Three years after the signing of the Ouagadougou Accords that paved the way for the 2010 presidential elections, the Ivoirians seemed eager to move on from the years of crisis, as shown by the voter turnout that reached 80 percent (Banégas 2011, 457). However, the elections opened up the bloodiest episode of violence, with a militarization of the state and society (Banégas 2011, 457). The year 2010 marked the end of the second – unelected – Gbagbo presidential term. After having commissioned opinion polls from the French firm TNS Sofres, Gbagbo was confident that he was in a position to win the elections (Piccolino 2012, 21). At the first round of the presidential elections on 28 October 2010, however, Gbagbo and Ouattara came ahead with 38 percent and 32 percent of the votes, respectively, which led to a runoff between the two candidates because neither of them had won the required threshold of 50 percent of the votes. Ouattara's Rassemblement des Républicains (RDR) and Bédié's PDCI joined forces for the second round, creating an alliance around the Houphouët-Boigny legacy. On 2 December 2010, the Commission Électorale Indépendante de Côte d'Ivoire (CEI) declared Ouattara the winner, with 54.1 percent of the votes, after a series of incidents at its headquarters.[8]

---

[8] The spokesperson for the Commission Électorale Indépendante de Côte d'Ivoire (CEI) began announcing the result of the election, but a pro-Gbagbo commission member tore the paperwork out of his hands in front of cameras. The video is available at www.youtube.com/watch?v=WjaWVyhs3qA.

Those results were immediately dismissed by the Constitutional Council – led by Gbagbo's loyalist Judge Yao Ndré – which invalidated 600,000 votes cast in the northern region, an Ouattara stronghold. The Constitutional Council thus declared Gbagbo the winner with 51.45 percent of the votes, which led to the unusual scenario in which the country had two presidents, each claiming his legitimacy (Rim 2012). Both men were sworn in and formed their governments (Akindès, Fofana, and Kouamé 2014, 248–249). It is worth noting that the AU, ECOWAS, UN, and Carter Center observers said that, despite some irregularities, the elections were generally free and fair, and certified that the results delivered by the CEI that declared Ouattara the winner were correct (Carter Center 2015).

In the aftermath of the elections, Ouattara at first pursued a legalistic battle, isolating Gbagbo internationally and through financial asphyxia. Most of the actors in the international community recognized Ouattara's victory and called on Gbagbo to step aside.[9] Ouattara and Soro (Soro was Gbagbo's prime minister in the unity government and had by that time defected to Ouattara's camp) retreated to the secured Golf Hotel in Abidjan. By February 2011, Gbagbo had found it difficult to pay his soldiers and his administration, leading to more defections (Banégas 2011, 463). In March 2011, Ouattara renamed Soro's Forces Nouvelles the Forces Républicaines de Côte d'Ivoire (FRCI) and launched an offensive at the end of March, which ended with the capture of Gbagbo on 11 April 2011 and his subsequent transfer to The Hague.

ALL INTERNATIONAL JUSTICE POLITICS ARE LOCAL

With the help of UN and French troops, the pro-Ouattara forces unseated Gbagbo and arrested him in 2011. The newly formed government faced a domestic challenge: a large portion of the Ivoirian population that was pro-Gbagbo viewed Ouattara as a leader imposed on them by the international community (Straus 2015). The Ouattara administration faced other challenges in the post-conflict era, such as restructuring the military forces; rebuilding the economic infrastructure; reestablishing social cohesion; and managing political inclusion, including the remnants of Gbagbo's FPI party (Straus 2015, 182–183). The Ouattara administration also put in place a transitional justice agenda, which included a disarmament, demobilization, and reconstruction program, integrating many of the former Gbagbo loyalists into the newly

---

9 For instance, the UN, the AU, the European Union (EU), and ECOWAS had all deployed a wide range of measures designed to make Gbagbo relinquish power (Banégas 2011, 458).

created national army. National reconciliation remained elusive, however, as the search for justice and accountability in the wake of the crisis both at home and through the ICC became enmeshed in the pursuit of political interests.

The Unfulfilled Promise of Transitional Justice

President Ouattara established the Dialogue, Truth, and Reconciliation Commission (Commission Dialogue, Vérité, et Reconciliation [CDVR]) on 13 May 2011, which operated until December 2014, when it submitted its final report to the president. The Ivoirian CDVR followed the long list of truth and reconciliation commissions that many African states implemented to address past human rights abuses.[10] President Ouattara appointed Charles Konan Bany to head the commission, whose mandate ranged from investigating the root causes of the crisis to documenting the crimes committed and identifying appropriate reparations for the victims. However, the Ivoirian transitional justice mechanism downplayed legal proceedings, focusing mostly on collecting testimonies from the victims (Straus 2015, 184). In total, the commission heard some 70,000 testimonies and held eighty public audiences (Calame 2015). The commission was marred by controversy that ultimately rendered its work ineffective, despite the 15 million euro allocated to its budget (Calame 2015). While its initial mandate was to last two years, the commission did not submit its final report until four years later. Its recommendations included a call for land reform, better regional development programs, restructuring of the national army, and establishment of "national days of memory and forgiveness" (Calame 2015). The final report is yet to be released to the public, however.

Among the many failures of the commission, one could note the lack of coordination between its work and the criminal investigations conducted by other branches of the government and the ICC investigations and prosecutions. Civil society organizations complained that they were not consulted by the commission, and the concerns of the population were not adequately taken into account (FIDH 2014). The chair of the commission, Charles Konan Bany, was a polarizing figure, having been a prime minister under Gbagbo and an adviser to Ouattara during the 2010 presidential elections. Konan Bany did not hide the fact that he held presidential ambitions and was eyeing a run in the 2015 presidential elections. Indeed, just two months

---

[10] Several African countries have set up truth and reconciliation committees since the 1990s, including Chad, Democratic Republic of Congo (DRC), The Gambia, Kenya, Liberia, Nigeria, Rwanda, Sierra Leone, South Africa, Togo, Tunisia, and Uganda, among others.

after submitting the final report to President Ouattara, Konan Bany declared his candidacy to the 2015 presidential elections, seeking the nomination of Bedié's PDCI. At the end of the CDVR mandate, the Ivoirian government announced that a special fund of 15 million euros would be established for victims' compensation. The president signed a decree on 24 March 2015, establishing the National Commission for Reconciliation and Compensation of Victims (Commission Nationale pour la Réconciliation et l'Indemnisation des Victimes, CONARIV).[11]

Ultimately, the truth and reconciliation commission had little to no effect on either truthseeking or transitional justice. The judiciary in Côte d'Ivoire remained partisan under Ouattara's presidency, carried a weak account- ability performance, and continued the Ivoirian political trajectory wherein "laws and courts [are] used by political power-holders to buttress and legitimise their authority" (Bovcon 2014, 186). Through such instrumentalization of the law and courts, Bédié sought to exclude Ouattara from the political sphere in 1994, and junta leader Guëï sought to exclude both Ouattara and Bédié in 2000. President Gbagbo followed the same path once he assumed power. The new approach during Gbagbo's presidency, however, was to reach out to the ICC through an ad hoc declaration in 2003 as a way to counter Soro's rebel troops and Ouattara allies, a strategy that Ouattara himself adopted against Gbagbo in 2011.

The Domestic Politics of Invoking the ICC

In the aftermath of the November 2010 elections, up to 3,000 civilians were killed, most of the abuses attributable to the pro-Gbagbo forces and militias (HRW 2011). However, pro-Ouattara forces – renamed Forces Républicaines when Ouattara launched an offensive to take over the country – also perpetrated large-scale atrocities (HRW 2011). For instance, a Human Rights Watch (2011, 5) investigation finds that "[i]n Duékoué,[12] the Republican Forces and allied militias massacred hundreds of people, pulling men they alleged to be pro- Gbagbo militiamen out of their homes and executing them ... Later, dur- ing the military campaign to take over and consolidate control of Abidjan, the Republican Forces again executed scores of men from ethnic groups aligned to Gbagbo ... and tortured others." Therefore, there are grounds to

---

[11] See Commission Nationale pour la Réconciliation et l'Indemnisation des Victimes (CONARIV) http://conariv.ci/

[12] Duékoué is a city in western Côte d'Ivoire.

believe that both pro-Gbagbo and pro-Ouattara forces committed war crimes – and likely crimes against humanity, which fall within the material jurisdiction of the ICC (HRW 2011, 5).

Although Côte d'Ivoire did not become a state party to the Rome Statute until February 2013, it had already accepted ICC's jurisdiction by lodging an ad hoc declaration during both Gbagbo and Ouattara presidencies under Article 12(3) of the Rome Statute. Côte d'Ivoire first accepted the ICC's jurisdiction in a declaration dated 18 April 2003. Under Article 12(3) of the Rome Statute, Gbagbo's then minister of foreign affairs, Mamadou Bamba, indicated that the government "accepts the jurisdiction of the Court for the purposes of identifying, investigating and trying the perpetrators and accomplices of acts committed on Ivorian territory since the events of 19 September 2002." It is clear that the Gbagbo regime wanted at the time the ICC to investigate the events stemming from the 2002 attempted coup led by the Soro's forces and subsequent rebellion that divided the country in half. However, the ICC prosecutor failed to take the investigation seriously, and the file remained dormant in The Hague. After the 2010 elections that saw the defeat of Gbagbo and his refusal to relinquish power, and the postelectoral violence that ensued, president-elect Ouattara sent a new letter to the ICC on 14 December 2010 in which he "confirms the declaration of 18 Avril 2003" and he engages Côte d'Ivoire "to fully cooperate and without delay with the ICC, especially regarding all the crimes and abuses perpetrated since Mars 2004" (République de Côte d'Ivoire 2010). In both instances, Côte d'Ivoire lodged an ad hoc declaration accepting ICC jurisdiction as a means to counter and incapacitate domestic political and military adversaries. In her opening statement of the Gbagbo and Blé Goudé trial, Prosecutor Bensouda emphasized the apolitical nature of the case and that the objective was not to settle the questions regarding the winner of the 2010 presidential elections. The reaction from this statement was a chorus of incredulous groans from Gbagbo's supporters in the public gallery of the courtroom (Rosenberg 2016b). As Gbagbo supporters and many Ivoirians see it, "the trial is the finale of a campaign that set out to oust Gbagbo as president with the help of France, a campaign waged first with hijacked elections and now with an instrumentalised ICC" (Rosenberg 2016b).

CÔTE D'IVOIRE'S AD HOC DECLARATIONS UNDER ARTICLE 12(3)

Approximately eighty-five states around the world have yet to ratify the Rome Statute. It follows then that the relationship between these states and the ICC – which investigates and prosecutes crimes that are of concern to the international community – matters a great deal. How does the ICC exercise jurisdiction over the nationals or over territories of nonparty states? In other words, what are the obligations of any of those states toward the ICC? As Chapter 4 of this book made clear, states that are not parties to the ICC can still be brought within the Court's jurisdiction through a UN Security Council (UNSC) resolution. The ICC may also have jurisdiction over nationals of nonparty states if the state in which the crime was committed is an ICC member state. The Court has jurisdiction also over nationals of state parties even if the crimes were committed in a nonparty state, as outlined in Article 12(2) of the Rome Statute.

Non-state parties to the Rome Statute can also lodge ad hoc declarations with the ICC Registrar, as outlined in Article 12(3) of the statute. Under such declaration, states agree to cooperate with the ICC, an obligation they would not otherwise have been subjected to because of their nonmember status. Declarations under Article 12(3) give the ICC jurisdiction that the Court may not have had otherwise. Much like the state referrals under Article 14 of the Rome Statute, there are reasons to believe that ad hoc declarations by non-state parties under Article 12(3) may be used more frequently in the future, and in ways that were not envisioned at the time the Rome Statute was drafted (Freeland 2006). Although the rationale for Article 12(3) is to extend the scope of the Court's jurisdiction by offering states an option to accept it on an ad hoc basis, it may also be used "as a tool to influence the political landscape and balance of power of a society in transition, or to eliminate political opponents in the context of an ongoing internal armed conflict" (Stahn, El Zeidy, and Olásolo 2005, 423).[13] The Ivoirian case is an example of the latter.

Côte d'Ivoire signed the Rome Statute on 30 November 1998 but did not ratify it until 15 February 2013. In 2003, however, while a nonparty state to the Rome Statute, Côte d'Ivoire lodged an ad hoc declaration with the Court by which it accepted the Court's jurisdiction for crimes committed in its territory since 19 September 2002 (Republic of Côte d'Ivoire 2003). Such an ad hoc

---

[13] To date, Uganda, Côte d'Ivoire, and Palestine have made ad hoc declarations to the ICC under Article 12(3). The minister of justice of the Palestinian Authority lodged a declaration under Article 12(3) of the Rome Statute on 21 January 2009 following an Israeli campaign in Gaza. The Ugandan declaration is in support of the self-referral that Uganda made against the Lord's Resistance Army (LRA). The declaration extends the temporal jurisdiction for the ICC given that Uganda ratified the Rome Statute on 14 June 2002, and it entered into force with respect to Uganda on 1 September 2002. The declaration gives the Court jurisdiction over crimes committed since the entry in force of the Rome Statute, on 1 July 2002.

declaration had gone unnoticed in international legal theory and practice up to that point (Stahn, El Zeidy and Olásolo 2005, 421). The registrar of the ICC confirmed that it had received a declaration under Article 12(3) from the government of Côte d'Ivoire, and in 2006, Prosecutor Ocampo said that he would send a mission to Côte d'Ivoire "when security permits, with the support of the UN" (ICC 2006). Three years later, in April 2009, the deputy prosecutor said that the situation in Côte d'Ivoire was "under analysis," and the prosecutor told the Assembly of States Parties in November 2009 that "preliminary examination" was underway (Schabas 2010b, 10). However, very little was done in Côte d'Ivoire during the early years of the declaration, and the situation had not been assigned to a pre-trial chamber, which would have provided the chamber's oversight of the prosecutor's preliminary examination and an early investigation of the situation. In any case, it appears that Prosecutor Ocampo did not take any concrete steps to open a preliminary examination of the situation in Côte d'Ivoire following the request that Gbagbo sent to the ICC registrar in 2003.

During the crisis following the 2010 election, and seven years after President Gbagbo "invited" the ICC, President Ouattara renewed the ad hoc declaration to the Court on 14 December 2010, and again on 3 May 2011, modifying the temporal jurisdiction of the investigation. In the December 2010 letter, Ouattara had promised cooperation with ICC investigations into "all crimes and acts of violence committed since March 2004." Five months later, in confirming his previous request, Ouattara asked the ICC to investigate "the gravest crimes committed since November 28, 2010" (République de Côte d'Ivoire 2010). These dates are important because they aim to have the ICC prosecutor focus on the crimes committed during the post-electoral crisis and, by extension, investigate the pro-Gbagbo forces and loyalists. The time frame outlined by Ouattara's letter excludes the 2002 northern rebellion and the subsequent conflict, therefore protecting Ouattara and Soro allies.

Following Ouattara's letters, the ICC prosecutor submitted a request to the Pre-Trial Chamber II to open a full investigation, limiting the proposed period under investigation to the postelection period, which is an indication of a desire to focus on crimes committed following the 2010 postelectoral crisis. On 21 December 2010, in the midst of the electoral crisis, Prosecutor Ocampo publicly put Ivoirian political leaders on notice, warning that "those … who are planning violence will end up in The Hague" (ICC 2010). As much as the successive ad hoc declarations made by the Gbagbo and Ouattara administrations were driven by domestic political calculations, the ICC prosecutor's statement during the crisis also resonated politically. As McGovern contends, "with one sentence, Moreno-Ocampo ensured that Gbagbo would reject any negotiated solution and instead fight to the end" (cited in Bellamy and Williams 2011, 837).

It is difficult to measure exactly the effect of Ocampo's warning to the Ivoirian leaders in the midst of the political crisis. Akhavan (2009, 624) argues that, in Côte d'Ivoire, "the mere threat of an ICC investigation contributed to preventing escalation of an inter-ethnic war" because it ended the broadcast of hatred programs on state-sponsored media. The lessening of civilian abuses, however, was due more to Ivoirian conceptions of justice than the pressure from external threats of prosecution because local political actors were aware that the blame of war crimes or crimes against humanity would strip them of their legitimacy as political actors, which led to some level of self-regulation (McGovern 2009). Indeed, discussion about human rights abuses has been political currency as much as debate about citizenship since 2000 because Ivoirian politicians have realized the usefulness of such accusations against their opponents (McGovern 2009, 70). Gbagbo's invitation to the ICC in 2003 was an attempt to recruit international allies to cast his enemies as illegitimate actors (McGovern 2009, 73).

Following Ouattara's request, the ICC prosecutor at first agreed to limit the temporal scope of its investigation to the postelectoral crisis starting on 28 November 2010. This raised questions regarding the impartiality of the Court because the postelectoral crisis that started in November 2010 is widely viewed as the result of Gbagbo losing the election and refusing to relinquish power.[14] From that prism then, and with the support of most of the international community, Ouattara forces are viewed as fighting the good fight to unseat Gbagbo, which is the will expressed by the majority of Ivoirian voters. Therefore, an ICC investigation that focuses solely on the aftermath of the elections would fail to take into consideration the decade of civil conflict that punctuated Ivoirian political history.[15]

As of June 2019, almost a decade later, it still remains to be seen whether individuals from the pro-Ouattara camp will ever be investigated or prosecuted by the ICC. In fact, Human Rights Watch (2011) has identified key individuals from the pro-Ouattara camp who were implicated in human rights abuses

---

[14] The ICC prosecutor later decided to extend the temporal scope of the investigation to the period between 19 September 2002 and 28 November 2010.

[15] Matt Wells of Human Rights Watch (HRW), for example, pointed to the ICC's "unfortunate early decision to 'sequence' its investigation" by first looking only at the crimes committed by the Gbagbo side (Bovcon 2014, 193).

during the crisis[16] in addition to the Gbagbo loyalists.[17] Domestically, military and civilian prosecutors had brought charges against at least 118 Gbagbo allies, whereas no member of the Ouattara side or Republican Forces has been arrested or charged for crimes committed during the conflict (HRW 2011, 8).

<h2 style="text-align:center">GBAGBO GOES TO THE HAGUE</h2>

Laurent Gbagbo became the first former head of state to stand trial before the ICC, in The Hague. Gbagbo and his former ally Blé Goudé – who was the leader of his party's youth wing and nicknamed the "street general" – each faced four counts of crimes against humanity for their alleged role in the violence that followed the 2010 presidential elections. Following the final assault on the presidential palace in Abidjan on 11 April 2011 by Ouattara's forces with the assistance of French troops, Gbagbo was captured and transferred to a prison in Bouaké; from there, he was later handed over to the ICC on 30 November 2011. Blé Goudé was transferred to ICC custody in The Hague in March 2014. The ICC Trial Chamber I decided to join the two cases into a single trial because of their similarity (ICC Trial Chamber I 2015, 2016).

The prosecutor's case relied on the accusation that Gbagbo used the armed forces and other youth militias to target Ivoirians that were perceived to be Ouattara supporters, mainly Ivoirians from the north, Muslims, and others labeled "Ivoirians of West African descent." The prosecution had identified thirty-eight incidents that took place in or around Abidjan to argue that pro-Gbagbo attacks were widespread and systematic; five of those thirty-eight incidents are the focus of the charges against Gbagbo and Blé Goudé (ICC Pre-Trial Chamber I 2014). At the opening statement of the trial, Prosecutor Bensouda said that she would prove to the Court that Gbagbo and Blé Goudé were responsible for the deaths of 142 people and the rape of twenty-four girls in Abidjan in five incidents between 27 November 2010 and 12 April 2011 (Maliti 2016a).

---

[16] These individuals include Captain Eddie Médi, commander of the Republican Forces March 2011 offensive; Commander Fofana Losséni, overall commander of the Republican Forces March offensive in the west; Commander Chérif Ousmane, head of the Republican Forces operations in Yopougon during the final battle of Abidjan; and Commander Ousmane Coulibaly, the longtime Forces Nouvelles zone commander in Odienné (HRW 2011).

[17] From the Gbagbo camp, HRW (2011) has identified Gbagbo, Blé Goudé, General Philippe Mangou (head of armed forces under Gbagbo), General Guiai Bi Poin (head of the security force unit Centre de Commandement des Opérations de Sécurité [Security Operations Command Center] CECOS), and General Bruno Dogbo Blé (head of the Republican Guard).

Gbagbo's lead lawyer, Emmanuel Altit, described the trial as "essential" for history and the people of Côte d'Ivoire (Maliti 2016c) while Prosecutor Bensouda said at the opening of the trial, "Let me re-emphasise that this trial is not driven by political considerations. Our mandate is strictly a legal one under the Rome Statute. Led by the evidence our independent investigations have collected, our purpose is to prosecute crimes committed during a period of post-election violence which took and destroyed the lives of so many men, women and children in Côte d'Ivoire."[18] As the proceedings in the courtroom unfolded, however, it was clear that all actors involved in the trial deployed political narratives that were deeply enmeshed with the unfolding of Ivoirian national politics (Ba 2015b). For instance, during the audience at the confirmation of charges at the ICC, Gbagbo made a statement in which he focused on Ivoirian domestic politics to claim that he followed the rule of law and upheld the constitution of his country. For Gbagbo, the ICC proceedings cannot be dissociated from the politics of Côte d'Ivoire.[19] In that regard, he stated, "Madam the Prosecutor has said a sentence that shocked me a bit, when she said that we are not here to discuss who won the elections and who did not win. But … we cannot discuss the post-electoral crisis without discussing how the elections unfolded … Because it is the one who did not win that has caused the troubles."

Gbagbo discussed the elections, noting that his decision to order a recount of the votes was warranted because the Constitutional Court documents show that in Bouaké, 100,000 votes were added to "[his] adversary."[20] The heart of the matter is the elections, Gbagbo argued. "When we were attacked in 2002,"[21] he claimed, "I did what was needed because I never believed that Côte d'Ivoire could solve its problems through war." He said that he had always favored dialogue, which is why he traveled all over Africa for peace talks with the rebellion. He gave as examples the peace negotiations, such as the Lomé talks, Marcoussis-Kleber, Accra I, Accra II, Accra III, Pretoria I, and Pretoria II. He said that in Pretoria in 2005 he asked President Thabo Mbeki to help him find a "legal solution for Alassane Ouattara to be a presidential candidate." And the legal solution was an amendment of the Ivoirian constitution by introducing Article 48, which he says "is similar to Article 16 of the French constitution.

---

[18] See Transcript of Trial Hearing, www.icc-cpi.int/Transcripts/oCR2016_00664.pdf.
[19] An earlier version of this section was previously published in Ba (2015a). Reproduced with permission of the publisher.
[20] Bouaké is the second largest city in Côte d'Ivoire and is located in Ouattara's stronghold.
[21] This is a reference to the failed coup attempt against Gbagbo in September 2002, which resulted in the portioning of the state and the rebel forces occupying the northern part of Côte d'Ivoire.

It gives extraordinary powers to the president, and that day, I took Article 48 of the Constitution, and I allowed Ouattara and Bédié to be candidates."[22]

Gbagbo's narrative at the ICC veered into a reflection on the meaning of a vote and democracy in the African context. Asking a rhetorical question, Gbagbo wondered how else a country like Côte d'Ivoire would pick a head of state, given its ethnic fractionalization. For him, democracy helped Côte d'Ivoire because it erased the ethnic fractionalization and allowed each citizen one vote. But for Gbagbo, democracy was not limited to elections; it required also the respect of the constitution. He asserted, "[I]t is because I respected the Constitution that they want to bring me here [at the ICC]."

At the Hague, Gbagbo deployed and explained his political legalist approach, which was consistent with the political legalist approach that he had adopted in Côte d'Ivoire since the beginning of the crisis.[23] One can easily notice the similarity between Gbagbo's lecture before the Court about democracy and the need for constitutional order and his speech at his swearing-in ceremony at the height of the postelectoral crisis, after the Constitutional Council had declared him the winner. The opening statement at his oath ceremony was,

> Today, I understand better why there are so many crises in Africa … People do not like to respect the law and the procedures that stem from it. There is no strong State, no strong Republic without laws and procedures … The only strong Republic is the one that stands on legally established rules. Since I have become president, I have realized that all the crises that we have known have come out from the non-respect of the law, of the jurisdiction and of the procedures that this law produces. (*Fraternité Matin*, 6/9/2010, cited in Piccolino 2014, 46)

As Piccolino (2014) shows, the words *law, legality, rules,* and *procedures* "recur in an almost obsessive fashion in this speech, especially in connection with democracy." In another speech, Gbagbo insisted that "all the troubles that we are witnessing today in Côte d'Ivoire have come out from the refusal of my rival to abide by the laws, the rules and the procedures applicable in our country" (cited in Piccolino 2014, 47). For Gbagbo, the rule of law and the respect of democratic procedures as outlined in the constitution are at the

---

[22] Article 16 of the French Constitution of the Fifth Republic was introduced in 1958 and gives "extraordinary powers" to the president in times of national crisis. See www.senat.fr/evenement/revision/texte_originel.html.

[23] It is worth noting that no member of the diplomatic corps based in Côte d'Ivoire attended Gbagbo's swearing-in ceremony at the presidential palace on 4 December 2010. But he still felt the need to clothe his claim to be the legitimately elected president with an enactment of a swearing-in ceremony before the constitutional court. See Piccolino (2014, 45).

heart of the Ivoirian crisis. Since the death of Houphouët-Boigny and the power struggle and political crises that have ensued, however, the manipulation of democracy in Côte d'Ivoire has played out to a large extent on the legal and constitutional terrain.[24]

Gbagbo was quick to represent the postelectoral crisis as a conflict between "legalists" and "those who have taken the road of illegality."[25] In the aftermath of the 2010 presidential elections, Gbagbo relied on the Constitutional Council to give himself legitimacy in the postelectoral crisis, which is a way for him to claim the legalistic approach that "has undeniable performative effects, compelling agents of the state (in particular the police) to respect 'institutional order' on pain of arrest for sedition" (Banégas 2011, 429). While in custody in The Hague awaiting trial, Gbagbo refuted his portrayal as a power-hungry tyrant whose refusal to concede defeat plunged his country into chaos (Gbagbo and Mattei 2014). Rather, Gbagbo described himself as the lawful, democratic leader whose efforts to reconcile his country were countered by the France-supported rebels (Rosenberg 2016a). As such, Gbagbo's discourse "combined the legalistic exaltation of state sovereignty, a fierce anticolonial nationalism, and religious overtones in portraying the Ivoirian crisis as a 'war of second independence' against a wide range of international enemies" (Piccolino 2012, 1). From Gbagbo's perspective, such enemies included first and foremost France. As his lawyer Emmanuel Altit asserted, the Gbagbo–Blé Goudé trial had a "fundamental" relationship to France (Panaïté 2016a). The ICC is not just the arena for domestic Ivoirian politics, however; the Court is indeed a political actor in Ivoirian politics as well.

THE ICC AS A LOCAL POLITICAL ACTOR

Not only did the Ivoirian state and its political actors displace the Ivoirian political arena to The Hague courtroom, the ICC became a political actor whose intervention deeply shaped politics in Côte d'Ivoire. It is important to

---

[24] In fact, Bédié was the first to manipulate the constitution to prevent his rival Ouattara from running by introducing the "born from an Ivoirian mother *and* father" clause in the constitution. Guéï's new constitution, which was passed through referendum, included Article 35. It was so vague that it was used to disqualify twelve candidates out of seventeen from the 2000 elections (Piccolino 2014, 25).

[25] Gbagbo said, "I remind you that the Independent Electoral Commission (IEC) is an administrative authority, while the Constitutional Council is the highest jurisdiction of Côte d'Ivoire. The two institutions are not comparable, and it is illegitimate to compare them. Their decisions are of a different nature. They have neither the same foundation nor the same impact... I have waited for the voice of law to be expressed... They want to scare us, but they cannot expect that the legalists will surrender to those who have taken the road of illegality" (quoted in Piccolino 2014, 61).

note, however, that the ICC itself is composed of many entities whose actions have different political effects. To that extent, the focus here is more on the OTP, which is the entryway for states to use the Court to pursue their interests. The ICC's judicial intervention in the Ivoirian crisis, dating from the early years of the rebellion when it failed to take action after Gbagbo's first invitation in 2003 to the issuance of arrest warrants for Laurent Gbagbo, Simone Gbagbo, and Charles Blé Goudé in 2011, is a major element in the political discourse and action in Côte d'Ivoire. The ICC will remain a main political actor in Côte d'Ivoire for years to come because any action it takes – or fails to take – will still resonate with the state and its political affairs.[26]

The argument that the ICC is also a political actor rests on the ways in which its intervention in Côte d'Ivoire, to date, notably the one-sided investigations and prosecution, played into the political agenda of the Ivoirian state under Ouattara. Having failed to intervene at Gbagbo's request in 2003 and later claiming a sequencing approach in the selective prosecution of Gbagbo and his allies, the OTP participated in Ouattara's strategy of outsourcing his adversaries to the ICC while at the same time capitalizing on the refusal to surrender Simone Gbagbo. The ultimate acquittal of Gbagbo and Blé Goudé will animate Ivoirian politics for years to come. With the next presidential elections slated for 2020 and Ouattara contemplating to run for a third – unconstitutional – term, all the key actors of the Ivoirian crisis for the past twenty-five years – Bédié, Ouattara, Soro, Gbagbo, and Blé Goudé – are in place again in a deeply divided and unreconciled country (Adele 2018; Ba 2019; Suma 2019).

A Not-So-Sequential Prosecution

Almost a decade has passed since the arrest of Gbagbo that ended the political crisis and the postelectoral violence in Côte d'Ivoire. The ICC prosecution has so far only facilitated Ouattara's efforts to settle scores with his adversary. The Ivoirian state, under Ouattara, is indeed the beneficiary of the ICC one-sided investigation and prosecution. As Eric-Aimé Semien, director of the Ivorian Observatory of Human Rights, noted, the ICC prosecuted only one side, even though "[a]ll the observers noted that the different crimes were committed from both sides" (cited in Birchall 2016). At a press conference before the start of the Gbagbo and Blé Goudé trial, Prosecutor Bensouda was asked about the one-sided investigations and prosecutions in Côte d'Ivoire, and she responded that it was due to a lack of resources and that in 2015 she

---

[26] One can make a similar argument in other situations in which the ICC intervened, such as the DRC with the removal of Bemba from the political scene. See Chapter 7.

had intensified investigations in the pro-Ouattara camp, without giving any more information (Maliti 2016b). The OTP claims that its investigations in Côte d'Ivoire were not one-sided but it merely used a sequential approach[27] – which meant focusing on the Gbagbo side and shifting later to the Ouattara side for investigations. Even with the benefit of doubt that the prosecutor's strategy may indeed be a sequential approach, it still poses many problems.

The cautious approach of the OTP in the Ivoirian case by prosecuting the Gbagbo side is explained by the knowledge that they could count on the Ivoirian state, under the control of Ouattara, for cooperation. The OTP's response to criticism about the one-sided investigation pointed to the adoption of a sequential approach, which implied an upcoming investigation and eventual prosecution of crimes committed by Ouattara's allies during the conflict. However, questions remain about when does the sequencing end and how does that reassure those who believe that this strategy is a mere cover for a selective investigation.[28] Rod Rastan, legal adviser in the ICC's OTP, responds, "So far, we [the Office of the Prosecutor] investigated only the Gbagbo side, but we said we will also investigate the pro-Ouattara side ... We will investigate both sides."[29] Rastan argues that just because a state self-refers to the ICC doesn't mean that it can dictate the conduct of the OTP.[30] At most, that just ensures that state's cooperation for the investigations.[31] Rastan's explained the OTP's sequential strategy in Côte d'Ivoire in these terms:

> In Côte d'Ivoire we decided to go after the pro-Gbagbo side first because it's a lot more readily available, most of the perpetrators in the Gbagbo side were already arrested or available to us. We had access to the presidential palace and all the files from the Gbagbo regime, so easy to build up a quick case. We considered that we would do the allegations against the Ouattara side in a subsequent phase, which would involve much more forensics. The criticism now can be why it's taking so long? That's fair enough, but we have always been committed to doing it.[32]

---

[27] Author's interviews with Dr. Rod Rastan, legal adviser in the ICC OTP, and Jennifer Schense, international cooperation adviser in the Jurisdiction, Complementarity and Cooperation Division of the OTP, The Hague, May 2014.

[28] Author's interview with Alpha Sesay, legal officer for Open Society Justice Initiative, The Hague, May 2014.

[29] Author's interview with Dr. Rod Rastan, legal adviser in the OTP, The Hague, May 2014.

[30] Author's interview with Dr. Rod Rastan, legal adviser in the ICC OTP, The Hague, May 2014.

[31] Author's interview with Jennifer Schense, international cooperation adviser in the Jurisdiction, Complementarity and Cooperation Division of the OTP, The Hague, May 2014.

[32] Author's interview with Dr. Rod Rastan, legal adviser in the ICC OTP, The Hague, May 2014.

The explanation that pragmatism guided the OTP because of readily available evidence against Gbagbo and his allies seems fair enough, but that does not explain why, a decade later, there is no evidence of investigation and prosecution of crimes committed by Ouattara's allies, despite the evidence gathered by human rights organizations (HRW 2011, 2014, 2015a). In any case, the investigation and prosecution of Gbagbo and Blé Goudé show again the extent to which the ICC is more readily available to pursue justice on behalf of the state rather than the victims of core crimes.

The perception of political bias in the ICC intervention in Côte d'Ivoire can even be traced to the period prior to the investigation and prosecution of the Gbagbo camp. It is clear that the Côte d'Ivoire file remained dormant in Ocampo's cabinets from 2003 to 2010, when Gbagbo was in power and had called in the ICC to investigate the pro-Ouattara rebellion. Then, after the 2010 elections, the swiftness with which Ocampo launched a full investigation and soon after issued arrest warrants for Laurent and Simone Gbagbo and Blé Goudé lends itself to criticism of lack of fairness and impartiality, and the cooperation of the Ivoirian state, which aligned with Ouattara's agenda.

THE CURIOUS CASE OF SIMONE GBAGBO

The ICC prosecutor charged Simone Gbagbo as an alleged indirect co-perpetrator with four counts of crimes of humanity, namely, murder, rape and other sexual violence, persecution, and other inhumane acts.[33] The warrant for her arrest was issued on 29 February 2012; it was unsealed on 22 November 2012 (ICC Pre-Trial Chamber III 2012). Unlike Laurent Gbagbo and Blé Goudé, however, Simone Gbagbo was not in ICC custody because Côte d'Ivoire has refused to surrender her to the Court (Ba 2015a). The Ivoirian state had introduced before the ICC a challenge to the admissibility of the case against Simone Gbagbo, seeking to try her before Ivoirian courts. However, ICC Pre-Trial Chamber I rejected the Ivoirian challenge on 11 December 2014 (ICC 2016c). When challenging the admissibility of a case before the ICC, the state must prove that it is able and willing to try the case before its domestic courts, and the domestic prosecution must concern the same person and the same conduct that the ICC is prosecuting. In its rejection of the admissibility challenge, the Pre-Trial Chamber judges argued that "Côte d'Ivoire's domestic authorities were not taking tangible, concrete and progressive steps aimed at

---

[33] See *The Prosecutor* v. *Simone Gbagbo*, "Alleged Crimes," www.icc-cpi.int/cdi/simone-gbagbo/pages/alleged-crimes.aspx.

ascertaining whether Simone Gbagbo is criminally responsible for the same conduct that is alleged in the case before the Court" (ICC Pre-Trial Chamber I 2014). The Court reasoned that, whereas the ICC's prosecutor intended to prosecute Simone Gbagbo for crimes against humanity, the Ivorian court convicted her for the domestic crimes of disturbing the peace, organizing armed gangs, and undermining state security (Heller 2016). By rejecting the admissibility challenge, the ICC chamber reminded the government of Côte d'Ivoire of its obligation to surrender Simone Gbagbo to the ICC. The ICC's Appeals Chamber upheld the Pre-Trial chamber's decision, ruling that the Simone Gbagbo case was admissible before the ICC, and therefore she must be extradited to The Hague.[34]

However, the Ouattara regime has instead opted to try Simone Gbagbo in Côte d'Ivoire, where in March 2015 she was convicted of undermining state security and disturbing the peace during the 2010 electoral crisis by distributing arms to pro-Gbagbo militias. She was subsequently sentenced to twenty years in prison, alongside eighty-two former Gbagbo allies who received various sentences (Reuters 2015). Because Simone Gbagbo was tried and convicted in Abidjan for crimes against the state, the Ivoirian authorities initiated a second trial against her, this time, for crimes against civilians, namely, crimes against humanity, which started in May 2016. These new charges against Simone Gbagbo, which mirrored the charges she would face at the ICC, were initiated by the Ivoirian state as a response to the rejection of the admissibility challenge by the ICC.

Despite the ICC's call for the extradition of Simone Gbagbo, President Ouattara has vowed that he will not send any more Ivoirians to The Hague. His decision underscores not only the inconsistent approach of the Ouattara administration toward the ICC but also underlines political calculations that underpin the decision not to send Simone Gbagbo to The Hague (Ba 2015). Ouattara's decision not to transfer any more Ivoirian citizens to the ICC deals a blow to the ICC prosecutor's assertion that it is investigating the pro-Ouattara side. This clearly signals to the OTP that it cannot count on the Ivoirian state's cooperation and compliance for its investigation and eventual prosecution of pro-Ouattara individuals. It is clear that, as far as the Ouattara camp and current Ivoirian government are concerned, the ICC's work in Côte d'Ivoire is done, and the case is closed with the Gbagbo–Blé Goudé trials. In August 2018, President Ouattara pardoned Simone Gbagbo – who was serving

---

[34] See Judgment on the appeal of Côte d'Ivoire against the decision of Pre-Trial Chamber I of 11 December 2014 entitled "Decision on Côte d'Ivoire's Challenge to the Admissibility of the Case against Simone Gbagbo," www.icc-cpi.int/CourtRecords/CR2015_06088.pdf.

her twenty-year sentence – along with some 800 people who were imprisoned in the aftermath of the electoral crisis (Maclean 2018).

GBAGBO AND BLÉ GOUDÉ ACQUITTED

On 15 January 2019, Trial Chamber I, by a majority ruling, acquitted Laurent Gbagbo and Charles Blé Goudé from all charges of crimes against humanity and ordered their release.[35] During the trial, which lasted two years, from January 2016 to January 2018, the prosecutor presented eighty-two witnesses and more than 4,500 items of evidence. In February 2018, however, presiding Judge Cuno Tarfusser ordered the prosecution to file a brief summarizing its case, based on which the defense could make submissions on subsequent proceedings, including whether or not to file a "no case to answer motion" (ICC Trial Chamber I 2018). The defense therefore seized that opportunity and filed a "no case to answer motion" asking for the acquittal and immediate release of both Gbagbo and Blé Goudé in July 2018. Instead of presenting their arguments, Gbagbo's and Blé Goudé's lawyers simply asked the Court to evaluate the evidence presented by the prosecutor and declare it insufficient to move forward with the trial. Judges typically grant a "no case to answer motion" if they determine that no reasonable chamber would find the defendant guilty based on the evidence that the prosecutor presented.

In the oral decision that rendered the acquittal of Gbagbo and Blé Goudé, presiding Judge Tarfusser said that "the Prosecutor … [h]as failed to demonstrate the existence of the alleged policy to attack the civilian population on the basis of the alleged pattern of violence and other circumstantial evidence [and] [h]as failed to demonstrate that the crimes as alleged in the charges were committed pursuant to or in furtherance of a State or organizational policy to attack the civilian population." In other words, the majority of the Chamber found that the evidence did not show there was a "common plan" to keep Gbagbo in power after the contested elections and that speeches by the two defendants did not constitute "ordering, soliciting, or inducing the alleged crimes" (ICC Trial Chamber I 2019). Without the existence of a state or organizational policy to attack civilians, and without the evidence of a link between Gbagbo and Blé Goudé speeches to the acts of violence, the majority of the Chamber ruled that the defendants were innocent of the charges of crimes against humanity (Ba 2019).

[35] ICC (2019). The prosecutor has appealed the acquittal judgment.

The acquittal of Gbagbo and Blé Goudé is indeed a stunning moment for international criminal justice and Ivoirian politics. To a large extent, the acquittal demonstrates the independence and integrity of the judges (Ba 2019; Batros 2019) because arguably the majority of the Chamber based its decision solely on the merits of the prosecutor's case and the fair trial rights of the defendants (Goldstone 2019). Yet the case was another major blow to the OTP that came on the heels of Bemba's acquittal and the termination of the proceedings against Kenyatta and Ruto. It shows that the ICC prosecutor has been fundamentally unable to prosecute not only state officials but even former ones successfully. The sober reality is that, after more than seventeen years of operation, the ICC has convicted only four individuals – all of them rebels or militia commanders – for atrocity crimes.

CONCLUSION

By not investigating and thus protecting members of the Ouattara regime and current officials of the Ivoirian state, the prosecutor has indeed deferred to politics. How could the ICC escape such criticism when the only defendants who faced justice are from the Gbagbo side of the conflict? Understandably, the very nature of international courts such as the ICC compels the prosecutor to manage careful relations with states to ensure their cooperation, which also points to the inherent political dimension of the tension between pursuing effective yet impartial prosecutions, which calls for a "tactical rapport" between the OTP and the state (Rosenberg 2017a, 2017b). The fact that the Ouattara administration was quick and eager to transfer Gbagbo and Blé Goudé to The Hague for them to face justice at the ICC while at the same time refusing to abide by the ICC ruling to extradite Simone Gbagbo is symptomatic of political calculations transposed to international justice, which is in turn used to address domestic political questions. There is little doubt that Ouattara and his camp had a lot to gain in terms of political stability by quickly outsourcing the trials of Gbagbo and Blé Goudé to The Hague. Getting rid of political opponents who still have a large political base and still wield a lot of political and social capital is a safer and smarter strategy for the Ouattara administration than putting them on trial at home. As Kersten (2016c) argues, the Ivoirian case raises the issue of a state choosing "to simply and (almost) immediately flip its detainees to the ICC in order to get rid of them and ensure that they are not near their former bases of power." In order to consolidate his political power, Ouattara found that his safer bet was to let the ICC handle his major political enemies. He was not the first one to use the ICC to outsource problems at home, as discussed in the previous chapters.

Self-referrals, as used by Uganda, Democratic Republic of Congo (DRC), and Central African Republic (CAR), are typical examples of outsourcing, although Ouattara's government was the first one to use the ICC to handle political opponents turned enemies rather than rebels or warlords.

Ultimately, Ouattara's outsourcing option was successful, especially given the swiftness with which the OTP acted in the initial phase of the investigation (it issued a warrant for the arrest of Gbagbo within only two months after it opened its investigations). Transferring Gbagbo and Blé Goudé away from the circles of power and political opposition helped Ouattara establish his rule and consolidate his power through the 2015 elections, which he won with a wide margin. With the ICC's acquittal of Gbagbo and Blé Goudé, however, and Ouattara's pardon for Simon Gbagbo, the same protagonists of the previous Ivoirian crisis are in place again: Ouattara, Gbagbo, Blé Goudé, and Simone Gbagbo. In addition are former president Bédié and former leader of the rebellion Soro, who have both recently distanced themselves from Ouattara, who is contemplating a run for a third unconstitutional presidential term in 2020. Thus, Côte d'Ivoire remains a deeply divided country that has not yet reconciled itself with its past.

7

International Justice in a World of States

Today, the weather outside is gloomy. Should we, by analogy, reflect that the Court is passing through a dark time? We certainly cannot deny that this is a difficult time.

Sidiki Kaba, President of the ICC Assembly of States Parties (ASP)[1]

INTRODUCTION

On 15 December 2015, more than a dozen years after it came into existence, the International Criminal Court (ICC) moved into its permanent premises, located in the dune landscape between the city of The Hague and the North Sea.[2] The king of the Netherlands presided over the inauguration ceremony, during which the UN Secretary General Ban Ki-moon said that the new home represented a "milestone in global efforts to promote and uphold human rights and the rule of law."[3] The president of the Assembly of States Parties (ASP), Senegalese Justice Minister Sidiki Kaba, remarked, "It is a historic day but also a day of hope for all victims of mass crimes in the world," and ICC

---

[1] Speech of the President of the Assembly of States Parties (ASP), Mr. Sidiki Kaba, 15th Session of the Assembly of States Parties, 16 November 2016.

[2] Since its inception in 2002, the ICC had been temporarily located in two buildings in The Hague. The ASP decided in 2007 that the Court should be provided with new, purpose-built premises. ICC President Judge Fernàndez de Gurmendi said on the day of the inauguration, "As a permanent institution, the ICC now has a permanent home. It offers essential features for the court to work more efficiently, provide protection for witnesses and victims, and ensure fair and transparent proceedings. As such, the new, purpose-built premises will greatly assist us in our mandate of providing justice to victims and helping to establish accountability for – and thus helping to prevent – the most serious international crimes." See "The ICC Has Moved to Its Permanent Premises," Press Release, ICC-CPI-20151214-PR1180, 14 December 2015.

[3] See "ICC Permanent Premises Officially Opened by His Majesty King Willem-Alexander of the Netherlands," 20 April 2016, www.icc-permanentpremises.org/news.

President Judge Silvia Fernàndez de Gurmendi announced that the Court was "here to stay" (Charania 2016).

Indeed, two decades after its creation, the ICC may well be here to stay, but "the day for hope for all victims of mass crimes in the world" is not upon us yet. The previous chapters in this book have provided ample evidence to support the argument that the Court has been utterly unable so far to achieve the ideals enshrined in the preamble of the Rome Statute because, in large part, it cannot resist being instrumentalized by states.

This concluding chapter goes beyond the four case studies to survey other states' interactions with the ICC in order to highlight the extent to which their actions support the analytical framework developed in this book. Second, it discusses the crisis in which both the Court and the international criminal justice regime are situated, and the need for a sober and humble acknowledgment of this reality.

STATES OF JUSTICE

This section surveys other cases of ICC intervention, highlighting similarities and patterns that inform the four themes discussed in this book (the strategic use of self-referrals, complementarity between national and international justice systems, the limits of state cooperation with the Court, and the strategic use of the ICC in domestic politics) alongside the four major case studies (Uganda, Libya, Kenya, and Côte d'Ivoire). The broader discussion shows the ways in which the key themes discussed in the previous chapters are relevant to other ICC interventions and engagement with states, within and beyond the African continent. Thus, this section illustrates how other states have also engaged the Court following the same patterns of behavior highlighted in the theoretical framework. By bringing into the study this universe of cases, this section highlights the ways in which the patterns of behavior of all these states are consistent with the theoretical framework developed in this book. It shows, for instance, the extent to which fragile or fragmented states, most with transitional or postcoup governments or those coming to power through highly contentious elections, immediately engage and cooperate with the ICC through self-referrals (Democratic Republic of Congo [DRC], Central African Republic [CAR], Mali, Gabon). States challenge the admissibility of cases to the Court to suit their interests or withdraw cooperation with the Court when their interests shift (DRC, Sudan). All these states would cooperate with the Court if they were assured that ICC jurisdiction would not extend to their own agents, while the Office of the Prosecutor (OTP) selectively engaged in investigations, cases, and pursuing suspects. When the states felt threatened by the

ICC, they either rallied their allies for support, exerted influence on the Court, or threatened to withdraw from the Rome Statute (Burundi, The Gambia, the Philippines). South Africa's decision to withdraw from the ICC appears to be the only outlier in this situation, but even in that case, one can argue that South Africa's interests as a regional power and standing in the African Union (AU) was under threat, which prompted the initial decision to leave the Court.

DRC

Similar to the other self-referrals to the ICC, the DRC situation also highlights the ability of African states to use international institutions in pursuit of their own political and security interests. The Congolese state – through self-referral and cooperation with the ICC when it suited its agenda and noncooperation where it lacked incentives to do so – shows the dynamic process of state actions vis-à-vis the ICC and how such actions are highly strategic and instrumental. Soon after Ocampo was sworn in as the first prosecutor of the ICC, he announced on 17 July 2003, that he had selected the Ituri district in northeastern DRC as "the most urgent situation" under his jurisdiction to be addressed (The New Humanitarian 2003). The OTP announced that evidence in its possession indicated that "5,000 civilians had been killed in Ituri between July 2002 and early 2003" and that such crimes "could constitute genocide, crimes against humanity or war crimes, and could thus fall within the jurisdiction of the ICC" (The New Humanitarian 2003). Shortly thereafter, during a speech before the ICC's ASP, Ocampo issued an invitation to the DRC, stating that, due the practical difficulties associated with the use of his *proprio motu* powers, his role "could be facilitated by a referral or active support from DRC" (ICC OTP 2004, 4). Responding to Ocampo's invitation and following on the footsteps of Uganda's Museveni, President Kabila subsequently referred the situation in the DRC to the ICC.

Citing an interview with the former Congolese minister of justice and human rights Emanuel Luzolo, Clark (2018, 60–61) argues that Congolese authorities had three main reasons when they issued the state referral to the ICC. First, they believed that they could use the ICC to bring a case of aggression against their neighbors who had invaded their country (there was a pending case to that effect at the International Court of Justice [ICJ]).[4] Second, Uganda

---

[4] On 23 June 1999, the Democratic Republic of Congo (DRC) filed at the International Court of Justice (ICJ) a case against Burundi, Uganda, and Rwanda "for acts of armed aggression committed … in flagrant breach of the United Nations Charter and of the Charter of the Organization of African Unity." See *Armed Activities on the Territory of the Congo (Democratic Republic of Congo v. Uganda)*, www.icj-cij.org/en/case/116.

referral in January 2004 spurred the DRC to do the same. As Luzolo told Clark (2018, 61), "We could see [the Ugandan government] thought *the refer-ral suited their purposes, especially in dealing with their military opponents*" [emphasis added]. Finally, Kabila saw the ICC referral as an opportunity to sideline Azarias Ruberwa and Jean-Pierre Bemba, the leaders of armed groups and vice presidents in the DRC coalition government, for their links to the atrocities in Ituri (Clark 2018, 62).

In the DRC, as in Uganda, the states' instrumental use and manipulation of the ICC was facilitated by ICC personnel's lack of understanding of the national and local political dynamics. As one ICC OTP official later admitted, "We probably didn't know enough about these countries when we went in – how politics worked, how to get governments to work with us, what their concerns were, what they were trying to achieve" (Clark 2018, 63). Because the situation in the DRC was triggered by a self-referral, a close working relationship between the government and the OTP was to be expected, which is in line with the analytical framework discussed throughout this book. That same close working relationship is also visible in the cases of Uganda, CAR, Mali, and Côte d'Ivoire.

The Congolese state cooperated closely with the ICC in the cases against the Ituri rebel leaders, namely, Thomas Lubanga, Germain Katanga, Mathieu Ngudjolo Chui, and Bosco Ntaganda.[5] In fact, following the ICC's conviction of Lubanga – the first ever conviction by the Court in March 2012, Ocampo announced that he would soon visit Kinshasa to meet Kabila and "thank him for his support" during the Lubanga investigations (Clark 2018, 74). The DRC government was instrumental in the Bemba case stemming from the CAR situa-tion. It is worth repeating that Bemba was President Kabila's main rival in the DRC. The DRC's cooperation with the ICC also resulted in the arrest and surrender to the Court of four suspects for witness tampering in the Bemba case (Wakabi 2016).

By assisting the ICC prosecutor, the Congolese state ensured that the investi-gations and prosecutions would focus on the Ituri province, the region most iso-lated from the Kabila regime's entanglements. As Clark (2018, 83) asserts, there is less clear evidence connecting Kabila to the atrocities in Ituri than in other provinces such as Katanga and North and South Kivu, "where government forces and Mai-Mai militias backed by Kabila are directly implicated in serious crimes."[6] The investigations in Ituri were more likely to preserve Kabila's

---

[5] With the assistance of the UN mission in DRC, the Congolese authorities arrested the rebel leaders in 2005 and handed them over to the ICC. Ntaganda surrendered himself to the US Embassy in Kigali in 2013.

[6] For an analysis of these conflicts and their various actors, see, for instance, ICG (2006), Nantulya (2017), Stearns et al. (2013). For a study of missed opportunities in ICC's interven-tion in DRC, see Kambale (2015).

interests and focus on atrocities committed by his adversaries, resulting in positive dividends for the Kabila regime. This allowed the Kabila regime to portray DRC as a law-abiding citizen of the international community. For instance, in a letter addressed to the ICC Registry in June 2009, Kabila's office stated, "[President Kabila] has demonstrated to the world his determination to fight resolutely against impunity by making the DRC to date an unequalled model of cooperation for the ICC" (cited in Clark 2018, 85). Kabila also told the *New York Times*, "There is no other country in Africa that has cooperated with the ICC like Congo. Out of the four people at the ICC, four are Congolese. That shows how cooperative we've been" (Gettleman 2009). All this evidence points to a state that has been strategic in its referral to the ICC and its level of cooperation with the Court while pursuing its security and political interests. As the arguments developed in this book show, the DRC case exemplifies the ability of African states to use international institutions in pursuit of their own interests.

CAR

In December 2004, the government of CAR referred to the ICC the situation in the country, and the ICC prosecutor subsequently opened a formal investigation in May 2007. The focus of the investigation was alleged war crimes and crimes against humanity committed in the context of the conflict in CAR since 1 July 2002 – the date of the entry into force of the Rome Statute – with the peak of violence in 2002 and 2003.[7] The CAR situation has produced one major case: that against former DRC vice president Jean-Pierre Bemba, whom the ICC would find guilty of command responsibility over two counts of crimes against humanity (murder and rape) and three counts of war crimes (murder, rape, and pillage). In June 2016, Trial Chamber III sentenced Bemba to eighteen years in prison. Bemba was later acquitted, however, by the Appeals Chamber on 8 June 2018 (ICC 2018b) and released from prison after having been in ICC custody for a decade.

The CAR investigation and prosecution of Bemba focused on the involvement of Bemba's Movement for the Liberation of the Congo (MLC) rebel group in the CAR conflict in 2002 and 2003, following a call for support from the then president Ange Felix Patassé to help fend off an attempted coup by

---

[7] This situation is typically referred to as CAR I, while another investigation (CAR II) covers crimes committed from 2012 onward. See ICC, "Central African Republic: Situation in the Central African Republic," ICC-01/05; and ICC, "Central African Republic II: Situation in the Central African Republic II," ICC-01/14.

his former army chief of staff, General Felix Bozizé.[8] Bozizé overthrew the Patassé regime in March 2003, subsequently dissolved the parliament, and drew up a new constitution. Yet Bozizé himself would face many rebellions, which plunged CAR into a protracted conflict and instability that spanned the following dozen years (Lombard 2016). In this context, the Bozizé government appealed to the ICC and referred the situation to the Court in 2004, in a bid to incapacitate Patassé's forces and allies (including Bemba's MLC), and gain the upper hand in the conflict to establish his regime. A decade later, the transitional government of CAR, led by President Catherina Samba-Panza, referred to the ICC a separate conflict between the Seleka rebels and anti-balaka forces, a situation known in ICC parlance as CAR II.[9]

Both CAR situations highlight the fraught and instrumental relations between fragile governments in volatile situations and the ICC, and also the prosecutorial focus on rebels rather than state actors. Indeed, as Clark (2018, 270) argues, "The ICC's interventions in CAR coincide not only with an ongoing civil war but major political upheaval, with no fewer than six presidents holding office in thirteen years. Both of the CAR state referrals were made by newly ensconced governments against their recently defeated military opponents." Bozizé's referral in December 2004 followed his taking power through a military coup a few months earlier; Samba-Panza's referral in May 2014 immediately followed her appointment as interim president.

As it has been the case with other self-referrals to the ICC, the OTP's investigation into Bemba's crimes was made possible by Bozizé's assistance and cooperation while president, especially given that the prosecution targeted his enemy's (Patassé) main ally. Across the border, in the DRC, President Kabila also assisted the OTP in investigating and prosecuting Bemba, who was also his main rival. In court, Bemba's defense team argued that the OTP's exclusive focus on Bemba and his MLC troops was due to its close working relationship with President Kabila (ICC Trial Chamber III).[10]

The political situations in both CAR and DRC are fluid and unstable, and newly established or fragile governments may be eager to refer situations to the ICC and cooperate with the OTP. Sustaining the cooperation with the ICC depends, however, on how the situations and interests of the parties

---

[8] ICC, OTP, "Central African Republic, Situation in the Central African Republic," ICC-01/05.

[9] ICC, OTP, "Central African Republic II, Situation in the Central African Republic II," ICC-01/14.

[10] ICC, Trial Chamber III, "Public Redacted Version of Closing Brief of Mr. Jean-Pierre Bemba Gombo," Situation in the Central African Republic, *The Prosecutor* v. *Jean-Pierre Bemba Gombo*, para. 6.

evolve over time. This explains why the CAR II situations did not warrant much cooperation, as did the investigation and prosecution of Bemba in the CAR I situation. Both situations in CAR highlight the fact that the prosecutions have focused solely on rebels: Bemba's MLC forces in CAR I and Seleka and anti-balaka rebels in CAR II.[11] This aligns with the analytical framework developed in Chapter 2, which highlights the ways in which state cooperation with the ICC is sustained as long as the target of the investigations is limited to rebels or political adversaries.

Mali

The ICC situation in Mali originated from a self-referral issued by the Malian authorities in the aftermath of the 2012 crisis and the subsequent Islamist takeover of the northern part of the country.[12] As a state party to the Rome Statute, Mali sent a referral letter to the ICC on 13 July 2012.[13] In the letter, the Malian minister of justice referred to grave violations of human rights and humanitarian law, including "summary executions of Malian soldiers, rape of women and girls, massacres of civil populations, recruitment of child soldiers, torture, [...] forced disappearances, destruction of symbols of the state, buildings, hospitals, tribunals, mayor's offices, schools, NGO [nongovernmental organization] headquarters, destruction of churches, mausoleums and mosques."[14] Having determined that the legal requirements were met,[15] the ICC OTP opened an investigation, which concluded that there was a reasonable basis to believe that war crimes were committed in Mali, notably murder, passing of sentences and carrying out of executions without due process, mutilations, cruel punishment, and torture (ICC 2013). On 18 September 2015, the ICC issued a warrant for the arrest of Al Mahdi

---

[11] There are currently two suspects in ICC custody in relation to the CAR II situation. Alfred Yekatom was surrendered to the Court on 17 December 2018. He is accused of commanding a militia within the Anti-Balaka movement and charged with war crimes and crimes against humanity. Patrice-Edouard Ngaïssona was arrested by French authorities and transferred to ICC custody on 23 January 2019. He was also a leader in the Anti-Balaka movement.

[12] For background analysis of the 2012 crisis, see, for instance, Wing (2013), Thurston and Lebovich (2013), Morgan (2012), Lecoq et al. (2012).

[13] See Mali referral letter to the ICC, www.icc-cpi.int/NR/rdonlyres/A245A47F-BFD1-45B6-891C-3BCB5B173F57/0/ReferralLetterMali130712.pdf.

[14] See Mali referral letter to the ICC, www.icc-cpi.int/NR/rdonlyres/A245A47F-BFD1-45B6-891C-3BCB5B173F57/0/ReferralLetterMali130712.pdf.

[15] ICC, OTP, "ICC Prosecutor Opens Investigation into War Crimes in Mali," Press Release, No ICC-OTP-20130116-PR869, www.icc-cpi.int/en_menus/icc/press%20and%20media/press%20releases/news%20and%20highlights/Pages/pr869.aspx.

in connection with war crimes of destruction of nine mausoleums and one mosque in Timbuktu.[16] Al Mahdi pleaded guilty to the charges and was sentenced to nine years in prison. Al Hassan, a second suspect in the Mali situation, was taken into ICC custody and transferred to The Hague on 31 March 2018 (ICC 2018c). In addition to the destruction of the religious and cultural monuments, he is also accused of having participated in the policy of forced marriages that victimized female inhabitants of Timbuktu and led to rape and sexual enslavement of girls and women (ICC 2018a).

The Mali situation at the ICC echoes the same features as those of Uganda, DRC, CAR, and Côte d'Ivoire. The self-referral was initiated by an interim government struggling for legitimacy in a highly fluid political and security environment. After the 2012 military coup that plunged the country into a political crisis and spurred the quick takeover of the northern half of the country by various armed groups, the Economic Community of West African States (ECOWAS) pressured the military junta to hand over power to a transitional civilian government led by interim president Dioncounda Traore. However, Traore struggled to assert his power and control over the state, at one point, even sustaining injuries after demonstrators attacked him in his office in May 2012 (BBC 2012). A few months later, a government of national unity, led by Cheikh Modibo Diarra, was formed amidst another power struggle between soldiers loyal to former junta leader Sanogo (known as the green berets) and the military elite force (known as the red berets) (LA Times 2012). In December 2012, Prime Minister Diarra resigned, hours after having been arrested by Sanogo's soldiers (Diallo 2012). All these events occurred while Mali had lost control over half of its territory at the hands of Islamist and rebel groups, while France mulled a military intervention to stop the Islamists from marching toward Bamako.

In this context, Mali, under interim president Traore, referred the situation in its northern territory to the ICC. As Louw and Maunganidze (2012) wrote at the time of the referral, "The self-referral [by Mali] could ... be characterized as an attempt by the interim government – which is weak and in search of support and legitimacy both locally and abroad – to put down the rebellion in the north, and eliminate opposition from those who might seek to destabilize a new government." The situation in Mali therefore aligns with other cases wherein interim, unelected, or illegitimate governments (Uganda, DRC, CAR, Côte d'Ivoire, Kenya, Gabon) tried to use the ICC in their quest for political legitimacy or to bolster their claims of statehood.

---

[16] ICC, "Situation in the Republic of Mali," ICC-01/12, www.icc-cpi.int/en_menus/icc/situations%20and%20cases/situations/icc0112/Pages/situation%20index.aspx.

Gabon

Gabon is also a case of an illegitimate government in an extremely volatile political environment in the wake of contested electoral results that reached out to the ICC with a self-referral in an attempt to incapacitate its political opposition and assert its grip on power. At a time when AU countries were contemplating a mass exodus from the Court, Gabon went in the opposite direction and issued a self-referral to the ICC on 20 September 2016 in a letter signed by Justice Minister Denise Mekamne Edzidzie (République Gabonaise 2016). In the referral letter, Gabon declares that following the 27 August 2016 presidential elections and the victory of the incumbent president, the leader of the opposition Jean Ping proclaimed himself president-elect and sparked riots. The letter cites Ping's utterances to "plunge [the country] in a long and deep period of instability" and "total chaos" as justifications for what it calls "an incitement to commit genocide" and crimes against humanity (République Gabonaise 2016, 4–6). The ICC prosecutor subsequently opened a preliminary examination in the situation in Gabon. A brief political history of Gabon and the context of the 2016 presidential election and its aftermath will help elucidate the reasons for the self-referral to the ICC.

Incumbent president Ali Bongo ascended to power in 2009 through controversial elections following the death of his father, Omar Bongo, who had ruled Gabon for over four decades.[17] On 27 August 2016, the leading opposition parties rallied behind Jean Ping during the presidential elections in an effort to defeat Ali Bongo and end the Bongo dynasty. In 2016, just like the 2009 elections, the Bongo family's grip on power was maintained through electoral manipulations, which was legitimized by the constitutional court. The court declared Ali Bongo president-elect with a victory margin of just 1.6 percent. Over the past few decades, Gabon's political system can be described as what Levitsky and Way (2010) call "competitive authoritarianism," which means that, although elections may be held regularly and in the absence of massive fraud, the incumbents violate the rules and tailor the system to create such an uneven playing field that it was virtually impossible for the opposition to win (Ba 2016a).[18]

---

[17] It's important to note that, at the death of Omar Bongo, Senate leader Rose Francine Rogombe was sworn in as interim president in April 2009, a position she held until after the October 2009 presidential elections.

[18] Indeed, Gabon's electoral system overwhelmingly favors the status quo easily and perpetuates incumbency. For instance, Gabon no longer has presidential term limits, which were abolished in 2003. And unlike many francophone African countries, Gabon has adopted the first-past-the-post system for presidential elections, which means the winner is required to obtain only a plurality of the votes. This allowed Ali Bongo to win the 2009 elections with only 42 percent of the vote.

A few days after the 2016 elections, the electoral commission declared Bongo the winner with 49.9 percent of the vote, compared to Ping's 48.2 percent. By any objective measure however, this razor-thin victory in Gabon is suspicious. The doubts on the credibility of these results were even heightened by the fact that, in Bongo's stronghold, in the Haut-Ogooué province, the turnout was reported to be 99.9 percent, with 95.5 percent of the votes credited to Bongo (Macé 2016). The European Union (EU) Election Observation Mission in Gabon immediately flagged those "evident abnormalities" (EU EOM 2016a) and further confirmed flaws that compromised the integrity of the electoral results (EU EOM 2016b, 5). Immediately after the publication of the results of the presidential elections, thousands of Ping's supporters held demonstrations in Libreville and other cities across the country, calling on Bongo to step down. Violent clashes occurred between the demonstrators and security forces, while the opposition parties and the EU called for a recount of the ballots. As the demonstrations and repression escalated, protesters set the parliament building on fire, and security forces stormed Ping's headquarters. The death toll during the days of unrest ranged from ten to fifty deaths, and hundreds were arrested (Freedom House 2018). In the end, the constitutional court, led by a longtime Bongo family ally, credited Bongo with 50.55 percent of the votes. Ping refused to accept the results and declared himself president-elect.

In this context, in September 2016, the Bongo regime wrote a self-referral letter to the ICC, demanding an investigation and accusing Ping of incitement to genocide and crimes against humanity, while all indicators indeed pointed to Ping's victory in the presidential elections. It is important to note, however, that Ping also welcomed the ICC intervention in Gabon's crisis, stating, "[W]e ask that Amnesty and the ICC Prosecutor to come to Gabon to bring to light the events that occurred on 31 August [2016]" (Ping 2016). Two years after Gabon's self-referral, the ICC prosecutor announced that she would not open an investigation, therefore closing the preliminary examination (ICC OTP 2018). The OTP concluded, "The information available does not provide a reasonable basis to believe that any crimes falling within the jurisdiction of the Court have been committed in the situation in Gabon" (ICC OTP 2018, 57). The Bongo regime ultimately failed to have the OTP investigate its main political adversary for incitement of genocide and crimes against humanity. The fact that it issued a self-referral letter in the context of highly contested electoral results, political violence, and repression points, however, to an illegitimate government trying to cling to power, which fits into the framework of the ways in which states strategically use – or, at the very least, try to use – the ICC for political ends.

Sudan

Sudan and Libya are currently the two ICC situations triggered by a UN Security Council (UNSC) referral. Following the UNSC referral of the situation in Darfur, the ICC prosecutor opened the first ever investigation into a state that was not a signatory of the Rome Statute. That investigation also led to the first arrest warrant to be issued against a sitting head of state, President Bashir of Sudan, on 4 March 2009.

Similar to the challenges faced by the ICC in regard to admissibility, cooperation, and complementarity in the other UNSC referral situation (Libya), the Sudan case highlights the limits of ICC's reach in contexts where the state is hostile to the Court's proceedings. From the onset, the ICC faced a barrage of hurdles from the Sudanese state (Barnes 2011; Nouwen 2014; Kersten 2016b; Clark 2018). ICC personnel was not permitted to travel to Sudan to conduct their investigation and collect evidence, and Sudan also obstructed the potential cooperation the OTP could receive from NGOs on the ground. On the day the ICC issued a warrant to arrest President Bashir, Sudan revoked the licenses of ten international humanitarian organizations, accusing them of spying on behalf of the Court. President Bashir explained that Sudan needed "to clear our country of any spies" (Rice 2009). Sudan also expanded immunities for state officials after the opening of the ICC investigations (Clark 2018, 274). These challenges resulted in the OTP relying on satellite imagery (Benjamin 2011; Sandalinas 2015), testimonies from Darfuri refugees, and even a collection of pictures drawn by Darfuri children depicting Janjaweed attacks in their villages as contextual evidence (Aradau and Hill 2013).

The Darfur situation and the warrant for Bashir's arrest also sparked the biggest confrontation between the ICC and the AU, leading the AU to call on its member states not to cooperate with the Court. Meanwhile, Bashir traveled to many countries without facing arrest, until he was eventually deposed during the April 2019 uprising in Sudan. Still, a decade after the first warrant was issued in the Sudan situation, the ICC has failed to secure the arrest and transfer of any state officials.[19] On the other hand, three Sudanese suspects – all of them rebels – had initially appeared before the Court after being summoned.[20]

---

[19] The state officials facing ICC arrest warrants are former president Bashir, former minister of state for humanitarian affairs Ahmed Haroun, former commander of the government-backed Janjaweed militia, and Minister of National Defense Mohammed Hussain.

[20] Abu Garda and Abdallah Banda from the Justice and Equality Movement (JEM) and Saleh Jerbo, a commander in the Sudan Liberation Movement. Pre-Trial Chamber I declined to confirm the charges against Abu Garda in February 2010. Although Banda appeared voluntarily before the Court during the pretrial phase, the Trial Chamber issued a warrant for his arrest on 11 September 2014 and he remains at large. The case against Mohamed Jerbo was terminated in 2013, following his death.

The Sudanese state actions in the face of the ICC's demands, the support from Sudan's allies and the AU, and the indifference of the UNSC resulted in Prosecutor Bensouda hibernating the Darfur situation in December 2014, telling the UNSC, "I'm left with no choice but to hibernate investigative activities in Darfur as I shift resources to other urgent cases" (UN News 2014). Once again, this case shows the extent to which a weaker state in the international system is able to stonewall the Court and shield its agents from prosecution, even when the ICC's jurisdiction was triggered by the UNSC.

Burundi

On 27 October 2017, Burundi became the first state in the world to withdraw from the Rome Statute. The withdrawal of a state party to the ICC takes effect a year after the state has notified the UN Secretary General of its intent, which Burundi had done during a period of a contentious relationship between the Court and a number of African states and the AU. Amid calls for or threats of mass withdrawals from the ICC, Burundi, The Gambia, and South Africa officially announced their intention to leave the Court. Upon Burundi's withdrawal, its presidential office spokesperson said, "The ICC has shown itself to be a political instrument and weapon used by the west to enslave other states," adding that by leaving the Court, Burundi "has defended its sovereignty and national pride" (The Guardian 2017).

Burundi's withdrawal has less to do with sovereignty and national pride, however, than an attempt by state officials to shield themselves from potential prosecution for war crimes and crimes against humanity. Similar to the cases of the Philippines and The Gambia, Burundi took steps to leave the Court amid a record of atrocities that implicated high-ranking officials within the state and the security forces, thus trying to preempt ICC jurisdiction for investigation. Despite Burundi leaving the ICC, however, the Pre-Trial Chamber III judges decided to grant the request of the ICC prosecutor to open an investigation into Burundi on 25 October 2017 – two days prior to the withdrawal going into effect – although the decision was under seal until November 2017 (ICC 2017).

Burundi's move to withdraw from the ICC was precipitated by the OTP's announcement of the opening of a preliminary examination on 25 April 2016, when it received information that, at the time, "430 persons had reportedly been killed, at least 3,400 people arrested and over 230,000 Burundians forced to seek refuge in neighboring countries."[21] In the authorization to open an

---

[21] ICC, "Burundi: Situation in The Republic of Burundi," ICC-01/17, www.icc-cpi.int/burundi.

investigation, the ICC chamber noted that, "according to estimates, at least 1,200 persons were allegedly killed, thousands illegally detained, thousands reportedly tortured, and hundreds disappeared. The alleged acts of violence have reportedly resulted in the displacement of 413,490 persons between April 2015 and May 2017." The chamber therefore decided that there was a reasonable basis for the prosecutor to proceed with an investigation "in relation to crimes against humanity, including: a) murder and attempted murder; b) imprisonment or severe deprivation of liberty; c) torture; d) rape; e) enforced disappearance; and f) persecution, allegedly committed in Burundi, and in certain instances outside of the country by nationals of Burundi, since at least 26 April 2015."

The crisis in Burundi and the subsequent heightened human rights abuses and atrocity crimes started with the announcement in April 2015 by the ruling National Council for the Defense of Democracy–Forces for Defense of Democracy (Conseil National pour la Défense de la Démocratie–Forces pour la Défense de la Démocratie, [CNDD–FDD]) that incumbent President Pierre Nkurunziza would seek a new presidential term despite the constitutional limits. Protests erupted in the capital Bujumbura and other cities, prompting members of the ruling party's youth leagues, known as the *Imbonerakure*, and government security forces to intervene, "kill[ing] and tortur[ing] scores of opposition political party members and other perceived opponents since the start of the crisis" (HRW 2017). Human Rights Watch (HRW) also reported that "some members [of the *Imbonerakure*] have raped the wives and daughters of opposition members, beat people to death with clubs, and tortured opponents" (Hartill 2017). President Nkurunziza's administration held a constitutional referendum in May 2018, which was set to increase the presidential terms to seven years, renewable once. However, that referendum resets the clock on Nkurunziza's tenure, enabling him to run for two more seven-year terms, in 2020 and 2027 – which could potentially extend his rule until 2034. In the aftermath of the referendum, Burundian authorities and ruling party youth continued to carry out "dozens of beatings, arbitrary arrests, disappearances, and killings against real and suspected political opposition members" (Human Rights Watch 2019a).

The UN Commission of Inquiry on Burundi, which was established in September 2016, found that "the serious human rights violations documented in the first year of its mandate, including crimes against humanity, persisted in 2017 and 2018," and the commission also drew attention to the "growing role" of the *Imbonerakure* and the responsibility of the Burundian government for the abuses. The UN Commission of Inquiry found that "members of the National Intelligence Service and the police, including high-ranking officials, were involved in the commission of a large number of human rights violations in 2017 and 2018" (UN HRC 2018). The commission reported that there are "reasonable grounds to believe that crimes against humanity have been committed in Burundi since April 2015," which of course would fall under the jurisdiction of the ICC. Meanwhile, the government of Burundi has refused to share information or cooperate with the UN Commission of Inquiry, even threatening legal action against its members, accusing them of "attempt[ing] to destabilize the country" (Shingiro 2017).[22] In this context, Burundi announced its withdrawal from the ICC.

At this moment, the situation in Burundi is still under investigation by the OTP, and no indictment has been made public yet. It is clear, however, that Burundi's security services and state officials would be primary targets for the investigation and potential prosecution. The move to withdraw from the Rome Statute and refusal to cooperate with the Court is a preemptive measure undertaken by the state to shield its agents from the Court, much like The Gambia and the Philippines had done.

The Gambia

Yahya Jammeh's twenty-two-year authoritarian rule in The Gambia came to an end in the aftermath of the December 2016 presidential elections. Despite having lost the elections to Adama Barrow, Jammeh clung to power and faced a threat of an ECOWAS military intervention to unseat him. Following mediation efforts, Jammeh agreed to step down in January 2017 and went into exile in Equatorial Guinea.[23] A few weeks before the presidential elections, however, Jammeh had announced that The Gambia would leave the ICC, following Burundi's and South Africa's announcements of withdrawal. In a statement on state television, Gambian Information Minister Sheriff Bojang said, "[The] ICC, despite being called International Criminal Court, is in fact an International Caucasian Court for the persecution and humiliation of people of color, especially Africans" (O'Grady 2016). The Gambia's position therefore echoes the often-heard accusation of the ICC being a colonial institution, unfairly targeting Africans. Bojang also lamented that "not a single Western war criminal has been indicted [by the ICC] (O'Grady 2016). It is clear that The Gambia's decision to withdraw from the ICC was not really motivated

---

[22] See Ambassador Albert Shingiro, 2017, "#Burundi has the right to bring to justice the authors of the biased report of the commiss° of inquiry for attempt to destabilize the country," 28 October, Twitter, https://twitter.com/AShingiro/status/924335815282618369.

[23] It's important to note that Equatorial Guinea is not a state party to the Rome Statute.

by the fact that the Court hadn't prosecuted Westerners. The Gambian regime, because of its repressive nature and its human rights violations committed over many years, could potentially land on the ICC docket. Indeed, Jammeh and his regime became much more repressive during his attempt to secure a fifth presidential term.

President Jammeh and Gambian security forces violations of human rights, including disappearances, torture, and arbitrary arrest, have long been documented (HRW 2016a). The crackdown on political dissent ramped up leading into the December 2016 presidential elections, with Jammeh threatening to bury his political opponents "nine-feet deep" (HRW 2016a). In September 2009, President Jammeh stated, "I will kill anyone who wants to destabilize this country. If you think that you can collaborate with so-called human rights defenders, and get away with it, you must be living in a dream world. I will kill you, and nothing will come out of it…We are ready to kill saboteurs" (HRW 2015b). In May 2008, Jammeh gave gay persons in The Gambia a twenty-four-hour ultimatum to leave the county, promising to "cut off the head" of any gay person found in the country (HRW 2015b). The March 2015 report by the UN's Special Rapporteur on torture described the widespread use of unacknowledged detention that facilitates "torture or summary execution or both." Jammeh also reinstated the death penalty when he came to power and since 2012, "prisoners sentenced to death have been executed in violation of their fundamental rights to due process" (HRW 2015b). In August 2012, Jammeh announced his intention to execute all forty-seven inmates in death row at the time. Despite the AU's appeal to withhold that decision, nine of the inmates were executed (Amnesty International 2012). These are but a few examples of the dismal record of the Jammeh regime on human rights.

After Jammeh's fall, President Barrow asserted that his priority was to set up a truth and reconciliation commission that would investigate and gather the facts about Jammeh's repressive regime. At this moment, it is not clear whether crimes committed under Jammeh's rule amount to crimes against humanity or meet the gravity threshold of the ICC's jurisdiction. In fact, in the months leading to the presidential elections, in light of mounting political repression, ICC Prosecutor Fatou Bensouda declined to open preliminary examination in The Gambia,[24] arguing, "What we at the ICC look for is war crimes, crimes against humanity and genocide, which is the mandate of the institution and this is what has to be understood…It has to be clear that the ICC is not a human rights court but a court that deals with specific crimes under the Rome Statue" (Jollof News 2016).

---

[24] Bensouda is a former advisor to Jammeh and former minister of justice in Jammeh's government.

Whether the alleged crimes committed under Jammeh's regime amount to those over which the ICC has jurisdiction or not, The Gambian state's decision to withdraw from the ICC fits the pattern of states preemptively leaving the Court because of egregious violations of human rights that may lead to investigation and prosecution of their officials and security agents. As Sprouse (2017) writes, "It should not come as much of a surprise that an authoritarian leader in a country with a record of violating international human rights law has decided to withdraw from the very institution which prosecutes human rights violations." The Gambia's withdrawal occurred in the context of a chorus asking for a mass exit of African countries from the ICC and the decisions of Burundi and South Africa to leave the Court, all of which provided cover for the Jammeh regime. This type of context helps The Gambian state to send the message that it is not trying to shield itself from the ICC; rather, it is leaving the Court because of the Court's bias against Africans. Upon taking office, however, President Barrow revoked his country's plan to withdraw from the ICC.

South Africa

South Africa's decision to withdraw from the Court does not fit the pattern seen in the other instances of states, such as Burundi, The Gambia, and the Philippines, leaving or attempting to leave the Court. The fallout between South Africa and ICC stemmed from South Africa's failure to arrest President Bashir of Sudan during an AU summit in Johannesburg in June 2015. South Africa faced a loyalty conflict between its commitment to the ICC and its obligation toward the AU; ultimately, it chose to prioritize its regional political reputation (Boehme 2017). South Africa's decision to withdraw from the Court was based on what it perceived as conflicting obligations with the ICC and other obligations to other states and the AU. In the instrument of withdrawal that South Africa's foreign minister sent to the UN Secretary General, she argues that her country's commitment to peaceful resolution of conflicts is "incompatible" with the Court's interpretation of states' obligations under the Rome Statute.[25] During President Bashir's visit to the AU summit in South Africa, local civil society groups had sued the government over its obligation to arrest Bashir given that South Africa had incorporated the Rome Statute into its own national laws. Although the South African government claimed

---

[25] See the "Instrument of Withdrawal," www.justsecurity.org/wp-content/uploads/2016/10/South-Africa-Instrument-of-Withdrawal-International-Criminal-Court.jpg.

that Bashir was protected by sovereign immunity under customary international law, the South African Supreme Court of Appeal ruled that the state had violated national laws for not having arrested Bashir (Ba 2016b).

South Africa's decision to withdraw from the ICC still was surprising given that Bashir had already left the country and was unlikely ever to return. Therefore, one must view South Africa's decision in light of the context of calls for mass withdrawal from many African states, years of tension between the AU and the ICC, and especially the fact that South Africa did not want to be beaten by Burundi to the "withdrawal line." Still, South Africa sped up its decision and process, only to lose to Burundi on the "withdrawal race" (Kersten 2016a). The South African cabinet met on 19 October 2016, just one day after President Nkurunziza of Burundi signed a presidential decree to leave the ICC, to draft South Africa's executive order withdrawing from the Court.

Therefore, even though the South African attempt to leave the ICC seemed to be an outlier in comparison to the Burundi, The Gambia, and the Philippines cases, it can still be explained as an attempt from the Zuma administration to free itself from fulfilling its ICC obligations and maintain its regional and strategic role as a leader on the African continent and in the AU. Ultimately, the attempt to withdraw from the ICC was abandoned because the domestic court ruled that the notice of withdrawal required a legislative process and the presidential cabinet lacked the power to enact the withdrawal unilaterally.

The Philippines

The Philippines had deposited its instruments of ratification of the Rome Statute on 30 August 2011, which granted ICC territorial jurisdiction over core crimes committed in the country from 1 November 2011 onward. The situation in the Philippines at the ICC is currently at the preliminary examination phase and focuses on "alleged crimes committed since at least 1 June 2016, in the context of the 'war on drugs' campaign."[26] The OTP announced the opening of the preliminary examination in February 2018, specifically, looking into the allegations that "thousands of persons have been killed for reasons related to their alleged involvement in illegal drug use or dealing." Many of the alleged killings resulted from clashes between or within gangs, but incidents of "extra-judicial killings in the course of police anti-drug operations" (ICC OTP 2018) were also reported. A month later, President Duterte announced that his country was withdrawing from the Rome Statute, and he threatened to have Fatou Bensouda arrested if she set foot in the Philippines

[26] See ICC, Preliminary Examination: The Philippines, www.icc-cpi.int/philippines.

(Cabato 2019). The Philippines became the second state effectively to withdraw from the ICC, after Burundi.[27]

Human rights organizations have called the Philippines' withdrawal a "futile attempt to evade international justice" (Amnesty International 2019). The decision by the Filipino state to leave the ICC is indeed a strategy to shield its agents from potential investigation and prosecution in relation to alleged crimes committed in the context of its war on drugs. Human Rights Watch (2019b) called the withdrawal Duterte's "bald-faced effort to protect himself from the court's reach [which] looks more like an act of desperation for a man who appears deeply implicated in alleged crimes against humanity." Indeed, since coming to power on 30 June 2016, President Duterte's war on drugs has led to the death of over 27,000 Filipinos (UN OHCHR 2019), a campaign that, according to human rights organizations, may amount to crimes against humanity.[28] President Duterte himself may be directly involved in the alleged crimes because "[he] has taken numerous steps to encourage the killing of people linked to using or trading drugs. He has issued and publicized 'kill lists' – setting out the names of drug suspects" (Amnesty International 2019). After the ICC withdrawal took effect, President Duterte's legal counsel and spokesperson said, "Should the ICC proceed with its undertakings relative to the Philippines [...] it can only mean that it is bent on interfering with the sovereignty of our Republic" (Cabato 2019).

If the OTP finds satisfactory preliminary evidence of core crimes in the Philippines that fall within the material jurisdiction of the ICC, it will seek an authorization from the Pre-Trial Chamber to open a formal *proprio motu* investigation. In that case, the focus of the investigation is likely to be on state officials and security forces. The Philippines would therefore be in a similar situation as Burundi and The Gambia (under the Jammeh regime). As explained in the analytical framework developed in Chapter 2, states in this category will withdraw from the Court, use threats of withdrawal to shield themselves from the investigation and potential prosecution, or take various steps to impede the work of the ICC's OTP. States that are not members of the ICC but face a similar situation (the United States, Israel, Myanmar, for instance) will use threats against the Court or its agents for the same purpose.

Is the ICC equipped to hold states responsible for the atrocity crimes that their agents commit and for failing to protect their citizens from such crimes? Or is the state-centered international justice system a smokescreen that shields

---

[27] Even after a state withdraws from the ICC, however, the Court retains jurisdiction over core crimes committed during the time in which that state was party to the Rome Statute. That is the case for both The Philippines and Burundi.

[28] See Human Rights Watch reports, www.hrw.org/tag/philippines-war-drugs.

states and their agents and criminalizes individuals deemed as enemies of the state instead? The reality is that states mold international institutions as instruments to further their interests. The arguments developed in this book point to an instrumental use of the international criminal justice system in ways that advance the political and security interests of the states. Indeed, all the cases discussed here show that the ICC is nearly incapable of successfully prosecuting high-ranking state officials.

A COURT IN PERMANENT CRISIS?

Since it started operating in 2002, the ICC has achieved only four convictions for core crimes – former Congolese rebel leaders Thomas Lubanga, Germain Katanga, and Bosco Ntaganda, and the guilty plea from Ahmad Al Mahdi for the war crimes of destruction of religious edifices in Mali.[29] To date, out of the eleven ICC situations under investigation, only one is located outside the African continent,[30] while eleven other situations are currently at the preliminary examination phase.[31] Indeed, the Court has had very limited success and has faced drastic failures over its short mandate. Yet, the Court has set its mark on global politics and conflict processes, especially in Africa, although there are still many "known unknowns" and "unknown unknowns" (Stahn 2015d, v). As there is little doubt that the ICC is here to stay, it is still unclear whether and to what extent the Court can overcome its many crises, as it enters its third decade of operation. The election of a new Chief Prosecutor in December 2020 may at least give some indication of where the OTP is headed. It is clear, however, that the Court is troubled and in crisis. Most of its shortcomings in the past tended to be imputed to the OTP and were often cast as a "teething problem" (Cassese 2006). Many preliminary examination situations have lingered for years, without much progress. There were issues of timing and delayed action in Darfur and in the conduct of investigations in Sudan,[32] and mistakes made in the Ugandan referral.[33]

---

[29] Ntaganda appealed his conviction in September 2019. Former DRC vice president Jean-Pierre Bemba's conviction was overturned by the Appeals Chamber in June 2018.

[30] This investigation concerns the 2008 conflict between Russia and Georgia regarding South Ossetia. See "Situation in Georgia," ICC-01/15, www.icc-cpi.int/georgia.

[31] The ongoing preliminary examinations cover Afghanistan, Bangladesh/Myanmar, Colombia, Guinea, Iraq/United Kindgom, Nigeria, Palestine, the Philippines, Ukraine, and Venezuela.

[32] As Professor Dov Jacobs said, "The Office of the Prosecutor has investigated Darfur without ever setting a foot there. I wonder how did they do it." Interview with the author, The Hague, May 2014.

[33] For instance, the press conference that Prosecutor Ocampo and President Museveni held together to announce the referral of the "situation concerning the LRA [Lord's Resistance Army]."

Charges were not confirmed at the pretrial phase in some cases, were withdrawn by the prosecutor, or were dropped. The collapse of the Kenyan cases and the acquittals of Bemba, Gbagbo, and Blé Goudé also point to structural deficiencies of the OTP and its apparent inability to conduct investigations and prosecute successfully most of the suspects of core crimes that it targets (Ba 2018; Ellis 2019).

Beyond the OTP, other organs of the Court, such as the chambers and the registrar, also exhibit deep flaws in their operations and conduct. The ICC is also criticized for its failure to take on "hard cases" that would threaten "powerful states" (Schabas 2015), which now goes beyond just the limitations of the OTP. For instance, after more than a decade of preliminary examination in Afghanistan, the OTP finally requested an authorization from the Pre-Trial Chamber to open an investigation, which would potentially cover alleged crimes committed by both Taliban fighters and American soldiers. Many legal scholars found the refusal of the chamber to grant the authorization – on the grounds that it would not be "in the interests of justice" – odd and troubling (Heller 2019c; Jacobs 2019a; Kersten 2019b; Raynor 2019).

There has also been many recent controversies related to ICC judges' integrity, independence, and conflicts of interest. These scandals include Judge Ozaki's acceptance of a position as Japan's ambassador to Estonia while trying to remain a part-time judge in the Court (Heller 2019b). A speech given by Judge de Brinchambaut at Peking University recently surfaced wherein he remarked that European countries fund the ICC while African states "provide the suspects" (Lingsma 2019). A number of ICC judges are suing their own Court at the International Labor Organization (ILO) for a pay raise (Simons 2019). Following all these troubling developments, four former presidents of the ICC's ASP have raised concerns about the health of the institution. They argued that the Court "needs fixing" in light of the "growing gap between the unique vision captured in the Rome Statute ... and some of the daily work of the Court" (Al Hussein et al. 2019). They added, "We are disappointed by the quality of some of its judicial proceedings, frustrated by some of the results, and exasperated by the management deficiencies that prevent the Court from living up to its full potential" (Al Hussein et al. 2019).

Although the international criminal justice system is geared toward upholding individual accountability for core crimes, it is embedded in an institutional framework that is prone to absolve states and their agents. Thus, states use the ICC strategically to shield themselves and their agents while facilitating the prosecution and demise of their adversaries. As the previous chapters have shown, states have indeed taken full advantage of the international criminal justice system to advance their security and political interests at the expense of furthering norms of criminal accountability. What is clear is that, beyond the ICC, however, the international criminal justice project itself is in crisis.

THE CRISIS OF INTERNATIONAL CRIMINAL JUSTICE

The ICC, as the first *permanent* international criminal court, has the most expansive array of rules and regulations in addition to the Rome Statute, which is its founding document, a product of long and arduous negotiations between stakeholders with competing interests. Because of its unique and complex architecture, the ICC comes with its own set challenges that ad hoc tribunals and hybrid courts did not face (Stahn 2015c). For instance, not being a UN court and lacking universal jurisdiction, the ICC's intervention must be triggered through one of the three mechanisms discussed in the previous chapters notably, through a state referral, UNSC referral, or the prosecutor's use of her proprio motu powers. States, and African ones especially, have been able to utilize these mechanisms and other levers to engage strategically with the Court in ways that were not anticipated. Those states, although they are weaker in the international system, are able to devise strategies that allowed them to use international justice norms and institutions to defeat – whether militarily or politically – their adversaries, be they opposition leaders, warlords, or rebel groups.

This instrumental use of norms of international justice shows that the argument of "justice cascade" may not be as convincing as previously thought. As Peskin (2017) asserts, the "downward flow of the justice cascade is often met by an uphill undercurrent of equal or greater force that can stop, delay, or divert the course of justice." The supposedly widespread adoption of norms of individual criminal accountability and prosecutions in the wake of massive violations of human rights may actually just be symptomatic of an instrumental adoption. In that sense then, norms are not adopted because states have been socialized in believing in the normative value of using prosecutions to respond to human rights abuses; rather, states use instruments at their disposal – domestic, hybrid, or international courts, in this case – to minimize the costs and maximize the benefits of delivering justice that is underlined by political calculations.

Yet mainstream accounts of the history of international criminal justice typically adopt a master narrative of progress – the journey "from Nuremberg to The Hague through Rome and beyond" (Vasilev 2019, 3). This journey charts the trajectory of humanity's progress, from the darkness of (international) lawlessness to the promise of a civilized era of justice, redress, and accountability. The ICC is viewed, as Payam Akhavan put it, as a central driver in "this civilizing process of introducing the rule of law into the cynical, sordid culture of international politics" (CBC Radio.2019). After all, even Prosecutor Bensouda (2016) declared that "The ICC ... meets needs for humanity's progress in the modern era; because without the ICC, we will regress into an even more turbulent world where chaos, volatility and violence take the upper hand as inevitable norms." With such a view of the ICC as central to humanity's progress, one fails to notice the extent to which the international justice project is flawed. This narrative fails to consider the serious critiques leveled against the Court and other institutions of the international criminal justice regime, and their ideology and instruments. It views crises of the international criminal justice project as simple bumps in the road toward a more perfect world of justice rather than the structural flaws rooted on the foundations of the project itself.

Although one may dismiss the language of crisis that is attached to discussions of the ICC as "a cliché [that] has mostly been used as a click-bait rather than an analytical lens" (Vasilev 2019, 3), it remains that, for international justice scholars, there is a whole field of critique that lays beyond the spectacular and episodic shortcomings of the Court, such as the scandals, acquittals, withdrawals, and so on. These events are indeed just the symptoms of what underpins the Court's organization, functions, and place in international justice and politics. Why is it, for instance, that the Court seems able to deliver justice only on behalf of states rather than for victims and communities affected by atrocity crimes? Victims and communities remain at the center of the Court's discourse because ICC officials and advocates are too quick and eager to elevate the category of "victims" to the status of the Court's *raison d'être*, the constituency on whose behalf the Court exists (Vasilev 2015).

Proponents of the Court may claim that, by its mere existence, the ICC has changed the world and has a positive impact on global politics and conflict processes. However, this line of argument overlooks potential harms that the Court causes with its actions or inactions. Ultimately, despite its aspirations and ideals, it remains that the "[the ICC] is an intergovernmental organization of limited competence in, unfortunately, every sense" (Guilfoyle 2019). As Mark Drumbl (2019) eloquently put it, "The question that we should really be asking is: what kind of utility can the ICC serve when it is abundantly clear that today it will never be able to achieve the goals that were initially placed on its shoulders?" This conversation will require honesty and contrition and accepting the realization that the ICC may never fulfil the promise that was placed upon it on the road to Rome. The Court itself may need to acknowledge that it can only deliver justice that is both political, selective, and partial. The ICC's version of justice is bound to the will of states and to the intricacies of global politics and power dynamics (Grovogui 2015). This means that the Court will have to scale down its ambitions and purpose, or risk perpetuating harm to victims and communities affected by violence.

Highlighting the crisis of international criminal justice does not necessarily mean that international courts are epiphenomenal. The ICC and other international and hybrid courts are at the center of power politics with wide-ranging implications. Even though empirical studies so far point to the fact that the ICC's involvement in ongoing conflicts does not dampen the level of mass atrocities committed (Branch 2007; Hillebrecht 2016; Kersten 2016b; Clark 2018), other scholarship shows that the Court can have a deterrent effect on some governments and those rebel groups that seek legitimacy (Grono and Wheeler 2015; Jo and Simmons 2017).[34] The ICC has also pushed the boundaries of international law, generating new jurisprudence on child soldiers, crimes against cultural property, and gender-based violence, for instance. Even African states have taken actions aimed at strengthening international justice, both in areas of investigations, prosecution, complementarity, and adjudication of international crimes.[35] Individual states have taken bold steps in incorporating the Rome Statute into domestic law, thus incorporating international crimes into their judicial architecture.

CONCLUSION

African states constitute the largest regional bloc in the ICC membership and show *prima facie* a widespread adoption of the norm of individual criminal accountability in the face of international crimes. But as this book has argued, such claim rests on shaky grounds if we consider the ways in which these states, although they appear to have adopted the norm, nonetheless devise strategies to circumvent it and bend the rules to fit their calculations. Joining the ICC and working with international tribunals can be a mere cost-benefit analysis for states that are eager to find avenues to prosecute their enemies while at the same time shielding their agents. For the various ICC situations across the African continent, the lack of expertise in domestic political contexts has allowed states to instrumentalize the Court, and at the community level, citizens have suffered the continued violence of foreign and alienating versions of justice (Clark 2018).

---

[34] Jo and Simmons (2017) find that, although ratification of the ICC may be associated with increased violence among rebel groups, prosecutorial deterrence exists – albeit marginally – as a result of ICC actions, not from ratification of ICC statutes.

[35] Such examples include the African Court of Human and Peoples' Rights, the Malabo Protocol aimed at establishing the future African Court of Justice and Human Rights, the ECOWAS Court of Justice, and so on.

The international criminal justice project emerged in the 1990s at a euphoric moment of the promise of liberalism, cosmopolitanism, and internationalism. With the end of the Cold War, and in the wake of genocide, ethnic cleansing, and mass atrocities, the international community resorted to creating international courts as the best way to achieve justice, accountability, and redress. This era was marked by the creation of ad hoc courts, hybrid tribunals, commissions of inquiry, and the ICC, the ultimate institution that many believed the world needed. Cheerleaders, proponents, and advocates for this regime view justice as a superior alternative, one that can transcend or, at the very least, mitigate the destructive effects of power politics and atrocity crimes. More than two decades later, however, this international criminal justice regime is less a system than a patchwork (Peskin 2017), where some states and conflicts remain outside the reach of these courts, and the impunity gap remains glaring. Accountability is not guaranteed, even when the ICC – or other courts – have jurisdiction over the alleged crimes. Indeed, the ICC is entangled in the wider web of political instrumentalization and strategic calculations, even from states that are presumed to be weaker in the international system.

The ICC, as a political agent and actor (an identity that it refuses to embrace), has shown, over its almost two decades of operation, signs that raise doubt about the viability of the international criminal justice project. Will the ICC disappear or be dislocated or repurposed? Or will it fade toward obsolescence at the margins of international justice? Is the future of international justice local? Or does international justice have a future at all? The issue of human rights, "the last utopia" (Moyn 2012) upon which international justice is anchored, certainly faces an uncertain future. Probably the future of international justice *is* local, and scholars and practitioners ought to pay more attention to local manifestations of justice and accountability, and justice in its various forms and conceptions, rather than the politics and intricacies of international criminal justice.

References

Adele, Alexis. 2018. "How Selective Justice Is Eroding Peace in Côte d'Ivoire." The New Humanitarian, 28 February. www.thenewhumanitarian.org/analysis/2018/02/28/how-selective-justice-eroding-peace-cote-d-ivoire.

AFP. 2016. "President Ouattara Says 'Won't Send Any More Ivorians to ICC'." 4 February. https://news.yahoo.com/president-ouattara-says-wont-send-more-ivorians-icc-195852503.html.

African Union. 2009a. "Decision on the Application by the International Criminal Court (ICC) Prosecutor for the Indictment of the President of the Republic of Sudan." Assembly/AU/Dec.222(XII), decision no. 14.

African Union. 2009b. "Decision on the Meeting of African States Parties to the Rome Statute of the International Criminal Court (ICC)." Doc. Assembly/AU/13(XIII).

African Union. 2011. "Decision on the Implementation of the Assembly Decisions on the International Criminal Court." Assembly/AU/Dec.366(XVII), decision no. 4.

African Union. 2013. "Decision on Africa's Relationship with the International Criminal Court (ICC)." Ext/Assembly/AU/Dec.1(Oct.2013). https://au.int/sites/default/files/decisions/9655-ext_assembly_au_dec_decl_e_0.pdf.

Akande, Dapo. 2012. "The Effect of Security Council Resolutions and Domestic Proceedings on State Obligations to Cooperate with the ICC." Journal of International Criminal Justice 10 (2): 299–324.

Akande, Dapo. 2019. "ICC Appeals Chamber Holds That Heads of State Have No Immunity under Customary International Law before International Tribunals." EJIL: Talk!, 6 May. www.ejiltalk.org/icc-appeals-chamber-holds-that-heads-of-state-have-no-immunity-under-customary-international-law-before-international-tribunals/.

Akhavan, Payam. 1995. "Enforcement of the Genocide Convention: A Challenge to Civilization." Harvard Human Rights Journal 8: 229–258.

Akhavan, Payam. 2005. "The Lord's Resistance Army Case: Uganda's Submission of the First State Referral to the International Criminal Court." American Journal of International Law 99 (2): 403–421.

Akhavan, Payam. 2009. "Are International Criminal Tribunals a Disincentive to Peace? Reconciling Judicial Romanticism with Political Realism." Human Rights Quarterly 31 (3): 624–654.

Akhavan, Payam. 2010. "Self-Referrals before the International Criminal Court: Are States the Villains or the Victims of Atrocities?" *Criminal Law Forum* 21 (1): 103–120.

Akhavan, Payam. 2011. "International Criminal Justice in the Era of Failed States: The ICC and the Self-Referral Debate." In *The International Criminal Court and Complementarity: From Theory to Practice*, eds. C.Stahn and M. M. E. Zeidy. Cambridge: Cambridge University Press, pp. 283–303.

Akindès, Francis. 2003. "Côte d'Ivoire: Socio-political Crises, 'Ivoirité' and the Course of History." *African Sociological Review* 7 (2): 11–28.

Akindès, Francis, and Moussa Fofana. 2011. "Jeunesse, idéologisation de la notion de « patrie » et dynamique conflictuelle en Côte d'Ivoire." In *Côte d'Ivoire: La réinvention de soi dans la violence*, ed. F. Akindès. Dakar: CODESRIA, pp. 213–249.

Akindès, Francis, Moussa Fofana, and Séverin Yao Kouamé. 2014. "The Hows and Whys of Mobilization in Côte d'Ivoire." In *Liberalism and Its Discontents: Social Movements in West Africa*, ed. N. S. Sylla. Dakar: Rosa Luxembourg Foundation, pp. 230–261.

Al Hussein, Prince Zeid Raad, et al. 2019. "The International Criminal Court Needs Fixing." Atlantic Council, 24 April. www.atlanticcouncil.org/blogs/new-atlanticist/the-international-criminal-court-needs-fixing.

Allen, Tim. 2006. *Trial Justice: The International Criminal Court and the Lord's Resistance Army*. London: Zed Books.

Allen, Tim and Koen Vlassenroot (eds). 2010. *The Lord's Resistance Army: Myth and Reality*. London: Zed Books.

Aloisi, Rosa. 2013. "A Tale of Two Institutions: The United Nations Security Council and the International Criminal Court." In *The Realities of International Criminal Justice*, eds. D. L. Rothe, J. Meernik, and P. Ingadottir. Leiden: Martinus Nijhoff Publishers, pp. 147–168.

Alter, Karen J. 2014. *The New Terrain of International Law: Courts, Politics, Rights.* Princeton, NJ: Princeton University Press.

Amnesty International. 2004. "Uganda: First Step to Investigate Crimes Must Be Part of a Comprehensive Plan to End Impunity." 30 June. Index number: AFR 59/001/2004. www.amnesty.org/download/Documents/92000/afr590012004en.pdf.

Amnesty International. 2012. "Executions in the Gambia: Giant Leap Backwards." Press release, 24 August. www.amnesty.org/en/press-releases/2012/08/executions-gambia-giant-leap-backwards/.

Amnesty International. 2019. "Philippines: Withdrawal from the ICC Must Spur UN Action." 17 March. www.amnesty.org/en/latest/news/2019/03/philippines-withdrawal-icc-spur-un-action/.

Anghie, Antony. 2005. *Imperialism, Sovereignty and the Making of International Law.* Cambridge: Cambridge University Press.

Aradau, Claudia, and Andrew Hill. 2013. "The Politics of Drawing: Children, Evidence, and the Darfur Conflict." *International Political Sociology* 7 (4): 368–387.

Arbour, Louise. 2011. "The Rise and Fall of International Human Rights." International Crisis Group, 27 August. www.crisisgroup.org/global/rise-and-fall-international-human-rights.

Arbour, Louise. 2014. "The Relationship between the ICC and the UN Security Council." *Global Governance* 20 (2): 195–201.

Arsanjani, Mahnoush H., and W. Michael Reisman. 2005. "The Law-in-Action of the International Criminal Court." *American Journal of International Law* 99 (2): 385–403.

Associated Press. 2011. "Obama Sends 100 Troops to Combat LRA in Uganda." *Guardian*, 14 October. www.theguardian.com/world/2011/oct/14/obama-sends-troops-uganda.

Ba, Oumar. 2015a. "The Court Is the Political Arena: Performance and Political Narratives at the International Criminal Court." *African Journal of International Criminal Justice* 2 (2): 174–189.

Ba, Oumar. 2015b. "The Trials and Tribulations of Simone Gbagbo." Africa Is a Country, 12 January. http://africasacountry.com/2015/01/the-trials-and-tribulations-of-simone-gbagbo/.

Ba, Oumar. 2016a. "Gabon's Presidential Election: Are the Opposition's Attempts at Unifying Too Little Too Late?" African Arguments, 22 August. https://africanarguments.org/2016/08/22/gabons-presidential-election-are-the-oppositions-attempts-at-unifying-too-little-too-late/.

Ba, Oumar. 2016b. "Why Is South Africa Withdrawing from the International Criminal Court? And Why Now?" Africa Is a Country, 23 October. https://africasacountry.com/2016/10/why-is-south-africa-withdrawing-from-the-international-criminal-court-and-why-now/.

Ba, Oumar. 2017. "International Justice and the Postcolonial Condition." *Africa Today* 63 (4): 44–62.

Ba, Oumar. 2018. "What Jean-Pierre Bemba's Acquittal by the ICC Means." Al Jazeera, 13 June. www.aljazeera.com/indepth/opinion/jean-pierre-bemba-acquittal-icc-means-180612121012078.html.

Ba, Oumar. 2019. "The International Criminal Court Just Acquitted the Former Ivory Coast President. What Happens Now?" *Washington Post*, 22 January. www.washingtonpost.com/news/monkey-cage/wp/2019/01/22/the-international-criminal-court-just-acquitted-the-former-ivory-coast-president-what-happens-now/.

Banégas, Richard. 2006. "Côte d'Ivoire: Patriotism, Ethnonationalism and Other African Modes of Self-Writing." *African Affairs* 105 (421): 535–552.

Banégas, Richard. 2011. "Post-Election Crisis in Côte d'Ivoire: The Gbonhi War." *African Affairs* 110 (440): 457–468.

Barnes, Gwen P. 2011. "The International Criminal Court's Ineffective Enforcement Mechanisms: The Case of President Omar al Bashir." *Fordham International Law Journal* 34 (6): 1585–1619.

Barnett, Michael, and Martha Finnemore. 1999. "The Politics, Power, and Pathologies of International Organizations." *International Organization* 53 (4): 699–732.

Bass, Gary. 2000. *Stay the Hand of Vengeance: The Politics of War Crimes Tribunals.* Princeton, NJ: Princeton University Press.

Bassiouni, M. Chérif. 2001. "Universal Jurisdiction for International Crimes: Historical Perspectives and Contemporary Practice." *Virginia Journal of International Law* 42 (1): 81–162.

Batros, Ben. 2019. "A Confusing ICC Appeals Judgment on Head of State Immunity." *Just Security*, 7 May.

BBC. 2012. "Mali President Traore Beaten Up by Protesters." 21 May. www.bbc.com/news/world-africa-18142488.

Bellamy, Alex J., and Paul D.Williams. 2011. "The New Politics of Protection? Côte d'Ivoire, Libya and the Responsibility to Protect." *International Affairs* 87 (4): 825–850.

Benjamin, Mark. 2011. "George Clooney's Satellites Build a Case Against an Alleged War Criminal." *TIME*, 3 December.

Bensouda, Fatou. 2012. "The ICC: A Response to African Concerns." Keynote Address at Institute for Security Studies. www.politicsweb.co.za/documents/the-icc-a-response-to-african-concerns--fatou-bens.

Bensouda, Fatou. 2013. "Address to the Assembly of State Parties." 12th Session of the Assembly of State Parties, 20 November.

Bensouda, Fatou. 2016. "Address at the First Plenary, Fifteenth Session of the Assembly of States Parties." The Hague, 16 November. https://asp.icc-cpi.int/iccdocs/asp_docs/ASP15/ASP15-Opening-Statement-Prosecutor-ENG.pdf.

Birchall, Jonathan. 2016. "Talking Justice: New Podcast Focuses on Gbagbo Trial." *International Justice Monitor*, 26 January. www.opensocietyfoundations.org/podcasts/talking-justice-the-trial-of-laurent-gbagbo.

Bjork, Christine, and Juanita Goebertus. 2011. "Complementarity in Action: The Role of Civil Society and the ICC in Rule of Law Strengthening in Kenya." *Yale Human Rights and Development Journal* 14 (1): 205–230.

Boehme, Franziska. 2017. "'We Chose Africa': South Africa and the Regional Politics of Cooperation with the International Criminal Court." *International Journal of Transitional Justice* 11 (1): 50–70.

Bosco, David. 2014. *Rough Justice: The International Criminal Court in a World of Power Politics*. Oxford: Oxford University Press.

Bovcon, Maja. 2009. "France's Conflict Resolution Strategy in Côte d'Ivoire and Its Ethical Implications." *African Studies Quarterly* 11 (1): 1–24.

Bovcon, Maja. 2014. "The Progress in Establishing the Rule of Law in Côte d'Ivoire under Ouattara's Presidency." *Canadian Journal of African Studies* 48 (2): 185–202.

Branch, Adam. 2007. "Uganda's Civil War and the Politics of ICC Intervention." *Ethics & International Affairs* 21 (2): 179–198.

Brown, Stephen, and Chandra Lekha Sriram. 2012. "The Big Fish Won't Fry Themselves: Criminal Accountability for Post-Election Violence in Kenya." *African Affairs* 111 (443): 244–260.

Bryman, Alan. 2012. *Social Research Methods*. 4th ed. Oxford: Oxford University Press.

Cabato, Regine. 2019. "Philippines Leaves International Criminal Court as Duterte Probe Is Underway." *Washington Post*, 18 March.

Cakaj, Ledio. 2016. *When the Walking Defeats You: One Man's Journey as Joseph Kony's Bodyguard*. London: Zed Books.

Calame, Hélène. 2015. "La Commission Dialogue Vérité et Réconciliation ivoirienne: une belle coquille vide? "*Institut des Hautes Etudes sur la Justice*, 5 October. http://ihej.org/wp-content/uploads/2015/10/La-Commission-Dialogue-Vérité-et-Réconciliation-ivoirienne-une-belle-coquille-vide-_.pdf.

Carroll, Rory, and Henley, Jon. 2004. "French Attack Sparks Riots in Ivory Coast." *Guardian*, 7 November. www.theguardian.com/world/2004/nov/08/france.westafrica.

Cassese, Antonio. 2006. "Is the ICC Still Having Teething Problems?" *Journal of International Criminal Justice* 4 (3): 434–441.

Cassese, Antonio. 2012. *Realizing Utopia: The Future of International Law*. Oxford: Oxford University Press.

CBC Radio. 2019. "Payam Akhavan on How to Fix the International Criminal Court." 26 April. www.cbc.ca/radio/thesundayedition/the-sunday-edition-for-april-28-2019-1.5112097/payam-akhavan-on-how-to-fix-the-international-criminal-court-1.5112175.

Chapman, Terrence L., and Stephen Chaudoin. 2012. "Ratification Patterns and the International Criminal Court." *International Studies Quarterly* 57 (2): 400–409.

Charania, Shehzad. 2016. "The International Criminal Court at 14." *Opinio Juris*, 4 August. http://opiniojuris.org/2016/08/04/the-international-criminal-court-at-14/.

Checkel, Jeffrey T. 1998. "The Constructivist Turn in International Relations Theory." *World Politics* 50 (2): 324–348.

Checkel, Jeffrey T. 2001. "Why Comply? Social Learning and European Identity Change." *International Organization* 55 (3): 553–588.

Chirot, Daniel. 2006. "The Debacle in Cote d' Ivoire." *Journal of Democracy* 17(2): 63–77.

Clark, Phil. 2011. "Chasing Cases: The ICC and the Politics of State Referral in the Democratic Republic of Congo and Uganda." In *The International Criminal Court and Complementarity: From Theory to Practice*, eds. C. Stahn and M. M. E. Zeidy. Cambridge: Cambridge University Press, pp. 1180–1203.

Clark, Phil. 2018. *Distant Justice: The Impact of the International Criminal Court on African Politics*. Cambridge: Cambridge University Press.

Clarke, Kamari Maxine. 2009. *Fictions of Justice: The International Criminal Court and the Challenge of Legal Pluralism in Sub-Saharan Africa*. Cambridge: Cambridge University Press.

Clarke, Kamari Maxine. 2015. "'We Ask for Justice, You Give Us Law': The Rule of Law, Economic Markets and the Reconfiguration of Victimhood." In *Contested Justice: The Politics of International Criminal Court Interventions*, eds. C. D. Vos, S. Kendall, and C. Stahn. Cambridge: Cambridge University Press, pp. 272–301.

Clarke, Kamari Maxine, and Koulen Sarah-Jane. 2014. "The Legal Politics of Article 16 Decision: The International Criminal Court, the UN Security Council and the Ontologies of a Contemporary Compromise." *African Journal of Legal Studies* 7 (3): 297–319.

Coffey, Amanda, and Paul Atkinson. 1996. *Making Sense of Qualitative Data: Complementary Research Strategies*. London: Sage Publications.

Coomans, Fons, Fred Grünfeld, and Menno T. Kamminga. 2010. "Methods of Human Rights Research: A Primer." *Human Rights Quarterly* 32 (1): 179–186.

Cryer, Robert. 2006. "Sudan, Resolution 1593, and International Criminal Justice." *Leiden Journal of International Law* 19 (1): 195–222.

Cryer, Robert. 2015. "The ICC and Its Relationship to Non-States Parties." In *The Law and Practice of the International Criminal Court*, ed. C. Stahn. Oxford: Oxford University Press, pp. 260–280.

Cutolo, Armando. 2010. "Modernity, Autochthony and the Ivorian Nation: The End of a Century in Côte d'Ivoire." *Africa* 80 (4): 527–552.

Dabbashi, Ibrahim. 2011. "Letter dated 21 February 2011 from the Charge d'Affaires a.i. of the Permanent Mission of the Libyan Arab Jamahiriya to the United Nations addressed to the President of the Security Council." United Nations Security Council. www.securitycouncilreport.org/atf/cf/%7B65BFCF9B-6D 27-4E9C-8CD3-CF6E4FF96FF9%7D/Libya%20S%202011%20102.pdf.

De Brito, Alexandra Barahona. 2010. "Transitional Justice and Memory: Exploring Perspectives." *South European Society and Politics* 15 (3): 359–376.

Diallo, Tiemoko. 2012. "Mali PM Quits after Arrest, May Hurt Intervention Plan." *Reuters*, 10 December. www.reuters.com/article/uk-mali-primeminister/mali-pm-quits-after-arrest-may-hurt-intervention-plan-idUKBRE8BA03R20121211.

Dolan, Chris. 2011. *Social Torture: The Case of Northern Uganda, 1986–2006*. New York and Oxford: Berghahn Books.

Drumbl, Mark. 2019. "Law Cannot Solve the Biggest Problems We Face." *Justice Info*, 16 July.

Du Plessis, Max. 2012. "Implications of the AU Decision to Give the African Court Jurisdiction over International Crimes." *Institute for Security Studies Paper* 235: 16.

Elias, Olufemi and Annelise Quast. 2003. "The Relationship Between the Security Council and the International Criminal Court in Light of Resolution 1422 (2002)." *Non-State Actors in International Law* 3 (2–3): 165–185.

Ellis, Mark. 2019. "The Latest Crisis of the ICC: The Acquittal of Laurent Gbagbo." *Opinio Juris*, 28 March. http://opiniojuris.org/2019/03/28/the-latest-crisis-of-the-icc-the-acquittal-of-laurent-gbagbo/.

Epstein, Helen C. 2017. *Another Fine Mess: America, Uganda, and the War on Terror*. New York: Columbia Global Reports.

EU EOM. 2016a. "La Mission continue à observer la poursuite du processus électoral." Press Release 160906_5, 6 September.

EU EOM. 2016b. "Rapport Final: Republique Gabonaise." 12 December. https://eeas.europa.eu/sites/eeas/files/gabon_moe_rapport_final_0.pdf.

Fairlie, Megan A., and Joseph Powderly. 2011. "Complementarity and Burden Allocation." In *The International Criminal Court and Complementarity*, eds. S.Carsten and M. M. El Zeidy. Cambridge: Cambridge University Press, pp. 642–682.

Ferstman, Carla, Kevin Jon Heller, Melinda Taylor, and Elizabeth Wilmshurt. 2014. "The International Criminal Court and Libya: Complementarity in Conflict." *International Law Programme Meeting Summary*. London: Chatham House.

FIDH. 2014. "Côte d'Ivoire: Choisir entre la justice et l'impunité – Les autorités ivoiriennes face à leurs engagements." Rapport, 11 December. www.fidh.org/fr/regions/afrique/cote-d-ivoire/16629-cote-d-ivoire-choisir-entre-la-justice-et-l-impunite.

Finnemore, Martha. 1996. *National Interests in International Society*. Ithaca, NY: Cornell University Press.

Finnemore, Martha, and Kathryn Sikkink. 1998. "International Norm Dynamics and Political Change." *International Organization* 52 (4): 887–917.

Förster, Till. 2013. "Insurgent Nationalism: Political Imagination and Rupture in Côte d'Ivoire." *Africa Spectrum* 48 (3): 3–31.

Freedom House. 2018. "Gabon Profile." 8 April 2019. https://freedomhouse.org/report/freedom-world/2018/gabon.

Freeland, Steven. 2006. "How Open Should the Door Be? – Declarations by Non-States Parties under Article 12(3) of the Rome Statute of the International Criminal Court." *Nordic Journal of International Law* 75 (2): 211–241.

Gaeta, Paola. 2004. "Is the Practice of 'Self-Referrals' a Sound Start for the ICC?" *Journal of International Criminal Justice* 2 (4): 949–952.

Gaeta, Paola. 2009. "Does President Al Bashir Enjoy Immunity from Arrest?" *Journal of International Criminal Justice* 7 (2): 315–332.

Gbagbo, Laurent, and Jean-François Mattei. 2016. *Pour la vérité et la justice*. Paris: Le poche du moment.

Gerring, John. 2008. "Case Selection for Case-Study Analysis: Qualitative and Quantitative Techniques." In *The Oxford Handbook of Political Methodology*, eds. Janet M.Box-Steffensmeier, Henry W. Brady, and David Collier. Oxford: Oxford University Press, pp. 645–684.

Gettleman, Jeffrey. 2009. "An Interview with Joseph Kabila." *The New York Times*, 3 April.

Glasius, Marlies. 2006. *The International Criminal Court: A Global Civil Society Achievement*. New York: Routledge.

Goldsmith, Jack. 2003. "The Self-Defeating International Criminal Court." *The University of Chicago Law Review* 70 (1): 89–104.

Goldston, James A. 2010. "More Candour about Criteria: The Exercise of Discretion by the Prosecutor of the International Criminal Court." *Journal of International Criminal Justice* 8 (2): 383–406.

Goldstone, Richard. 2019. "Acquittals by the International Criminal Court." *EJIL: Talk!*, 18 January. www.ejiltalk.org/acquittals-by-the-international-criminal-court/.

Goodin, Robert E., James G. March, and Johan P. Olsen. 2011. "The Logic of Appropriateness." In *The Oxford Handbook of Political Science*. Oxford University Press.

Grah Mel, Frederic. 2003. *Félix Houphouët-Boigny I: Le fulgurant destin d'une jeune proie (?–1960)*. Paris: Maisonneuve & Larose.

Grah Mel, Frederic. 2010. *Félix Houphouët-Boigny: L'Epreuve du Pouvoir (1960–1980)*. Paris: Karthala.

Grono, Nick, and Anna de Courcy Wheeler. 2015. "The Deterrent Effect of the ICC on the Commission of International Crimes by Government Leaders." In *The Law and Practice of the International Criminal Court*, ed. C. Stahn. Oxford: Oxford University Press, pp. 1225–1244.

Grovogui, Siba. 2002. "Regimes of Sovereignty: International Morality and the African Condition." *European Journal of International Relations* 8 (3): 315–338.

Grovogui, Siba. 2008. "The Secret Lives of the Sovereign: Rethinking Sovereignty as International Morality." In *The State of Sovereignty: Territories, Laws, Populations*, eds. D. Howland and L. S. White. Bloomington: Indiana University Press, pp. 261–275.

Grovogui, Siba. 2013. "Deferring Difference: A Postcolonial Critique of the 'Race Problem' in Moral Thought." In *Postcolonial Theory and International Relations: A Critical Introduction*, ed. Sanjay Seth. New York: Routledge, pp. 106–123.

Grovogui, Siba. 2015. "Intricate Entanglement: The ICC and the Pursuit of Peace, Reconciliation and Justice in Libya, Guinea, and Mali." *Africa Development* 40 (2): 99–122.

Grugel, Jean, and Nicola Piper. 2007. *Critical Perspectives on Global Governance: Rights and Regulations in Governing Regimes.* New York: Routledge.

Guilfoyle, Douglas. 2019. "Reforming the International Criminal Court: Is It Time for the Assembly of States Parties to Be the Adults in the Room?" *EJIL: Talk!*, 8 May.

Gurber, Thomas. 2013. "Letter to the Security Council." 5 October 2018. www.news.admin.ch/NSBSubscriber/message/attachments/29293.pdf.

Haig, Brian D. 1995. "Grounded Theory as Scientific Method." *Philosophy of Education* 28 (1): 1–11.

Hansen, Thomas Obel. 2012. "The International Criminal Court in Kenya: Three Defining Features of a Contested Accountability Process and Their Implications for the Future of International Justice." *Australian Journal of Human Rights* 18 (2): 187–217.

Hartill, Lane. 2017. "A Vile Side of Ruling Party Youth League Members." HRW Dispatches, 7 April.

Hartmann, Christof. 2017. "ECOWAS and the Restoration of Democracy in the Gambia." *Africa Spectrum* 52 (1): 85–99.

Helfer, Laurence R., and Erik Voeten. 2014. "International Courts as Agents of Legal Change: Evidence from LGBT Rights in Europe." *International Organization* 68 (1): 77–110.

Heller, Kevin Jon. 2016. "Radical Complementarity." *Journal of International Criminal Justice* 14 (3): 637–665.

Heller, Kevin Jon. 2019a. "Can the PTC Review the Interests of Justice?" *Opinio Juris*, 12 April. http://opiniojuris.org/2019/04/12/can-the-ptc-review-the-interests-of-justice/.

Heller, Kevin Jon. 2019b. "Judge Ozaki Must Resign – Or Be Removed." *Opinio Juris*, 29 March.

Heller, Kevin Jon. 2019c. "A Thought Experiment about Complementarity and the Jordan Appeal Decision." *Opinio Juris*, 9 May.

Hillebrecht, Courtney. 2012. "Implementing International Human Rights Law at Home: Domestic Politics and the European Court of Human Rights." *Human Rights Review* 13 (3): 279–301.

Hillebrecht, Courtney. 2014. "The Power of Human Rights Tribunals: Compliance with the European Court of Human Rights and Domestic Policy Change." *European Journal of International Relations* 20 (4): 1100–1123.

Hillebrecht, Courtney. 2016. "The Deterrent Effects of the International Criminal Court: Evidence from Libya." *International Interactions* 42 (4): 616–643.

Hobbs, Patricia. 2015. "Contemporary Challenges in Relation to the Prosecution of Senior State Officials before the International Criminal Court." *International Criminal Law Review* 15 (1): 76–100.

Höhn, Sabine. 2014. "New Start or False Start? The ICC and Electoral Violence in Kenya." *Development and Change* 45 (3): 565–588.

Hopgood, Stephen. 2013. *The Endtimes of Human Rights.* Ithaca, NY: Cornell University Press.

Hozic, Aida. 2014. "The Origins of 'Post-Conflict.'" In *Post-Conflict Studies: An Interdisciplinary Approach*, eds. C. Gagnon and K. Brown. New York: Routledge.

Human Rights Watch. 2004. "ICC: Investigate All Sides in Uganda." Human Rights Watch, 4 February. www.hrw.org/news/2004/02/04/icc-investigate-all-sides-uganda.

Human Rights Watch. 2011. "'They Killed Them Like It Was Nothing': The Need for Justice for Côte d'Ivoire's Post-Election Crimes." Human Rights Watch, 5 October.

Human Rights Watch. 2013. "Syria and the International Criminal Court." Human Rights, 7 February 2020. www.hrw.org/sites/default/files/related_material/ Q%26A_Syria_ICC_Sept2013_en_0.pdf.

Human Rights Watch. 2014. "Côte d'Ivoire: ICC Seeking Militia Leader." Human Rights Watch. www.hrw.org/news/2013/10/03/cote-d-ivoire-icc-seeking-militia-leader.

Human Rights Watch. 2015a. "Making Justice Count: Lessons from the ICC's Work in Côte d'Ivoire." Human Rights Watch, 4 August.

Human Rights Watch. 2015b. State of Fear: Arbitrary Arrests, Torture, and Killings." Report. 16 November. www.hrw.org/report/2015/09/16/state-fear/arbitrary-arrests-torture-and-killings.

Human Rights Watch. 2016a. "More Fear Than Fair: Gambia's 2016 Presidential Election." Report. 2 November. www.hrw.org/report/2016/11/02/more-fear-fair/ gambias-2016-presidential-election.

Human Rights Watch. 2016b. "World Report 2015: Syria." Human Rights Watch, 7 February 2020. www.hrw.org/sites/default/files/related_material/syria_8.pdf.

Human Rights Watch. 2017. "ICC: New Burundi Investigation." 9 November. www.hrw.org/news/2017/11/09/icc-new-burundi-investigation.

Human Rights Watch. 2018. "World Report: Syria." www.hrw.org/world-report/2018/ country-chapters/syria.

Human Rights Watch. 2019a. "Burundi: Rampant Abuses Against Opposition." 12 June. www.hrw.org/news/2019/06/12/burundi-rampant-abuses-against-opposition.

Human Rights Watch. 2019b. "Philippines Pullout from ICC Won't Block Justice for 'Drug War': President Duterte Could Still Face Prosecution by International Criminal Court." Dispatches, 18 March.

Huneeus, Alexandra. 2007. "Norms Trickling Down: Of Judges, the Justice Cascade, and Pinochet Era Cases in Chile." *Santa Clara Journal of International Law* 5: 352–392.

Hurd, Ian. 1999. "Legitimacy and Authority in International Politics." *International Organization* 53 (2): 379–408.

Hurd, Ian. 2007. "Breaking and Making Norms: American Revisionism and Crises of Legitimacy." *International Politics* 44 (2–3): 194–213.

ICC. 1998. *Rome Statute of the International Criminal Court.* www.icc-cpi.int/nr/ rdonlyres/ea9aeff7-5752-4f84-be94-0a655eb30e16/0/rome_statute_english.pdf.

ICC. 2004a. "Decision Assigning the Situation in Uganda to Pre-Trial Chamber II." ICC-02/04–1, 5 July. www.icc-cpi.int/pages/record.aspx?uri=271808.

ICC. 2004b. "ICC – Prosecutor Receives Referral of the Situation in the Democratic Republic of Congo." ICC-OTP-20040419-50, 19 April. www.icc-cpi.int/Pages/ item.aspx?name=prosecutor+receives+referral+of+the+situation+in+the+demo cratic+republic+of+congo.

ICC. 2004c. "The Office of the Prosecutor of the International Criminal Court Opens Its First Investigation." ICC-OTP-20040623-59, 23 June. www.icc-cpi.int/ Pages/item.aspx?name=the+office+of+the+prosecutor+of+the+international+cr iminal+court+opens+its+first+investigation.

ICC. 2004d. "President of Uganda Refers Situation Concerning the Lord's Resistance Army (LRA) to the ICC." ICC-20040129-44, 29 January. www.icc-cpi.int/Pages/item.aspx?name=president+of+uganda+refers+situation+concerning+the+lord_s+resistance+army+_lra_+to+the+icc.

ICC. 2006. "Sixth Diplomatic Briefing of the International Criminal Court: Compilation of Statements." 23 March. www.legal-tools.org/doc/b65c5d/pdf/.

ICC. 2010. "Statement by ICC Prosecutor Luis Moreno-Ocampo on the Situation in Côte d'Ivoire." Press Release, ICC-OTP-20101221-PR617, 21 December. www.icc-cpi.int/Pages/item.aspx?name=pr617.

ICC. 2013. "Situation in Mali: Article 53(1) Report." 16 January. www.icc-cpi.int/itemsDocuments/SASMaliArticle53_1PublicReportENG16Jan2013.pdf.

ICC. 2015. "Kenyatta Case: Trial Chamber V(B) Terminates the Proceedings." ICC-CPI-20150313-PR1099, 13 March. www.icc-cpi.int/Pages/item.aspx?name=pr1099.

ICC. 2016a. "ICC Permanent Premises Officially Opened by His Majesty King Willem-Alexander of the Netherlands." 7 February 2020. www.icc-cpi.int/Pages/item.aspx?name=pr1208&ln=en.

ICC. 2016b. "Ruto and Sang Case: Trial Chamber V(A) Terminates the Case without Prejudice for Re-prosecution in Future." ICC-CPI-20160405-PR1205, 5 April. www.icc-cpi.int/pages/item.aspx?name=pr1205.

ICC. 2016c. "Simone Gbagbo Case: ICC Pre-Trial Chamber I Rejects Côte d'Ivoire's Challenge to the Admissibility of the Case and Reminds the Government of Its Obligation to Surrender Simone Gbagbo." ICC-CPI-20141209-PR1075, 11 December. www.icc-cpi.int/pages/item.aspx?name=pr1075.

ICC. 2016d. "Trial Hearing." ICC-02/11-01/15-T-9-ENG ET WT-28-01-2016. www.icc-cpi.int/Transcripts/oCR2016_00664.pdf.

ICC. 2017. "ICC Judges Authorize Opening of an Investigation Regarding Burundi Situation." Press Release, ICC-CPI-20171109-PR1342. www.icc-cpi.int/Pages/item.aspx?name=pr1342.

ICC. 2018a. "Al Hassan Ag Abdoul Aziz Ag Mohamed Ag Mahmoud Makes First Appearance before ICC." Press Release, ICC-CPI-20180404-PR1377, 4 April. www.icc-cpi.int/Pages/item.aspx?name=pr1377.

ICC. 2018b. "ICC Appeals Chamber Acquits Mr Bemba from All Charges of War Crimes and Crimes against Humanity." Press Release, ICC-CPI-20180608-PR1390, 8 June. www.icc-cpi.int/Pages/item.aspx?name=pr1390.

ICC. 2018c. "Mandat d'arrêt à l'encontre d'Al Hassan Ag Abdoul Aziz Ag Mohamed Ag Mahmoud." Document No. ICC-01/12-01/18-2, 31 March. www.icc-cpi.int/itemsDocuments/CR2018_01863_FRA.PDF.

ICC. 2019. "ICC Trial Chamber I Acquits Laurent Gbagbo and Charles Blé Goudé from All Charges." ICC-CPI-20190115-PR1427, Press Release, 15 January. www.icc-cpi.int/Pages/item.aspx?name=pr1427.

ICC Appeals Chamber. 2011. "Judgment on the Appeal of the Republic of Kenya against the Decision of Pre-Trial Chamber II of the 30 May 2011 Entitled "Decision on the Application by Government of Kenya Challenging the Admissibility of the Case Pursuant to Article 19(2)(b) of the Statute." ICC-01/09-02/11-274, 30 August. www.icc-cpi.int/pages/record.aspx?uri=1223134.

ICC Appeals Chamber. 2014a. "Judgment on the Appeal of Libya against the Decision of Pre-Trial Chamber I of 31 May 2013 Entitled 'Decision on the Admissibility of the Case against Saif Al-Islam Gaddafi'." ICC-01/11-01/11-547-Red, 21 May. www.icc-cpi.int/pages/record.aspx?uri=1779877.

ICC Appeals Chamber. 2014b. "Judgment on the Appeal of Mr Abdullah Al-Senussi against the Decision of Pre-Trial Chamber I of 11 October 2013 Entitled 'Decision on the Admissibility of the Case against Abdullah Al-Senussi'." ICC-01/11-01/11-565, 24 July. www.icc-cpi.int/pages/record.aspx?uri=1807073.

ICC OTP. 2003a. "Paper on Some Policy Issues before the Office of the Prosecutor." 7 February 2020. www.legal-tools.org/doc/f53870/pdf.

ICC OTP. 2003b. "Second Assembly of State Parties to the Rome Statute of the International Criminal Court, Report of the Prosecutor of the ICC." 8 September. www.icc-cpi.int/NR/rdonlyres/C073586C-7D46-4CBE-B901-0672908E8639/143656/LMO_20030908_En.pdf.

ICC OTP. 2004. "Report of the Prosecutor of the ICC, Second Assembly of States Parties to the Rome Statute of the International Criminal Court." 8 September.

ICC OTP. 2005. "Joint Statement by ICC Chief Prosecutor and the Visiting Delegation of Lango, Acholi, Iteso and Madi Community Leaders from Northern Uganda." Press Release, ICC-OTP-20050416-99-En, 16 April.

ICC OTP. 2009a. "Agreed Minutes of the Meeting between Prosecutor Moreno-Ocampo and the Delegation of the Kenyan Government." 3 July. www.legal-tools.org/doc/27d6b9/pdf/.

ICC OTP. 2009b. "ICC Prosecutor Receives Materials on Post-Election Violence in Kenya." Press Release, ICC-OTP-20090716-PR438.

ICC OTP. 2013. "Notification of the Removal of Witness from the Prosecution's Witness List and Application for Adjournment of the Provisional Trial Date." 19 December. www.icc-cpi.int/iccdocs/doc/doc1703998.pdf.

ICC OTP. 2018a. "Situation in the Gabonese Republic: Article 5 Report." 21 September. www.icc-cpi.int/itemsDocuments/180921-otp-rep-gabon_ENG.pdf.

ICC OTP. 2018b. "Statement of Prosecutor of the International Criminal Court, Fatou Bensouda, on Opening Preliminary Examinations into the Situations in the Philippines and in Venezuela." 8 February. www.icc-cpi.int/Pages/item.aspx?name=180208-otp-stat.

ICC Pre-Trial Chamber I. 2009. "Decision on the Prosecution's Application for a Warrant of Arrest against Omar Hassan Al Bashir." ICC-02/05-01/09-3, 4 March. www.icc-cpi.int/pages/record.aspx?uri=639096.

ICC Pre-Trial Chamber I. 2011. "Decision on the Prosecutor's Application Pursuant to Article 58 as to Muammar Mohammed Abu Minyar GADDAFI, Saif Al-Islam GADDAFI and Abdullah AL-SENUSSI." ICC-01/11, 27 June. www.icc-cpi.int/CourtRecords/CR2011_08499.PDF.

ICC Pre-Trial Chamber I. 2013. "Public Redacted-Decision on the Admissibility of the Case against Saif Al-Islam Gaddafi." ICC-01/11-01/11-344-Red, 31 May. www.icc-cpi.int/Pages/record.aspx?docNo=ICC-01/11-01/11-344-Red.

ICC Pre-Trial Chamber I. 2014. "Decision on the Confirmation of Charges against Laurent Gbagbo." ICC-02/11-01/11, 12 June. www.icc-cpi.int/CourtRecords/CR2015_04777.PDF.

ICC Pre-Trial Chamber II. 2010. "Decision Pursuant to Article 15 of the Rome Statute on the Authorization of an Investigation into the Situation in the Republic of Kenya." ICC-01/09-19, 31 March. www.legal-tools.org/doc/338a6f/pdf/.

ICC Pre-Trial Chamber II. 2011. "Situation in the Republic of Kenya: Decision on the Prosecutor's Application for Summons to Appear for William Samoei Ruto, Henry Kiprono Kosgey, and Joshua Arap Sang." ICC-01/09-01/11-1, 8 March. www.icc-cpi.int/pages/record.aspx?uri=1037044.

ICC Pre-Trial Chamber II. 2014a. "Decision on the Cooperation of the Democratic Republic of Congo Regarding Omar Al Bashir's Arrest and Surrender to the Court." ICC-02/05-01/09-195, 9 April. www.icc-cpi.int/pages/record.aspx?uri=1759849.

ICC Pre-Trial Chamber II. 2014b. "Decision on the Cooperation of the Democratic Republic of Congo Regarding Omar Al Bashir's Arrest and Surrender to the Court." 9 May. www.icc-cpi.int/CourtRecords/CR2014_03452.pdf.

ICC Pre-Trial Chamber II. 2015. "Decision Pursuant to Article 15 of the Rome Statute on the Authorization of an Investigation into the Situation in the Republic of Kenya." ICC-01/09-19, 31 March. www.legal-tools.org/doc/338a6f/pdf/.

ICC Pre-Trial Chamber III. 2012. "Warrant of Arrest for Simone Gbagbo." ICC-02/11-01/12, 29 February. www.icc-cpi.int/CourtRecords/CR2012_03549.PDF.

ICC Trial Chamber I. 2015. "Decision on Prosecution Requests to Join the Cases of *The Prosecutor* v. *Laurent Gbagbo* and *The Prosecutor* v. *Charles Blé Goudé* and Related Matters." ICC-02/11-01/15/, 11 March. www.icc-cpi.int/Pages/record.aspx?docNo=ICC-02/11-01/15-1&ln=en.

ICC Trial Chamber I. 2016. "Decision on Prosecution Requests to Join the Cases of *The Prosecutor* v. *Laurent Gbagbo* and *The Prosecutor* v. *Charles Blé Goudé* and Related Matters." ICC-02/11-01/15-1, 11 March. www.icc-cpi.int/pages/record.aspx?uri=1939590.

ICC Trial Chamber I. 2018. "Order on The Further Conduct of The Proceedings." ICC-02/11-01/15, 7 February 2020. www.icc-cpi.int/CourtRecords/CR2018_00949.PDF.

ICC Trial Chamber I. 2019. Transcript No ICC-02/11-01/15-T-234-ENG. www.icc-cpi.int/Transcripts/CR2019_00134.PDF.

ICC, Trial Chamber III. 2016. "Public Redacted Version of Closing Brief of Mr. Jean-Pierre Bemba Gombo." ICC-01/05-01/08-3121-Red, 22 April. www.icc-cpi.int/Pages/record.aspx?docNo=ICC-01/05-01/08-3121-Red.

ICC Trial Chamber V. 2013. "Decision on the Withdrawal of Charges against Mr. Muthaura." ICC-01/09-02/11-696, 18 March. www.icc-cpi.int/pages/record.aspx?uri=1568411.

ICC Trial Chamber V. 2016. "Decision on Defense Applications for Judgments of Acquittal." ICC-01/09-01/11, 5 April. www.legal-tools.org/doc/41dc5f/pdf/.

International Court of Justice. 1999. "Requête Introductive d'Instance: Activités armées sur le territoire du Congo (République Démocratique du Congo c. Ouganda)." International Court of Justice. www.icj-cij.org/files/case-related/116/7150.pdf.

International Court of Justice. 2002. "Arrest Warrant of 11 April 2000, *Democratic Republic of Congo* v *Belgium*." International Court of Justice, 7 February 2020. www.icj-cij.org/en/case/121/judgments.

International Crisis Group (ICG). 2006. "Katanga: The Congo's Forgotten Crisis." Africa Report No 103.

Jacobs, Dov. 2015. "The Frog That Wanted to Be an Ox: The ICC Approach to Immunities and Cooperation." In *The Law and Practice of the International Criminal Court*, ed. C. Stahn. Oxford: Oxford University Press, pp. 281–302.

Jacobs, Dov. 2019a. "ICC Pre-Trial Chamber Rejects OTP Request to Open an Investigation in Afghanistan: Some Preliminary Thoughts on an Ultra Vires Decision." *Spreading the Jam*, 12 April.

Jacobs, Dov. 2019b. "You Have Just Entered Narnia: ICC Appeals Chamber Adopts the Worst Possible Solution on Immunities in the Bashir Case." *Spreading the Jam*, 6 May.

Jalloh, Charles Chernor. 2012. "Situation in the Republic of Kenya." *The American Journal of International Law* 106 (1): 118–125.

Jalloh, Charles Chernor. 2013. "Kenya vs. The ICC Prosecutor." *Harvard International Law Journal* 53: 269–285.

Jessberger, Florian, and Julia Geneuss. 2012. "The Many Faces of the International Criminal Court." *Journal of International Criminal Justice* 10 (5): 1081–1094.

Jo, Hyeran, and Beth A. Simmons. 2017. "Can the International Criminal Court Deter Atrocity?" – Corrigendum. *International Organization* 71 (2): 419–421.

Johnston, Alastair Iain. 2001. "Treating International Institutions as Social Environments." *International Studies Quarterly* 45 (4): 487–515.

Jollof News. 2016. "Gambian Activists Disappointed at ICC's Refusal to Investigate Jammeh.", *Jollof News*, 3 June. https://jollofnews.com/2016/06/03/gambian-activists-disappointed-at-iccs-refusal-to-investigate-jammeh/.

Kagwanja, Mwangi. 1998. *Killing the Vote: State Sponsored Violence and Flawed Elections in Kenya*. Nairobi: Kenya Human Rights Commission.

Kambale, Pascal Kalume. 2015. "A Story of Missed Opportunities: The Role of the International Criminal Court in the Democratic Republic of Congo." In *Contested Justice: The Politics of International Criminal Court Interventions*, eds. C. D. Vos, S. Kendall, and C. Stahn. Cambridge: Cambridge University Press, pp. 171–197.

Kastner, Philipp. 2012. *International Criminal Justice in Bello?* Leiden: Martinus Nijhoff.

Katzenstein, Peter. 1998. *Cultural Norms and National Security, Police and Military in Postwar Japan*. Ithaca, NY: Cornell University Press.

Kaye, David. 2013. "The Council and the Court: Improving Security Council Support of the International Criminal Court." *UC Irvine Law School Review* . Research Paper No 2013-127. https://sites.uci.edu/internationaljustice/files/2013/05/The-Council-and-the-Court-FINAL.pdf.

Keck, Margaret E., and Kathryn Sikkink. 1998. *Activists beyond Borders: Advocacy Networks in International Politics*. Ithaca: Cornell University Press.

Kelle, Udo. 2007. "The Development of Categories: Different Approaches in Grounded Theory." In *The SAGE Handbook of Grounded Theory*, eds. A. Bryant and K. Charmaz. Los Angeles: Sage Publications, pp. 191–214.

Kendall, Sara. 2014. "'UhuRuto' and Other Leviathans: The International Criminal Court and the Kenyan Political Order." *African Journal of Legal Studies* 7 (3): 399–427.

Keohane, Robert. 1982. "The Demand for International Regimes." *International Organization* 36 (2): 332–355.

Keohane, Robert. 1984. *After Hegemony: Cooperation and Discord in the World Political Economy.* Princeton, NJ: Princeton University Press.

Kersten, Mark. 2014. "A Fatal Attraction?: Libya, the UN Security Council and the Relationship between R2P and the International Criminal Court." In *Mobilizing International Law for "Global Justice,"* eds. J. Handmaker and K. Arts. Cambridge: Cambridge University Press, pp. 142–162.

Kersten, Mark. 2015a. "Between Justice and Politics: The ICC's Intervention in Libya." In *Contested Justice: The Politics of International Criminal Court Interventions,* eds. C. D. Vos, S. Kendall, and C. Stahn. Cambridge: Cambridge University Press, pp. 456–478.

Kersten, Mark. 2015b. "The Lesson the ICC Shouldn't Learn in the Wake of Kenyatta." *Justice in Conflict,* 7 December. http://justiceinconflict.org/2014/12/07/the-lesson-the-icc-shouldnt-learn-in-the-wake-of-kenyatta/.

Kersten, Mark. 2016a. "Hold Your Horses, ICC Complementarity." *Justice in Conflict,* 21 June.

Kersten, Mark. 2016b. *Justice in Conflict: The Effects of the International Criminal Court's Interventions on Ending Wars and Building Peace.* Oxford: Oxford University Press.

Kersten, Mark. 2016c. "Some Thoughts on South Africa's Withdrawal from the International Criminal Court." *Justice in Conflict,* 26 October.

Kersten, Mark. 2019a. "Perceptions of Justice: When and How the ICC Should Meet with 'Bad' Leaders." *Justice in Conflict,* 21 February.

Kersten, Mark. 2019b. "Whither the Aspirational ICC, Welcome the 'Practical' Court?" *EJIL: Talk!,* 22 May. www.ejiltalk.org/whither-the-aspirational-icc-welcome-the-practical-court/.

Kissinger, Henry A. 2001. "The Pitfalls of Universal Jurisdiction." *Foreign Affairs* 80 (4): 86–96.

Kitchen, J. Coleman, and Jean-Paul Paddack. 1990. "The 1990 Franco-African Summit." *CSIS Africa Notes,* Number 115.

Kiyani, Asad. 2019. "Elisions and Omissions: Questioning the ICC's Latest Bashir Immunity Ruling." *Just Security,* 8 May.

Koremenos, Barbara. 2008. "When, What, and Why Do States Choose to Delegate?" *Law and Contemporary Problems* 71 (1): 151–192.

Koremenos, Barbara, Charles Lipson, and Duncan Snidal. 2001. "The Rational Design of International Institutions." *International Organization* 55 (4): 761–799.

Krasner, Stephen D. 1983. *International Regimes.* Ithaca, NY: Cornell University Press.

Krasner, Stephen D. 1999. *Sovereignty: Organized Hypocrisy.* Princeton, NJ: Princeton University Press.

Krasner, Stephen D. 2004. "Sharing Sovereignty: New Institutions for Collapsed and Failing States." *International Security* 29 (2): 85–120.

Kratochwil, Friedrich, and John Gerard Ruggie. 1986. "International Organization: A Sate of the Art on an Art of the State." *International Organization* 40 (4): 753–775.

Kress, Claus. 2004. "'Self-Referrals' and 'Waivers of Complementarity': Some Considerations in Law and Policy." *Journal of International Criminal Justice,* 2 (4): 944–948.

LA Times. 2012. "Mali Soldiers Tortured, Abducted 'Red Berets,' Rights Groups Say." 30 July. https://latimesblogs.latimes.com/world_now/2012/07/mali-soldiers-tortured-abducted-red-berets-rights-groups-say.html.

Labuda, Patryk. 2019. "Perceptions of Justice: Continuing the Conversation on Managing Perceptions at the ICC." *Justice in Conflict*, 7 March.

Lake, David A., and Mathew D. McCubbins. 2006. "The Logic of Delegation to International Organization." In *Delegation and Agency in International Organizations*, eds. D. G. Hawkins, D. A. Lake, Daniel L. Nielson, and M. J. Tierney. Cambridge: Cambridge University Press, pp. 341–368.

Lamony, Stephen. 2014. "Rwanda and the ICC – Playing Politics with Justice." *African Arguments*, 21 October.

Lecoq et al. 2012. "One Hippopotamus and Eight Blind Analysts: A Multivocal Analysis of the 2012 Political Crisis in the Divided Republic of Mali." *Review of African Political Economy* 40 (137): 343–357.

Levitsky, Steven and Lucan A. Way. 2010. *Competitive Authoritarianism: Hybrid Regimes after the Cold War*. Cambridge: Cambridge University Press.

Levy, Daniel. 2010. "Recursive Cosmopolitization: Argentina and the Global Human Rights Regime." *The British Journal of Sociology* 61 (3): 579–596.

Lingsma, Tjitske. 2019. "ICC Judges at Centre of Controversy." *Justice Info*, 16 May.

Lombard, Louisa. 2016. *State of Rebellion: Violence and Intervention in the Central African Republic*. London: Zed Books.

Louw, Antoinette, and Ottilia Anna Maunganidze. 2012. "The Decision by the Government of Mali to Refer the Situation in the Country Has Several Implications for the Country, Africa and the ICC." *ISS Today*, 24 July.

Lutz, Ellen, and Kathryn Sikkink. 2001. "The Justice Cascade: The Evolution and Impact of Foreign Human Rights Trials in Latin America." *Chicago Journal of International Law*, 2(1): 1–33.

Lynch, Colum. 2014. "U.S. to Support ICC War Crimes Prosecution in Syria." *Foreign Policy*, 7 May.

Lynch, Gabriella. 2014. "Electing the 'Alliance of the Accused': The Success of the Jubilee Alliance in Kenya's Rift Valley." *Journal of Eastern African Studies* 8 (1): 93–114.

Macé, Célian. 2016. "Dans le Haut-Ogooué, le score de Bongo trop gros pour être vrai." *Liberation*, 1 September.

Maclean, Ruth. 2018. "Ivory Coast President Pardons 800 People Including Ex-First Lady." *Guardian*, 7 August. www.theguardian.com/world/2018/aug/07/ivory-coast-president-pardons-800-people-ex-first-lady-simone-gbagbo.

Maliti, Tom. 2014a. "Prosecutor Withdraws Seven Witnesses in Kenyatta Case in Past Year." *International Justice Monitor*, 16 January.

Maliti, Tom. 2014b. "Witness Denies Making Statement to Prosecution." *International Justice Monitor*: Open Society Foundation. www.ijmonitor.org/2014/09/witness-denies-making-statement-to-prosecution/.

Maliti, Tom. 2014c. "Witness Narrates His Frustrations with ICC Protection Program." *International Justice Monitor*. www.ijmonitor.org/2014/11/witness-narrates-his-frustrations-with-icc-protection-program/.

Maliti, Tom. 2014d. "Witness Says Promise of 'Good Life' Induced False Claims." *International Justice Monitor*. www.ijmonitor.org/2014/09/witness-says-promise-of-good-life-induced-false-claims/.

Maliti, Tom. 2014e. "Witness Says Three People Coached Him to Implicate Ruto and Sang." *International Justice Monitor*. www.ijmonitor.org/2014/09/witness-says-three-people-coached-him-to-implicate-ruto-and-sang/.

Maliti, Tom. 2015a. "Prosecution Calls Its Own Witness 'Thoroughly Unreliable and Incredible,'" *International Justice Monitor*, 21 January.

Maliti, Tom. 2015b. "Witness 727 Has Been Hiding, His Lawyer Says." 26 March. www.ijmonitor.org/2015/03/witness-727-has-been-in-hiding-says-his-lawyer/.

Maliti, Tom. 2016a. "Prosecution and Defense Exude Confidence before Start of Gbagbo and Blé Goudé Trial." *International Justice Monitor*.

Maliti, Tom. 2016b. "Prosecutor: We Have Evidence to Prove Case against Gbagbo and Blé Goudé." *International Justice Monitor*.

Maliti, Tom. 2016c. "Prosecutor Withdraws Seven Witnesses in Kenyatta Case in Past Year." *International Justice Monitor*, 16 January.

Mamdani, Mahmood. 2009. *Saviors and Survivors: Darfur, Politics, and the War on Terror*. New York: Pantheon Books.

Manirakiza, Pacifique. 2009. "L'Afrique et le système de justice pénale internationale." *African Journal of Legal Studies* 3 (1): 21–52.

Marchall, Ruth. 2005. "La France en Côte d'Ivoire: l'interventionnisme à l'épreuve des faits." *Politique Africaine* 98: 21–41.

McAuliffe, Padraig. 2013. "The Roots of Transitional Accountability: Interrogating the 'Justice Cascade.'" *International Journal of Law in Context*, 9 (1): 106–123.

McDougall, Carry. 2019. "Perceptions of Justice: The ICC Shouldn't Have to Justify Meetings with Government Officials Not Wanted by the Court." *Justice in Conflict*, 26 February.

McGovern, Mike. 2009. "Proleptic Justice: The Threat of Investigation as Deterrent to Human Rights Abuses in Côte d'Ivoire." In *Mirrors of Justice: Law and Power in the Post-Cold War Era*, eds. K. M. Clarke and M. Goodale. Cambridge: Cambridge University Press, pp. 67–86.

McGovern, Mike. 2011. *Making War in Côte d'Ivoire*: Chicago: University of Chicago Press.

Mégret, Frédéric. 2015. "In Whose Name?: The ICC and the Search for Constituency." In *Contested Justice: The Politics of International Criminal Court Interventions*, eds. C. D. Vos, S. Kendall, and C. Stahn. Cambridge: Cambridge University Press, pp. 23–45.

Mégret, Frédéric, and Marika Giles Samson. 2013. "Holding the Line on Complementarity in Libya: The Case for Tolerating Flawed Domestic Trials." *Journal of International Criminal Justice* 11 (3): 571–589.

Meyer, Christoph O. 2005. "Convergence Towards a European Strategic Culture?: A Constructivist Framework for Explaining Changing Norms." *European Journal of International Relations* 11 (4): 523–549.

Moghalu, Kingsley Chiedu. 2006. *Global Justice: The Politics of War Crimes Trials*. Westport, CT: Praeger Security International.

Moravcsik, Andrew. 2000. "The Origins of Human Rights Regimes: Democratic Delegation in Postwar Europe." *International Organization* 14 (2): 217–252.

Moravcsik, Andrew. 2008. "The New Liberalism." In *The Oxford Handbook of International Relations*, eds. C. Reus-Smit and D. Snidal. Oxford: Oxford University Press, pp. 234–254.

Morgan, Andy. 2012. "The Causes of the Uprising in Northern Mali." *Think Africa Press*, 6 February. http://thinkafricapress.com/mali/causes-uprising-northern-mali-tuareg.

Moyn, Samuel. 2012. *The Last Utopia: Human Rights in History.* Cambridge, MA: Harvard University Press.

Mue, Njonjo, and Judy Gitau. 2015. "The Justice Vanguard: The Role of Civil Society in Seeking Accountability for Kenya's Post-Election Violence." In *Contested Justice: The Politics of International Criminal Court Interventions*, eds. C. D. Vos, S. Kendall, and C. Stahn. Cambridge: Cambridge University Press, pp. 198–218.

Mueller, Susanne D. 2014. "Kenya and the International Criminal Court (ICC): Politics, the Election and the Law." *Journal of East African Studies* 8 (1): 25–42.

Mutua, Makau. 2008. *Kenya's Quest for Democracy: Taming Leviathan.* New York: Lynn Rienner Publishers.

Mutua, Makau. 2016. "Africans and the ICC: Hypocrisy, Impunity and Perversion." In *Africa and the ICC: Perceptions of Justice*, eds. Kamari M. Clarke, Abel S. Knottnerus, and Eefje de Volder. Cambridge: Cambridge University Press, pp. 47–60.

Nantulya, Paul. 2017. "A Medley of Armed Groups Play on Congo's Crisis." *Africa Center for Strategic Studies Spotlight*, 25 September.

Nielson, Daniel L., and Michael J. Tierney. 2003. "Delegation to International Organizations: Agency Theory and World Bank Environmental Reform." *International Organization* 57(2): 241–276.

Nouwen, Sarah M. H. 2011. "Complementarity in Uganda: Domestic Diversity or International Imposition?" In *The International Criminal Court and Complementarity: From Theory to Practice*, eds. C. Stahn and M. M. E. Zeidy. Cambridge: Cambridge University Press, pp. 1120–1154.

Nouwen, Sarah M. H. 2014. *Complementarity in the Line of Fire: The Catalysing Effect of the International Criminal Court in Uganda and Sudan.* Cambridge: Cambridge University Press.

Nouwen, Sarah M. H., and Wouter G. Werner. 2010. "Doing Justice to the Political: The International Criminal Court in Uganda and Sudan." *European Journal of International Law* 21 (4): 941–965.

Odigie, Brown. 2017. "In Defense of Democracy: Lessons from ECOWAS' Management of the Gambia's 2016 Post-Election Impasse." *The African Centre for the Constructive Resolution of Disputes*, Policy and Practice Brief No 4.

O'Grady, Siobhán. 2016. "Gambia Is the Latest Country to Leave the ICC." *Foreign Policy*, 26 October.

Olsen, Tricia D., Leigh A. Payne, and Andrew G. Reiter. 2010. *Transitional Justice in Balance: Comparing Processes, Weighing Efficacy.* Washington, DC: US Institute of Peace.

Panaïté, Antoine. 2016a. "Emmanuel Altit: The Gbagbo/Blé Goudé Trial Has a 'Fundamental' Relationship to France." *International Justice Monitor*, 16 March.

Panaïté, Antoine. 2016b. "Laurent Gbagbo Allegedly Made 'Shocking' Statements, According to Witness N'Guessan." *International Justice Monitor*, 28 June.

Papillon, Sophie. 2010. "Has the United Nations Security Council Implicitly Removed Al Bashir's Immunity?" *International Criminal Law Review*, 10 (2): 275–288.

Perelman, Marc. 2015. "Investigations against Pro-Ouattara Camp to Begin Mid-2015, Says ICC Chief Prosecutor." *France 24*, 31 March. www.france24.com/en/20150331-interview-fatou-bensouda-icc-chief-prosecutor-investigations.

Peskin, Victor. 2008. *International Justice in Rwanda and the Balkans: Virtual Trials and the Struggle for State Cooperation.* Cambridge: Cambridge University Press.

Peskin, Victor. 2009. "Caution and Confrontation in International Criminal Court's Pursuit of Accountability in Uganda and Kenya." *Human Rights Quarterly* 31 (3): 644–691.

Peskin, Victor. 2017. "Things Fall Apart: Battles of Legitimation and the Politics of Noncompliance and African Sovereignty from the Rwanda Tribunal to the ICC." In *The Legitimacy of International Criminal Tribunals*, eds. Nobuo Hayashi and Cecilia M. Bailliet. Cambridge: Cambridge University Press, pp. 401–425.

Piccolino, Giulia. 2012. "David against Goliath in Côte d'Ivoire?: Laurent Gbagbo's War against Global Governance." *African Affairs* 111 (442): 1–23.

Piccolino, Giulia. 2014. "Ultranationalism, Democracy and the Law: Insights from Côte d'Ivoire." *The Journal of Modern African Studies* 52 (1): 45–68.

Ping, Jean. 2016. "Nous demandons à @amnesty et au Procureur de @IntlCrimCourt de venir au #Gabonfaire tte la lumière sur les événements perpétrés le 31/8 #13." 29 September. Tweet.

Pitts, M. Christopher. 2014. "Being Able to Prosecute Saif al-Islam Gaddafi: Applying Article 17(3) of the Rome Statute to Libya." *Emory International Law Review* 27 (2): 1291–1339.

Pollack, Mark A. 1997. "Delegation, Agency, and Agenda Setting in the European Community." *International Organization* 51 (1): 99–134.

Powell, Emilia Justyna. 2013. "Two Courts Two Roads: Domestic Rule of Law and Legitimacy of International Courts." *Foreign Policy Analysis* 9 (4): 349–368.

Raynor, Keith. 2019. "A Reality-Check: The Need for Reform and a Culture Change at the ICC." *Justice in Conflict*, 17 June. https://justiceinconflict.org/2019/06/17/a-reality-check-the-need-for-reform-and-a-culture-change-at-the-icc/#more-7855.

Reichertz, Jo. 2007. "Abduction: The Logic of Discovery in Grounded Theory." In *Handbook of Grounded Theory*, eds. A. Bryant and K. Charmaz. London: Sage Publications, pp. 214–228.

Republic of Côte d'Ivoire. 2003. "Declaration Accepting the Jurisdiction of the International Criminal Court." 7 February 2020. www.icc-cpi.int/NR/rdonlyres/74EEE201-0FED-4481-95D4-C8071087102C/279844/ICDEENG.pdf.

République de Côte d'Ivoire. 2010. "Confirmation de la Declaration de Reconnaissance." NR 0039-PR-du 14/12/2010. www.icc-cpi.int/NR/rdonlyres/498E8FEB-7A72-4005-A209-C14BA374804F/0/ReconCPI.pdf.

République Gabonaise. 2016. "Requête aux fins de renvoi d'une situation par un état partie auprès du procureur de la Cour Pénale Internationale." 20 September. www.icc-cpi.int/iccdocs/otp/Referral-Gabon.pdf.

Reuters. 2006. "Rebel Chief in Uganda Says He Wants Peace." 25 May.

Reuters. 2007. "Uganda's President Hopes Rebels Choose 'Soft Landing.'" 4 June.

Reuters. 2015. "Ivory Coast Jails Ex-First Lady for 20 Years over Poll Violence." 10 May.

Rice, Xan. 2009. "Sudan's President Orders All Foreign Aid Groups to Leave Country within a Year." *Guardian*, 16 March.

Rim, Yejoon. 2012. "Two Governments and One Legitimacy: International Responses to the Post-Election Crisis in Côte d'Ivoire." *Leiden Journal of International Law* 25 (3): 683–705.

Roach, Steven C. 2013. "How Political Is the ICC?: Pressing Challenges and the Need for Diplomatic Efficacy." *Global Governance: A Review of Multilateralism and International Organizations* 19 (4): 507–523.

Rodman, Kenneth A. 2013. "Justice Is Interventionist: The Political Sources of the Judicial Reach of the Special Court for Sierra Leone." In *The Realities of International Criminal Justice*, eds. D. L. Rothe, J. D. Meernik, and T. Ingadottir. The Hague: Martinus Nijhoff.

Rodman, Kenneth A. 2015. "Intervention and the 'Justice Cascade': Lessons from the Special Court for Sierra Leone on Prosecution and Civil War." *Human Rights Review* 16 (1): 39–58.

Roht-Arriaza, Naomi, and Javier Mariezcurrena (eds.). 2006. *Transitional Justice in the Twenty-First Century: Beyond Truth versus Justice*. Cambridge: Cambridge University Press.

Rosenberg, Sophie. 2016a. "A Portrait from The Hague: All You Need to Know about What Laurent Gbagbo Wants You to Know." *Justice in Conflict*, 20 January.

Rosenberg, Sophie. 2016b. "Disbelief and Division at the ICC: Inside the Laurent Gbagbo Trial." *The Conversation*, 16 February.

Rosenberg, Sophie. 2017a. "Le procès Gbagbo-Blé Goudé pour crimes contre l'humanité: Contestation de la crise ivoirienne à la Haye." *Afrique Contemporaine* 3–4 (263–264): 268–270.

Rosenberg, Sophie. 2017b. "The International Criminal Court in Côte d'Ivoire: Impartiality at Stake?" *Journal of International Criminal Justice*, 15 (3): 471–490.

Ruteere, Mutuma, and Kamau Wairuri. 2015. "Explaining and Mitigating Election-Related Violence and Human Rights Violations in Kenya." In *Kenya's 2013 General Elections: Stakes, Practices, Outcomes*, eds. K. Njogu and P. W. Wekesa. Nairobi: Twaweza Communications, pp. 112–123.

Sandalinas, Jordi. 2015. "Satellite Imagery and Its Use as Evidence in the Proceedings of the International Criminal Court." *German Journal of Air and Space Law* 64 (4): 666–675.

Schabas, William A. 2008. "Prosecutorial Discretion v. Judicial Activism at the International Criminal Court." *Journal of International Criminal Justice* 6 (4): 731–761.

Schabas, William. 2010a. *The International Criminal Court: A Commentary on the Rome Statute*. Oxford: Oxford University Press.

Schabas, William. 2010b. "The International Criminal Court and Non-Party States." *Windsor Yearbook of Access to Justice* 28 (1): 1–21.

Schabas, William. 2011a. *An Introduction to the International Criminal Court*. Cambridge: Cambridge University Press.

Schabas, William. 2011b. "The Rise and Fall of Complementarity." In *The International Criminal Court and Complementarity: From Theory to Practice*, eds. C. Stahn and M. M. E. Zeidy. Cambridge: Cambridge University Press, pp. 150–164.

Schabas, William. 2013. "The Banality of International Justice." *Journal of International Criminal Justice* 11 (3): 545–551.

Schabas, William. 2015. "Selecting Situations and Cases." In *The Law and Practice of the International Criminal Court*, ed. C. Stahn. Oxford: Oxford University Press, pp. 365–381.

Scheffer, David. 2013. *All the Missing Souls: A Personal History of the War Crimes Tribunals*. Princeton, NJ: Princeton University Press.

Schimmelfennig, Frank. 2005. "Strategic Calculation and International Socialization: Membership Incentives, Party Constellations, and Sustained Compliance in Central and Eastern Europe." *International Organization* 59 (4): 827–860.

Schumann, Anne. 2013. "Songs of a New Era: Popular Music and Political Expression in the Ivorian Crisis." *African Affairs* 112 (448): 440–459.

Shingiro, Albert. 2017. "#Burundi Has the Right to Bring to Justice the Authors of the Biased Report of the Commiss of Inquiry for Attempt to Destabilize the Country." 28 October. Twitter. https://twitter.com/AShingiro/status/924335815282618369.

Sikkink, Kathryn. 1996. "The Emergence, Evolution, and Effectiveness of the Latin American Human Rights Network." In *Constructing Democracy: Human Rights, Citizenship, and Society in Latin America*, edited by Elizabeth Jelin and Eric Hershberg, 59–84. Boulder, CO: Westview Press.

Sikkink, Kathryn. 2008. "The Role of Consequences, Comparison and Counterfactuals in Constructivist Ethical Thought." In *Moral Limit and Possibility in World Politics*, edited by Richard M. Price, 83–111. Cambridge: Cambridge University Press.

Sikkink, Kathryn. 2011. *The Justice Cascade: How Human Rights Prosecutions Are Changing World Politics*. New York: W. W. Norton & Co.

Sikkink, Kathryn, and Carrie Booth Walling. 2007. "The Impact of Human Rights Trials in Latin America." *Journal of Peace Research* 44 (4): 427–445.

Simmons, Beth A. 2009. *Mobilizing Human Rights: International Law in Domestic Politics*. Cambridge: Cambridge University Press.

Simmons, Beth A., and Allison Danner. 2010. "Credible Commitments and the International Criminal Court." *International Organization* 64 (2): 225–256.

Simons, Marlise. 2019. "In The Hague's Lofty Judicial Halls, Judges Wrangle Over Pay." *New York Times*, 20 January. www.nytimes.com/2019/01/20/world/europe/hague-judges-pay.html.

Simpson, Gerry J. 2004. *Great Powers and Outlaw States: Unequal Sovereigns in the International Legal Order*. Cambridge: Cambridge University Press.

Smith, Stephen. 2003. "La politique d'engagement de la France à l'épreuve de la Côte d'Ivoire." *Politique Africaine* 89: 112–126.

Song, Sang-Hyun. 2014. "Separate Opinion of Judge Sang-Hyun Song." ICC.

Soro, Guillaume. 2005. *Pourquoi je suis devenu un rebelle: La Côte d'Ivoire au bord du gouffre*. Paris: Hachette.

Sprouse, Ian. 2017. "The Gambia's Unsurprising Renunciation of the ICC, or the So-Called 'International Caucasian Court.'" *Africa at LSE*, 11 October.

Sriram, Chandra Lekha. 2003. "Revolutions in Accountability: New Approaches to Past Abuses." *American University International Law Review* 19 (2): 310–429.

Stahn, Carsten. 2012. "Libya, the International Criminal Court and Complementarity." *Journal of International Criminal Justice* 10 (2): 325–349.

Stahn, Carsten. 2015a. "Admissibility Challenges before the ICC: From Quasi-Primacy to Qualified Deference?" In *The Law and Practice of the International Criminal Court*, ed. C. Stahn. Oxford: Oxford University Press, pp. 228–259.

Stahn, Carsten. 2015b. "Justice Civilisatrice?: The ICC, Post-colonial Theory, and Faces of 'the Local.'" In *Contested Justice: The Politics of International Criminal Court Interventions*, eds. C. D. Vos, S. Kendall, and C. Stahn. Cambridge: Cambridge University Press, pp. 46–84.

Stahn, Carsten. 2015c. "More Than a Court, Less Than a Court, Several Courts in One?: The International Criminal Court in Perspective." In *The Law and Practice of the International Criminal Court*, ed. C. Stahn. Oxford: Oxford University Press, pp. lxxxiii–c.

Stahn, Carsten, Mohamed M. El Zeidy, and Héctor Olásolo. 2005. "The International Criminal Court's Ad Hoc Jurisdiction Revisited." *The American Journal of International Law* 99 (2): 421–431.

Stearns, Jason, Judith Verweijen, and Maria Eriksson Baaz. 2013. *The National Army and Armed Groups in the Eastern Congo: Untangling the Gordian Knot of Insecurity.* London: Rift Valley Institute.

Straus, Scott. 2015. "Challenges, Debates, and Reflections on the "Post" in "Post-conflict" Côte d'Ivoire: An Introduction." *Canadian Journal of African Studies* 48 (2): 181–184.

Straziuso, Jason. 2013. "Africa vs ICC: Quotes on Court before Kenya Trial." *Associated Press*, 11 October.

Struett, Michael J. 2008. *The Politics of Constructing the International Criminal Court: NGOs, Discourse, and Agency.* New York: Palgrave Macmillan.

Subotic, Jelena. 2009. *Hijacked Justice: Dealing with the Past in the Balkans.* Ithaca, NY: Cornell University Press.

Sudan Tribune. 2006. "Ugandan President Doubts Rebels Seriousness for Peace." 20 November.

Sudan Tribune. 2007. "Kony Must Disarm to Get Amnesty." 4 December.

Suma, Mohamed. 2019. "Côte d'Ivoire's Continued Struggle for Justice and Reconciliation." *International Center for Transitional Justice*, 30 January. www.ictj.org/news/cote-d'ivoire's-continued-struggle-justice-and-reconciliation.

The Carter Center. 2015. *International Election Observation Mission in Côte d'Ivoire – Final Report.* www.cartercenter.org/resources/pdfs/news/peace_publications/election_reports/cote-diviore-2010-2011-elections-final-rpt.pdf.

The Guardian. 2017. "Burundi Becomes First Nation to Leave International Criminal Court." 27 October.

The New Humanitarian. 2003. "DRC: International Criminal Court Targets Ituri." 17 July. https://reliefweb.int/report/democratic-republic-congo/drc-international-criminal-court-targets-ituri.

The New Humanitarian. 2005. "Uganda: Interview with President Yoweri Museveni." 9 June. www.thenewhumanitarian.org/report/54853/uganda-interview-president-yoweri-museveni.

The New Humanitarian. 2013. "Rebel Amnesty Reinstated in Uganda." 30 May. www.thenewhumanitarian.org/news/2013/05/30/rebel-amnesty-reinstated-uganda.

The New Vision. 2006a. "LRA Amnesty Limited." 6 July.

The New Vision. 2006b. "Uganda: We Can't Arrest Kony, Says Minister Kivejinja." 3 July.

The New Vision. 2007. "Ugandan Government Rejects Rebel Demand for 2m Dollars." The New Vision, 27 July.

The New Vision. 2013. "Museveni Salutes Kenyans for Rejecting ICC Blackmail." 9 April. www.newvision.co.ug/news/641494-museveni-salutes-kenyans-for-rejecting-icc-blackmail.html.

Thurston, Alex, and Andrew Lebovich. 2013. "A Handbook on Mali's 2012–2013 Crisis." *Institute for the Study of Islamic Thought (ISITA)'s Working Paper series*, No. 13-001.

Timmermans, Stefan, and Iddo Tavory. 2012. "Theory Construction in Qualitative Research: From Grounded Theory to Abductive Analysis." *Sociological Theory* 30 (3): 167–186.

Toh, Alain, and Richard Banégas. 2006. "La France et l'Onu devant le « parlement » de Yopougon." *Politique africaine* 104 (4): 141–158.

Towns, Ann. 2010. *Women and States: Norms and Hierarchies in International Relations.* Cambridge: Cambridge University Press.

Tutu, Desmond. 2013. "In Africa, Seeking a License to Kill." *New York Times*, 10 October. www.nytimes.com/2013/10/11/opinion/in-africa-seeking-a-license-to-kill.html.

Uganda. 2000. "Amnesty Act." 7 February 2020. https://ulii.org/node/23788.

Uganda. 2007. "Agreement on Accountability and Reconciliation." https://peace-maker.un.org/uganda-accountability-reconciliation2007.

UN Security Council. 2005. "Resolution 1593 (2005)." S/RES 1593 (2005), 7 February 2020. www.icc-cpi.int/NR/rdonlyres/85FEBD1A-29F8-4EC4-9566-48EDF55CC587/283244/N0529273.pdf.

UN Security Council. 2011a. "Letter dated 21 February 2011 from the Charge d'Affaires a.i. of the Permanent Mission of the Libyan Arab Jamahiriya to the United Nations addressed to the President of the Security Council." *UN Doc S/2011/102.*

UN Security Council. 2011b. "Resolution 1970 (2011)." Un Doc. S/RES/1970 (2011). www.undocs.org/S/RES/1970%20(2011).

United Nations. 2011c. "In Swift, Decisive Action, Security Council Imposes Tough Measures on Libyan Regime, Adopting Resolution 1970 in Wake of Crackdown on Protesters." UN Doc. SC/10187/REV.1, 28 February. www.un.org/press/en/2011/sc10187.doc.htm.

United Nations. 2011d. "Report of the Secretary-General's Panel of Experts on Accountability in Sri Lanka." 7 February 2020. www.un.org/News/dh/infocus/Sri_Lanka/POE_Report_Full.pdf.

United Nations. 2014. "Referral of Syria to International Criminal Court Fails as Negative Votes Prevent Security Council from Adopting Draft Resolution." UN Doc. SC/11407, 22 May. www.un.org/press/en/2014/sc11407.doc.htm.

UN HRC. 2018. "Report of the Commission of Inquiry on Burundi." A/HRC/39/63, 10–28 September. www.ohchr.org/Documents/HRBodies/HRCouncil/CoIBurundi/ReportHRC39/A_HRC_39_63_EN.pdf.

UN OHCHR. 2007. "Making Peace Our Own: Victims' Perceptions of Accountability, Reconciliation and Transitional Justice in Northern Uganda." 7 February 2020. www.refworld.org/docid/46cc4a690.html.

UN OHCHR. 2019. "High Commissioner Bachelet Calls on States to Take Strong Action against Inequalities." 6 March. www.ohchr.org/EN/NewsEvents/Pages/DisplayNews.aspx?NewsID=24265&LangID=E.

United Nations News. 2014. "Security Council Inaction on Darfur 'Can Only Embolden Perpetrators' – ICC Prosecutor." 12 December. https://news.un.org/en/story/2014/12/486172-security-council-inaction-darfur-can-only-embolden-perpetrators-icc-prosecutor.

US Congress. 2004. "Northern Uganda Crisis Response Act." 7 February 2020. www.congress.gov/108/plaws/publ283/PLAW-108publ283.pdf.

US Department of State. 2001. "Statement on the Designation of 39 Organizations on the USA PATRIOT Act's 'Terrorist Exclusion List,'" 6 December.

Ušacka, Anita. 2014. "Dissenting Opinion of Judge Anita Ušacka." ICC-01/11-01/11-547-Anx2. 7 February 2020. www.icc-cpi.int/pages/record.aspx?uri=1779879.

van de Merve, Hugo. 2009. "Delivering Justice during Transition: Researcher Challenges." In *Transitional Justice: Challenges for Empirical Research*, eds. H. van de Merve, V. Baxter, and A. Chapman. Washington, DC: USIP Press, pp. 115–142.

van der Wilt, Harmen. 2015. "Self-Referrals as an Indication of the Inability of States to Cope with Non-States Actors." In *The Law and Practice of the International Criminal Court*, ed. C. Stahn. Oxford: Oxford University Press, pp. 210–227.

Vasiliev, Sergey. 2015. "Victim Participation Revisited: What the ICC Is Learning about Itself." In *The Law and Practice of the International Criminal Court*, ed. C. Stahn. Oxford: Oxford University Press, pp. 1133–1202.

Vasilev, Sergey. 2019. "The Crises and Critiques of International Criminal Justice." In *The Oxford of International Criminal Law*, eds. Kevin Jon Heller et al. (Forthcoming 2020). https://papers.ssrn.com/sol3/papers.cfm?abstract_id=3358240.

Vaubel, Robert. 2006. "Principal-Agent Problems in International Organizations." *The Review of International Organizations* 1 (1): 125–138.

Verduzco, Deborah Ruiz. 2015. "The Relationship between the ICC and the United Nations Security Council." In *The Law and Practice of the International Criminal Court*, ed. C. Stahn. Oxford: Oxford University Press, pp. 30–64.

Vinjamuri, Leslie. 2015. "The ICC and the Politics of Peace and Justice." In *The Law and Practice of the International Criminal Court*, ed. C. Stahn. Oxford: Oxford University Press, pp. 13–29.

Vinjamuri, Leslie, and Jack Snyder. 2004. "Advocacy and Scholarship in the Study of International War Crime Tribunals and Transitional Justice." *Annual Review of Political Science*, 7 (1): 345–362.

Vos, Christian De, Sara Kendall, and Carsten Stahn (eds.). 2015. *Contested Justice: The Politics and Practice of International Criminal Court Interventions*. Cambridge: Cambridge University Press.

Vreeland, James. 2008. "Political Institutions and Human Rights: Why Dictatorships Enter into the United Nations Convention against Torture." *International Organization* 62 (1): 65–101.

Wakabi, Wairagala. 2016. "Bemba and Four Associates Convicted for Witness Tampering." *International Justice Monitor*, 19 October.

Waki Commission. 2008. *Report*. https://reliefweb.int/sites/reliefweb.int/files/resources/15A00F569813F4D549257607001F459D-Full_Report.pdf.

Walker, Angela. 2014. "The ICC versus Libya: How to End the Cycle of Impunity for Atrocity Crimes by Protecting Due Process." *UCLA Journal of International Law and Foreign Affairs* 18 (2): 303–354.

Wierda, Marieke, and Michael Otim. 2011. "Courts, Conflict and Complementarity in Uganda." In *The International Criminal Court and Complementarity: From Theory to Practice*, eds. C. Stahn and M. M. E. Zeidy. Cambridge: Cambridge University Press, pp. 1155–1179.

Wing, Susanna. 2013. "Making Sense of Mali." *Foreign Affairs*, 20 January.

Wolf, Thomas P. 2015. "From Sinners to Saints?: The ICC and Jubilee's Triumph in Kenya's 2013 Election." In *Kenya's 2013 General Election: Stakes, Practices, and Outcomes*, eds. K. Njogu and P. W. Wekesa. Nairobi: Twaweza Communications, pp. 162–197.

Index

CPSIA information can be obtained
at www.ICGtesting.com
Printed in the USA
BVHW031806100822
644286BV00005B/41